*Social History in Perspective* is a series of in-depth studies of the many topics in social, cultural and religious history for students. They also give the student clear surveys of the subject and present the most recent research in an accessible way.

## PUBLISHED

John Belchem *Popular Radicalism in Nineteenth-Century Britain*
Simon Dentith *Society and Cultural Forms in Nineteenth-Century England*
Harry Goulbourne *Race Relations in Britain since 1945*
Tim Hitchcock *English Sexualities, 1700–1800*
Sybil M. Jack *Towns in Tudor and Stuart Britain*
Helen M. Jewell *Education in Early Modern England*
Hugh McLeod *Religion and Society in England, 1850–1914*
Christopher Marsh *Popular Religion in the Sixteenth Century*
Michael A. Mullett *Catholics in Britain and Ireland, 1558–1829*
John Spurr *English Puritanism, 1603–1689*
W. B. Stephens *Education in Britain, 1750–1914*
David Taylor *Crime, Policing and Punishment in England, 1750–1914*
N. L. Tranter *British Population in the Twentieth Century*
Ian D. Whyte *Scotland's Society and Economy in Transition, c.1500–c.1760*

## FORTHCOMING

Eric Acheson *Late Medieval Economy and Society*
Ian Archer *Rebellion and Riot in England, 1360–1660*
Jonathan Barry *Religion and Society in England, 1603–1760*
A. L. Beier *Early Modern London*
Sue Bruley *Women's Century of Change*
Andrew Charlesworth *Popular Protest in Britain and Ireland, 1650–1870*
Richard Connors *The Growth of Welfare in Hanoverian England, 1723–1793*
Geoffrey Crossick *A History of London from 1800 to 1939*
Alistair Davies *Culture and Society, 1900–1995*
Martin Durham *The Permissive Society*
Peter Fleming *Medieval Family and Household England*
David Fowler *Youth Culture in the Twentieth Century*
Malcolm Gaskill *Witchcraft in England, 1560–1760*
Peter Gosden *Education in the Twentieth Century*
S. J. D. Green *Religion and the Decline of Christianity in Modern Britain, 1880–1980*

*Titles continued overleaf*

Please note that a sister series, *British History in Perspective*, is available which covers all the key topics in British political history.

# Race Relations in Britain Since 1945

Harry Goulbourne

First published in Great Britain 1998 by
**MACMILLAN PRESS LTD**
Houndmills, Basingstoke, Hampshire RG21 6XS and London
Companies and representatives throughout the world

A catalogue record for this book is available from the British Library.

ISBN 0–333–62114–X hardcover
ISBN 0–333–62115–8 paperback

First published in the United States of America 1998 by
**ST. MARTIN'S PRESS, INC.,**
Scholarly and Reference Division,
175 Fifth Avenue, New York, N.Y. 10010

ISBN 0–312–21583–5

Library of Congress Cataloging-in-Publication Data
Goulbourne, Harry.
Race relations in Britain since 1945 / Harry Goulbourne.
p.   cm. — (Social history in perspective)
Includes bibliographical references (p.        ) and index.
ISBN 0–312–21583–5 (cloth)
1. Great Britain—Race relations—History—20th century.   2. Great
Britain—Social conditions—1945–   I. Title.   II. Series.
DA125.A1G62   1998
305.8'00941—dc21                                          98–17282
                                                              CIP

This book is printed on paper suitable for recycling and made from fully managed and
sustained forest sources.

10   9   8   7   6   5   4   3   2   1
07   06   05   04   03   02   01   00   99   98

Printed in Hong Kong

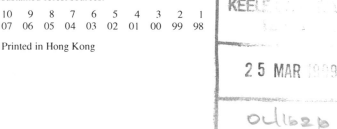

# Contents

*For SM*
*who, whilst suffering the chill of early wintry wakenings,*
*provided support*

# Acknowledgements

I wish to thank the many individuals who helped to make this book possible. These include Professor Jeremy Black, who kindly invited me to write the book for the series in which it now appears. Although we have never met, Jeremy has provided encouragement at the points when it was necessary and has exercised much patience over my varying delivery deadlines. My editors at Macmillan, Beverley Tarquini and Jonathan Reeve, provided me with useful critical comments from readers of my initial outline, revised outline and draft of the book; thanks are also due to these various unknown readers and to Valery Rose whose comments have helped to sharpen my thinking on, and presentation of, the subject discussed in this book. I am also grateful to my colleagues Harry Cowen and Ian Jones and their students for providing the opportunity to discuss aspects of relevant draft chapters. My managerial colleagues Dr Peter Noyes, Dr Peter Easy, Elaine Cutting and Paul Taylor have been generous in providing me with the time for completing this work. I am grateful to Ann Shaw and Beryl Pine-Coffin of the Centre for Research in Ethnic Relations, University of Warwick, for their help in finding my way around the invaluable collection they have assembled over the years. Chapter 6 draws upon research conducted by Veena Vasista under my direction during the academic year 1994/5 as part of a wider project, and I am grateful to Veena as well as all the individuals working in race relations research and policy who kindly discussed their work with her. I am particularly grateful to my colleague Professor Mary Chamberlain for her comments on the broad subject discussed here.

My special thanks to Selina Goulbourne for overall reading and criticism and for detailed comments and clarification of the legal situation in British race relations. I benefited from our sons' critical comments and pointed questions about much of what I took for granted, and from their newly acquired habit of coming home from apparently rigorous undergraduate life to do some work at their desks.

None the less, after taking account of the variety of influences which go into the completion of a book, I remain responsible for all the shortcomings as well as the views expressed in the discussion that follows.

# Preface

In a recent polemical article the political theorist Bernard Crick argued that because there 'is no such thing as race, only the destructive and false belief in the concept' it behoves us to 'throw the R-word away' (*New Statesman*, 18 November 1996, p. 49). Struck by Crick's certainty and by the brevity and sharpness of the piece rather than the force of the argument, I decided to use it as the basis of a discussion at a third-year sociology seminar on the notion of a field of race relations. The essential question was whether the notion of such a field of social and historical study is universally shared by social scientists and historians. To my surprise, most of the students agreed with Crick's position and turned on writers who, like me, are inclined to use the term, albeit with all the necessary qualifications. Like Crick, the students were of the view that there is no such thing as 'race', apart from the human race, and they therefore felt that the concept has no place in social life or explanatory value in sociological and historical analyses of human affairs. Moreover, like Crick the students suggested that by utilising the dangerous concept of race in national legislation and in popular and academic discourses, Parliament, campaigners for racial equality and academics contribute to the longevity of a palpable fallacy against which they purport to fight. By the end of the seminar I knew that there was a democratic majority of the group who opposed my argument and supported Crick and others who proffer a view that seems to me to run in the face of reality.

This reality is not that humanity can be properly divided into racial categories. Rather, it is that however false the claim to natural racial differentiation within the human species may be, it is a sociological fact that people's beliefs, attitudes and behaviour, as well as the socio-economic and political structures we establish, are informed by such differentiation. To say that this differentiation is merely perceptual is beside the point. After all, it is our perceptions which inform and significantly structure the forms of social action we engage in on a daily basis. It is not necessary to employ the argument by analogy to clarify the point. But for social analysts and historians not to seek to understand, and lawmakers not to legislate about, the relations which arise between groups of people perceived to be racially differentiated in a social order would be similar to saying that since men and women are all members of humanity their differential status and treatment in society are of no relevance. We know that this form of argument is absurd. But when it comes to racial differential status and treatment by society, it is a little surprising that it is often people who regard themselves to be socially and politically progressive who express the desire to bury their heads in the sand – perhaps because of their well-intentioned egalitarian hearts – and ignore what is painfully obvious to those who suffer the inequalities and the burden of racial differentiation. Groups and individuals placed on the deficit side of the racial or colour-line can have little sympathy with the absurdities of the supposed colour blindness on the part of those who, structurally if not through individual choice, benefit from being placed on the privileged side of the colour-line.

At the beginning of the twentieth century the distinguished African-American sociologist, intellectual and Pan-Africanist W. E. B. DuBois ended the second chapter of the most famous of his many books, *The Souls of Black Folk* (1903), with the prophetic words 'The problem of the twentieth century is the problem of the colour-line.' For a time in the 1980s the work of William Julius Wilson (1978) and others seemed to suggest that this was no longer the case, at least in the USA. But it is instructive that Bill Clinton, the last elected US president this century, also chose to stress in his Inaugural Address in January 1997 that the future of American society is still pivoted – notwithstanding significant changes over the last forty years or so – on the 'colour-line'.

The argument advanced here is that there are such things as race relations, and that in Britain these are best understood against a background of empire and decline and within a context of migration and the development of what is generally regarded as a British multi-cultural society. The stress is placed on post-World-War-Two migration from the colonies to the United Kingdom and the catalytic role black and brown people played in the process of Britain redefining her identity and place as a post-imperial nation-state. Thus, whilst the focus is on the last four or five decades, the background to the period is the colonial/imperial past which is larger than the story of Island Britain. The discussion is informed by what is not a popular view amongst those who would wish to argue that there have always been race relations in Britain. My general view is that whilst relations between different European groups or between different groups of white people gave rise to patterns of discrimination, the emergence of the notion of racial differentiation

and the subsequent race relations or relations between races arose out
of the dramatic contact and integration of Africans and Asians in the
world that Europe, and in this instance Britain, built. Some of the forms
of discrimination exercised against the Jews and the Irish were often as
vicious, and sometimes more so than those forms of discrimination and
oppression established by dominant whites (Anglo-Scots in the first
instance) against peoples of different pigmentation with origins in Africa and Asia through slavery, indentureship and colonialism. But, as
will be shown in Chapter 1, whilst exclusion on the basis of colour or
race shares much with exclusion on the basis of nationality, culture or
religion it may be a mistake to collapse them together, as is sometimes
done with the best of intentions. The point may be expressed in another
way: more often than not, attempts to collapse together all forms of injustice in society lie in the desire to effect a basis for unity of opposition
or resistance to oppression. Such unity is, of course, necessary and desirable, but it does not require analytical compromise.

Another potentially contentious underlying assumption here is that
this discussion is not a comprehensive or exhaustive account of British
race relations. As I suggest throughout the discussion that follows, the
impressive body of literature that has developed around a common set
of social problems generally described as race relations makes it unnecessary for another account setting out the empirical details of this sub-
field which have become fairly familiar to students, policy-makers and
others. Thus, whilst it is usual in books on British race relations to have
whole chapters on each of the more problematic areas of national life
such as education, employment, housing or the judicial system, in this
discussion these and other problem areas are treated in a single chapter.
Another example of a departure from normal practice is the relative
absence of an uninterrupted chronology of events, and I am aware that
for those who see history mainly in chronological terms this may be
unacceptable. My response is that the detailed chronicle of the emergence and development of the issues of British race relations may be
found elsewhere, and from time to time I point the enquiring reader in
the appropriate direction; the comparative bibliography at the end of
the book will also be useful to the newcomer to the subject as well as to
most who are well versed in British race relations from an exclusively
island perspective.

What this discussion offers is a broad view of a number of salient aspects of race relations as they have developed and the discussion sets
these within a wider context than has been the case in many recent studies of the British situation. To begin with, the sub-field of race relations

studies in Britain as elsewhere is multi-disciplinary in nature, and contributions to the understanding of these relations have come from sociology, politics, psychology, social geography, policy studies, literature,
and law as well as from history. Indeed, Chapter 6 is a discussion of how
this sub-field of study started in post-imperial Britain within the social
sciences, particularly sociology. This is an area awaiting further research. The discussion in  Chapter 1 highlights the multi-disciplinary
nature of race relations analysis. Drawing on discussions in sociology,
social anthropolology, and political analysis the chapter commences
the analysis of British race relations with a recognition that the definition of the sub-field is a matter of contestation. Chapter 2 draws largely
on the historical literature, but also on social geography and migration
studies to arrive at a general depiction of the imperial and post-imperial
backgrounds to contemporary British race relations theory and practice. There is here more than the usual genuflection to these aspects of
the background by a handful of writers who, unfortunately, have not
gone on to take the trouble to acquaint themselves with the relevant literature in the post-colonial world as they do with the writings of their
colleagues in Britain. In Chapter 4 I draw a distinction between long-
standing problems in race relations (such as education, employment
and housing) and what are relatively new problems (such as care for the
elderly, health issues and the adoption of children). The old problems
which characterised the period of immigration from the 1950s have not
been resolved, nor have they gone away. But different problems are
emerging as new minority ethnic groups are integrated into British society and problems of the multi-cultural society become more 'normal'
in the sense that the new minorities experience much the same problems as members of the indigenous population. Given the central role
that the law and Parliament have played in defining and determining
the scope of race relations, Chapter 5 concentrates on some of the
strengths and weaknesses of the law, principally the Race Relations Act
1976. This measure may now require overhauling, as lawyers and others have argued. It remains, however, to be seen whether in the last years
of the century the reforming New Labour government of Tony Blair
and Home Secretary Jack Straw will be as radical as the old Labour
government of Harold Wilson and Home Secretary Roy Jenkins who,
with his advisor Anthony Lester, had the farsightedness and courage to
tackle what some see as a major cancer of British society.

In the USA, President Clinton has highlighted the need for Americans of all colours to overcome the divide or cancer of the 'colour-line' as
the twentieth century comes to an end and a new millennium beckons

(see, for example, *The Times*, 16 June 1997, p. 13). This has been seen by some of his critics to be nothing more than a president in his second term groping for an issue over which to make a lasting mark on his country's history. But in this instance motive can be set aside if the desired result is achieved. Similarly, the vision of a multi-coloured society in which the colour-line is not the determinant factor in the pattern of relations between groups of people may be Utopian, but in British race relations a degree of this Utopian optimism may again need the support of the state at the highest level. The last chapter picks up, therefore, the general theme of this book, namely the need to see the patterns and direction of British race relations within a broad historical perspective.

HARRY GOULBOURNE

# 1   The Question of a Field of Race Relations

## Introduction

The inelegance with which we nearly always place the word race in inverted commas when writing about race relations illustrates our unease in dividing people into racial categories. This unease is a recognition that the social relations we describe as racial have been seen as highly problematic since the 1939–45 war against Nazi Germany. But our discomfiture is increasingly felt in an age of mass migration and the greater participation of nearly if not all countries and communities in the global economy. In Britain, the problematic of race and ethnic relations has spawned an impressive body of literature concerned with both academic and policy issues, and this corpus of literature may be said to set the parameters of the field of British race and ethnic relations. None the less, there still are surprisingly few attempts made to define a set of social relations which may be unambiguously designated as the field of race relations. Indeed, it often appears that the search for a definition of this field and its historical beginnings is a futile enterprise. The result is that commonsensical understandings and vague historical markers are the best we can hope for. The principal aim of this chapter is to suggest, therefore, what we have in mind when we speak about race relations and what these relations might mean in the historical and sociological contexts of post-imperial Britain.

## The Question of Definition

Despite the lack of specific definition, it is none the less a commonplace for people to speak about race or ethnic relations in somewhat unequivocal terms. In other words, we have come to think about race relations in much the same ways as we might think of industrial relations. However, when we speak of the relations that characterise the structural arrangements and social behaviour found in industry, we have in mind

1

something like the difficulties which inevitably emerge between employers and employees. Before the rise of employee ownership of shares or partnership in companies, it used to be easy to imagine what kinds of problems there were likely to be between employers and employees. We not incorrectly assumed that industrial relations had the potential to be conflictual or harmonious, because the relationship between employer and employee essentially was based on what Karl Marx described as the fundamentally irreconcilable interests of capital and labour. Despite the changes in ownership and control of capital that Dahrendorf (1959) spoke about long before the present complex situation regarding ownership and control, the structures of industrial relations may still be seen as means to ensure the necessary peaceful conditions for the production and exchange of goods. A product of capitalist modes of production and exchange of goods and services, industrial relations are not left entirely to the vagaries of individual interests or the invisible hand of the market that liberal economists spoke about in their attack on mercantilism at the beginning of the last century. Even regimes, such as the Conservative governments of Margaret Thatcher and John Major from 1979 to 1997, that are ideologically committed to non-intervention in economic relations, will employ the instruments of the state to set the terms on which competition takes place.

The notion of there being a structure of relations between people of different races does not have the relative straightforwardness that the concept of industrial relations implies. But we none the less tend to entertain notions of difference, conflict and reconciliation when we speak of relations between the races into which humanity is perceived to be divided, and to this extent there may be some resemblances between the two fields. Indeed, as we shall see in Chapter 5, there has developed in Britain a fairly clear structure of race relations law and management established by the state which in many respects parallels the structure of industrial relations. These identifiable structures of relations between groups of people deemed to be of different racial or ethnic backgrounds are generally taken to be the substance of race relations. In short, some people are wont to take for granted the existence of a field of race and ethnic relations, because for them it is self-evident not only that there are important racial differences, but also that biological differentiation denotes social, psychological and cultural differences. For people who hold such views it is relatively easy to proceed to describe specific structures and patterns of individual and collective behaviour as being the stuff of which race and ethnic relations in Britain are made. But there is considerable disagreement over the meaning of race relations and consequently there have been several attempts to define and clarify the field in Britain and elsewhere (see, for example, Rex, 1983; Rex and Mason, 1988; Schermerhorn, 1970; van den Berghe, 1967). It is not, of course, necessary to go through the large body of literature that has grown up around the subject. However, in order to convey the importance of questions about race and racism in the twentieth century generally and specifically in Britain during the last four or so de:ades, it is helpful briefly to highlight aspects of the discussion in the literature.

It may be useful to start with Michael Banton's suggestion that 'three major models of racial friction' (Banton, 1967, p. 7) have contributed to the understanding of race relations. One of the founding fathers of British race relations study, Banton outlines these models to be, first, the approach of race relations from the perspective of ideology; second, the concept of prejudice; and, third, the concept of discrimination (ibid., pp. 7–11). Each of these, he suggested, may be deployed to address different problems, such as colonial domination, anti-semitism and customary behaviour in a society. He correctly attributes the first approach to those Marxists who tend to see racism as an ideology advanced in the interests of the dominant capitalist class and racist behaviour (racialism) being promoted to the same class end. There is an abundance of examples in the literature on race relations in Britain (for example, Miles, 1989, 1993), but there are also those who attempt to construct a more nuanced Marxist approach (see, for example, Solomos and Back, 1994, 1995a and b). The concept of prejudice is sometimes used to account for forms of behaviour determined by preconceived and generalised notions about groups other than our own. Alport's work is often referred to as exemplifying this kind of approach (Allport, 1958). Finally, Banton suggests that discrimination, based on the notion of social relationships, may be for or against a social group, and is not necessarily reprehensible. About these three approaches he makes the following sensible observations and distinctions:

> Discrimination may be caused by other things than an attitude of prejudice. Prejudiced people do not give vent to their feelings in all situations; sometimes the possibility of punishment for doing so appears too threatening, and prejudice does not produce discrimination. Similarly, discriminators and prejudiced people often do not subscribe to a racist ideology, and people who do are not always prejudiced or likely to discriminate. The three factors are often associated in particular situations but they are in principle independent. (Banton, 1967, p. 9)

The late M. G. Smith also summarised the many theories of race relations in a similar manner: psychological or socio-psychological theories; race relations as the effects of economic order and motivation; and theories of race relations being determined by a universal principle. The first of these emphasise concepts of prejudice and discrimination and study individual motivations and opinions of one group about another. The second category of writers are likely to emphasise race relations as relations of inequality and colonial exploitation, ignoring other examples of these situations. Under the 'universal principle' category Smith grouped the work of van den Berghe on the socio-biology of race, Banton's rational choice theory, and Park's race relations cycle (Smith, 1988, p. 199). I will return to some of these writers and their theories later in this discussion.

At this point it is important to note that the understanding of race and ethnic relations as being based on, or arising from, actual racial difference was rejected by most biologists in the years after World War Two. It was entirely appropriate for biologists to do so, because from the late nineteenth century they had been largely responsible for propagating the notion that there are fundamental differences between groups of people so that they constituted different races. There was something of a dialectical relationship between, first, Charles Darwin's theory of human biological evolution; second, the emergence and development of social Darwinism in the late nineteenth and early twentieth centuries as propagated largely through the organistic sociology of Herbert Spencer (see Spencer, 1967, 1972) in Britain, and in the USA the more culturally understood sociology of William Sumner (see, Sumner, 1959, 1963); and, finally, the rejection of this mode of thought in the aftermaths of World War Two. The rejection of biological racism, however, came only after there was a clear and unambiguous demonstration of the large-scale destruction to which the ideology of racial difference could lead. The fascist experience under Adolf Hitler in Germany in the 1930s and 1940s, which resulted in the annihilation of millions of Jews and other vulnerable minorities, such as travellers, and World War Two engulfing Europe, led to UNESCO in the 1960s providing leadership in debunking the notion of race as a scientific concept (Ashley, 1972; Rex, 1983). Largely because the Holocaust occurred in Europe, and partly because the struggles for human rights had been greatly advanced by the 1950s – particularly in European colonies in Africa, Asia and the Caribbean – racialist ideas lost their official intellectual, pseudo-scientific and political sanctions.

But when the ideology of race was used, albeit without scientific sanction, from the seventeenth to the nineteenth centuries to justify mass annihilation of indigenous peoples in what are today the Americas, there was little understanding on the part of dominant Europeans that the logic of racialism could be dangerous. Indeed, before the pretension of scientific sanction of racism, leading Christian denominations provided the necessary justifications for racist thought and practice, as in the case of the enslavement of West Africans in the Caribbean and the Americas from the seventeenth century. The eventual abolition of the slave trade in 1807 and Emancipation in 1838–40 in the British empire were, as Williams (1964) argued, more the outcomes of the realisation that slavery was uneconomical and the emergence of *laissez-faire* economic philosophy, than the result of philanthropic action. Thus, whilst the speeches and activities of William Wilberforce and his fellow abolitionists were important in the abolition of slavery, anti-mercantalist economic arguments such as Adam Smith's influential *The Wealth of Nations*[1] constituted a powerful blow to the system.

But historically and sociologically the earlier religious and the later pseudo-scientific justifications of ideologies of racial superiority and inferiority between groups of human beings played out a political drama in the heart of Europe. This occurred at a historical conjuncture when Europe was in imperial decline. Once biologists decreed that the so-called racial differences between groups are of far less significance than the overwhelming similarities between them, racialism lost a powerful ally. This might not have meant much, but for the combination of historical factors: European decline at the point of the continent's most dramatic demonstration of the dangers of racialism in the late 1930s and early 1940s; the emergence of two, in many ways dissimilar, world powers, the USA and the USSR, with differing ideologies that both proclaimed to varying degrees the right of self-determination and anti-racism (provided the realisation of these aspirations were not too close to home); and, finally, the demand throughout the colonial world for political independence. These developments delivered what amounted to a major blow to both the validity of the concept and the practice of European racial superiority, and therefore to the notion that one group of humanity is superior to others and has an inalienable right politically to rule other groups and socially dominate them.

There is no suggestion here that racism is exclusive to Europe or to the expansion and export of European institutions and practices to other parts of the world. It is common knowledge that racialist ideas of superiority and inferiority exist in very many societies from China to Russia to Africa and elsewhere, and there is no need to argue the point here. In other words, the strong view found in both popular and sociological discussions that 'Britain is a racist society', implying that other societies are not, is highly ahistorical and does not make sociological sense. Racism is not uniquely British, European or American. With respect to relations between different groups of human beings, the difference with European world expansion was the accompanying idea – powerfully supported by what the late Thomas Kuhn (1970) would have called 'conventional' or 'ordinary science' – that the white groups of humanity were innately superior to others. But the strength and longevity of European ideas globally during the last three or so centuries warrant these observations and give continuing force to them even as we approach what may be seen as the end of the Euro-American century.

Racist or racialist ideas have not lost their hold on individuals and society. To be sure, the idea of racial difference has been used positively to suggest human variety and resource. Indeed, to a degree and as we will see later in this chapter, notions of racial and cultural pluralism as expressed in the ideology of multi-culturalism celebrate racial difference. It has even been suggested that there is a certain romance in the activity of categorising people along racial lines (Allen, 1971, p. x). As we approach the end of the twentieth century, and the memories of the Holocaust and World War Two fade, revisionist historians and neo-fascists in Europe are propagating the idea of racial difference as the significant indicator of the place and worth of different groups of people. The importance, therefore, of race in human affairs during the modern period from the seventeenth century, but particularly during the nineteenth and twentieth centuries, cannot be overstressed.

Ideas of racial difference and the usual accompanying notion of superiority and inferiority, existed before they had their pseudo-scientific justifications. They have existed and are likely to continue long after losing such justifications. Moreover, for some social scientists the differences signalled by phenotype (observable physical variations in colour, shape and structure) indicate real, fundamental, variations which they continue to express as racial division. For example, M. G. Smith was of the view that there are indeed distinct, immutable races into which humankind are divided. For him, races were 'those varieties of mankind characterised by distinctive sets of gross heredity phenotypical features' (Smith, 1988, p. 190). Race relations for Smith were therefore those relations that exist between peoples of different 'racial stocks', such as between Africans and Europeans in the West, and as an anthropologist he distinguished between Negroes, Asiatic Mongols, Caucasians, Australian Aborigines, Amerindians, Pygmies, Bushmen and others. Smith's point should not be confused with the theories of racialists who hold that such differences make for superiority and inferiority, and he stressed that

> There have never been any 'pure' races since raciation – the process by which races evolve, change and come into being – is an essential aspect of human evolution and proceeds within isolated populations as well as by miscegenation. (Smith, 1988, p. 189)

Ethnic relations Smith defined as relations between people of the same racial group but 'who feel themselves, and are felt by others, to differ ethnically by virtue of their differing descent and culture' (ibid., p. 190). There are several situations in which racial and ethnic differences occur simultaneously, as among Europeans and different racial groups of Africans in that continent. The tendency by sociologists to collapse together racial and ethnic relations was unacceptable to Smith, and he viewed the biologists' rejection of the concept of race to be purely ideological because they cannot dismiss the physical differences that obtain between groups of people born to different parents. He argued that the replacement of 'biological race' with 'sociological race' not only leads to confusion but also defies the obvious in nature and human society, because different groups do not beget children of another kind but reproduce themselves in much the same ways as other species in the animal world.

History and social science cannot, therefore, ignore the obvious physical differences between groups of humanity; what the historian and social theorist should reject is the view that such differences denote differences in value or equality and that such natural differences connote superiority and inferiority between groups of people. Even less can social science ignore the sociological fact that people and the institutions they construct around social beliefs and action continue to distinguish between human groups in terms of racial and ethnic categories. What groups of people believe about their relations with other groups of people cannot be dismissed as unimportant, or being what some Marxists and others would describe as merely ideological. People do act on their beliefs and such collective behaviour is part and parcel of the structure of social action. Even so, it is an important aspect of the value system of the liberal or radical social scientist that the belief about so-called racial difference is an insufficient starting point from which to describe social reality. This is fairly well established in much of what may be taken to be British race relations theory and practice historically and contemporaneously. Colour and other physical variations do present external and visible differences, but among most liberal and radical historians and social theorists these are not taken to be differences in the value or worth attributed to people.

This position apparently is strongly held amongst Marxists. From Karl Marx's analysis of what he saw as the antagonism between owners of capital and workers who have to sell their labour in order to make a living, it has been variously argued that race relations are an ideological construction by the capitalist classes to enable the easier exploitation of workers, the creators of surplus value. In this view, racism has been constructed in order to hide the fundamental contradiction between capital and labour by the capitalist class. Perhaps the most well-known general statement of this view is Oliver Cromwell Cox's *Caste, Class and Race* (1959). Cox examined relations between black and white people in the United States and compared the situation there with that of the caste system in India. His conclusions were that as restricted and unacceptable as relations between black and white groups were, a situation of class rather than caste obtained in the USA. Whereas the caste system was broadly accepted in India, black people did not accept their subordinate position in the American social order. Myrdal (1944) had argued a few years earlier that white Americans could not reconcile black exclusion with the tenets of American democracy. For Cox, race relations arose as a result of colonialism and slavery in the Americas, because groups of people were exploited for their labour power on the basis of their perceived race. In this view, capitalist exploitation of labour power is intertwined with racial domination and subordination. It is assumed that this may be taken to constitute the legitimate concerns of people who want to understand those matters generally described as race relations. Clearly, Cox is referring here to just one of several historical situations. And whilst for the discussion about British race relations it is this historical context that is of overwhelming relevance, it is a mistake to assume that all race and ethnic relations can be confined to those between black and white in the Anglo-American world.

In Britain, the work of Robert Miles is perhaps the best example of an extended and elaborate attempt to deny that from a Marxist position there can be a field or sociology of race relations. Miles contends that the 'use of "race" (and "race relations") as analytical concepts disguises the social construction of difference, presenting it as somehow inherent in the empirical reality of observable or imagined biological difference' (Miles, 1993, p. 48). Miles sees the aim of his Marxism therefore to 'deconstruct' race and separate it from 'racism', but, the language aside, this is no more or less than what most liberal and even conservative post-World-War-Two social scientists, from whom Miles wishes to distinguish himself, seek to do. The tendency to reduce the historical experiences of Africans and capital in the West to a merely imagined situation is indeed reification and mystification of an order that would make Georg Frederick Hegel's idealist philosophy look like crude empiricism.

If I understand this line of reasoning, it would appear that the interesting aspect of the argument arises from one reading of Marx's analysis of surplus value[2]. But the attempt to understand race relations from this point in Marx's work shows the limitation, not the relevance, of the theory of surplus value to the analysis of those social relations we generally regard as having to do with groups of people distinguished by racial or ethnic differentiation. Marx's theory of surplus value is set out in the first volume of his seminal work, *Capital*, and is premised on the view that the free worker who freely sells his labour power to the capitalist produces surplus value that is taken from him in a situation of equality. In the free market place, where the capitalist and the labourer first meet in Marx's account, a contract is entered into by free agents, but the amount that the labourer produces is more than had been bargained for by the parties. This surplus is appropriated by the capitalist and, for Marx, this act of appropriation defines exploitation of the worker. The extent to which the labourer produces surplus is the extent to which the capitalist is increasing his rate of exploitation/surplus, but this is also dependent on other factors as other volumes of *Capital* go on to show. The vital elements in this model of capitalist relations are freedom (of both labour and capital); contracts openly arrived at in a situation of apparent equality; the exclusive ownership of capital by one party and the ownership of only labour power by the other; and the alienation of this labour power by the labourer when it is sold. The labourer's freedom is only partial, because his only means of livelihood is his labour power; he is divorced from the land and ownership of any means of production.

In some Marxist analyses, this simple model, or ideal type, that Marx devised to illustrate the exploitative relationship between capital and labour is transformed into a dogma. The dogma holds that since slaves were, by definition, unfree labourers they did not produce surplus and, by extension, there was no exploitation involved in the relationship. Hindess and Hurst (1975) went to some lengths to demonstrate this thesis, describing slavery in the Caribbean as a pre-capitalist mode of production and, whilst there is no acknowledgement of Hindess and Hurst, this appears to be Miles' view too. The historical fact that slave labour in the Caribbean provided Britain with the necessary capital to fuel the Industrial Revolution, as Williams (1964) argued, counts for nothing in this mechanistic deployment of Marx. Of equal importance to Williams' work is that of Sidney Mintz who pointed out that the rational organisation of labour on a large-scale, that became characteristic of capitalist production, first occurred in the production of sugar in the Caribbean during slavery (Mintz, 1993; Mintz and Price, 1992). Moreover, through this large-scale production of commodities for the European market, Africans in the Caribbean became the first people in the modern world to be effectively divorced from pre-capitalist social relations or traditions. This was not a matter of choice. The slave trade and slavery were amongst the most barbaric and inhumane systems constructed in the modern age (see, for example, Elkins, 1963) and the Western world has still not addressed this aspect of its recent past which remains an essential element of the present.[3]

These historical facts are a problem for Marxist theory. Some Marxists are willing to recognise this whilst others believe that the model or ideal type, which was constructed to explain the phenomenon of the rise of modern capitalism, is itself the phenomenon. Not unlike religious sects, this latter kind of Marxists struggles to force sociological fact to fit preconceived notions of the past and conspires to arrest, or freeze, history. Since for this kind of Marxist, as slaves fail to qualify as free labourers then their labour was not exploited. The conclusion drawn by Miles is that there is no basis for a sociology of race relations. But, of course, Marx's theory could be equally taken to suggest that since the capitalist comes to own the very labour power of the individual, the early capitalist enjoyed the highest rate of surplus from each producer under slavery. But Marx saw legal and political rights to be important for the capitalist market place to function; for the individual divorced from the land and deprived of any other independent means of a livelihood, the only thing that remains to the individual, as Marx puts it, is his hide to take to market. Under plantation slavery in the Caribbean the early capitalist dispensed with these rights and enjoyed the total surplus. Of course, this suggestion would be rejected by any self-respecting Marxist familar with *Capital.* After all, the plantation capitalist had to care for his slave as part of what Marx would have called 'fixed capital', and this meant being directly responsible for reproducing the slave's labour power.[4] The point here, however, is that suggestive as Marx's model of capitalist relations may be, the labour theory of value of itself does not explain the historical facts of plantation slavery in the Caribbean and North America.

There has, therefore, long been a dissenting Marxist view from the dogmatic and uncreative Marxism which appears to see its main tasks as being to place Europe's historical experience, particularly that of the working classes, in a position of privilege over the experiences of other peoples. The dissenting view holds that whilst class may be an enormously important variable in the relations between groups in capitalist societies, class analysis does not adequately account for domination on the basis of a real or an ascribed racial identity. This has been true for Cox's work, but particularly so in the thinking of those activists who sought to apply Marx's social and political theories in a creative manner to the situations of exploitation and domination of black people in the Western world. During the period of black radicalism in the late 1960s and early 1970s, in both the USA and Britain, many black spokespersons stressed this view; they argued that in the Western world, and particularly in predominantly white Anglo-American societies, racists regard colour difference as a basis for superiority and inferiority and as a basis for the more effective exploitation of labour (Hall *et al.*, 1978). Following the influential work of Hamilton and Carmichael (1967) radicals argued that although black individuals in Britain and North America experience individual acts of racism, it is the institutional nature of racism that is more pestiferous.[5] Consequently, as Hamilton and Carmichael argued, the individual black person can often find that their progress is not unhindered by their colour; it is their group or community that is discriminated against. At the level of more systematic general social theory, M. G. Smith's notion of differential incorporation is of relevance in understanding the political sociology of race relations in the context being discussed here. Before, considering Smith's work however, I want, first, to turn to the typologies presented by Park and Rex, and, second, outline my own understanding of ethnic mobilisation and relate these to multi-culturalism, pluralism and corporation theories.

## Race Relations 'Cycle' and 'Situations' in Park and Rex

Long before race relations became a field of study in Britain, Robert Park's work in the USA had suggested an approach to the subject. As he stated in his brief autobiographical note, his interest in sociology started with a reading of Goethe's *Faust*; like Faust, Park wanted to see the world. His work as a journalist had enabled him to see the world, particularly cities, and he came to believe that sociology was what he called the 'big news', that is 'the long-term trends which recorded what is actually going on rather than what, on the surface of things, merely seems to be going on' (Park, 1950, p. ix). Already in the 1920s, when racialist ideas enjoyed great respectability, Park developed a progressive, if over-optimistic, theory of race relations based on what he and his collaborator, Ernest Burgess, called a 'race relations cycle'. This involved four processes or basic components: contacts, competition, accommodation and eventual assimilation. Park argued that contacts between what he could only see as races, lead to competition through to accomodation between the races and then assimilation.[6] He suggested that where distinct races become aware of their differences and where people develop racial consciousness, race relations exist. Where, however, as in Brazil, there were several races but no consciousness of racial differences, there were no race relations to speak of. In other words, the mere existence of different racial groups does not denote a situation of race relations.

Park suggested two levels of understanding race relations. In the first place there is the sense in which 'the expression race relations seems to describe merely the sentiments and attitudes which racial contacts invariably provoke and for which there is, apparently, no more substantial basis than an existing state of the public mind' (Park, 1950, p. 82). Frequently when we speak of race relations in Britain, it is this general sense of the term that we have in mind. But there need not be any view that contact between groups will 'invariably provoke', as Park thought and as many politicians and public figures in British life suggest whenever issues about minority ethnic communities are discussed.

The second level of understanding race relations, and of far greater significance, involves a

> wider universe of discourse, in which it includes all the relations that ordinarily exist between members of different ethnic and generic groups which are capable of provoking race conflict and race consciousness or of determining the relative status of the racial groups of which a community is composed.   (Park, 1950, p. 82)

This inclusive definition of race relations involves a wide range of situations, including what Park described as 'all those situations in which some relatively stable equilibrium between competing races has been achieved and in which the resulting social order has become fixed in custom and tradition' (ibid.). For him, the notion of race relations also encompassed, first, 'relations which are not now conscious or personal, though they have been' in the past, and, second, 'relations which are fixed in and enforced by the custom, convention, and the routine of an expected social order of which there may be at the moment no very lively consciousness' (ibid., p. 83). His work is replete with historical examples of the first in Europe and elsewhere, although his primary concern was with the situation in the United States between Europeans and Africans.

Park correctly observed that groups naturally seek to preserve their distinct identities, the actual or perceived traits which separate or differentiate, but he believed that in a democratic social order where ties of the market are more important for the individual than ties of kinship, groups would lose their distinctiveness. He saw this as part of the process whereby 'civilisation, not merely here but elsewhere, has evolved, drawing into the circle of its influence an ever widening circle of races and peoples' (ibid., p. viii). What most social scientists and biologists would today see as Park's mistaken acceptance of distinct races of humanity should not distract from what would then have been a progressive view, namely, that although he expected that contact between different groups of people would lead to conflict, he also believed that assimilation – then considered a desirable goal of social policy – would be the eventual result, and presumably minimise conflict on the basis of racial difference. This was an over-optimistic or naive view of the development of race relations in the USA and on a world scale. After all, the confidence he and others had in the market, or Marx had in capitalism as a mode of production, to do away with traditional life and work was misplaced, even although the economy has become increasingly global and integrated.

It is interesting that although John Rex's influential typology of 'a race relations situation' is similar to Park's 'cycle of race relations', Rex made no mention of Park's work in this respect. But instead of making any comparison and before pointing to the strengths and weaknesses of Rex's model, it is worth reminding ourselves of the specific characteristics he outlined as being essential to 'a race relations situation'. In the 1970 edition of his book, *Race Relations in Sociological Theory*, he defines a race relations situation to be where three elements are present:

(i) a situation of differentiation, inequality and pluralism as between groups; (ii) the possibility of clearly distinguishing between such groups by their physical appearance, their culture or occasionally merely by their ancestry; (iii) the justification and explanation of this discrimination in terms of some kind of implicit or explicit theory, frequently but not always of a biological kind.   (Rex, 1983, p. 30)

These features of a race relations situation were differently stated in the 1983 edition of his book, thus:

(i) that it was a necessary but not sufficient condition of a race relations situation that there should be a situation of severe competition, exploitation, coercion or repression; (ii) that this situation occurred between groups rather than individuals, with only limited possibilities of mobility from one group to the other; (iii) that the intergroup structure so produced was rationalised at the ideological level by means of a deterministic theory of human attributes, of which the most important type historically had been based upon biological and genetic theory.    (Rex, 1983, p. viii)

Elsewhere in the text and in other essays Rex has elaborated this depiction of a field of race relations, but has also sensibly pointed out that this typology is only tentative and open to discussion. His approach is posited as a comprehensive coverage of a range of situations including colonial, frontier, free and unfree labour conditions, cultural diversity, closure, the metropolis and so forth. After a masterly coverage of some relevant literature, Rex concluded that he had demonstrated 'there is a distinct field of race relations studies' (ibid., p. 160). The reputation that his model has enjoyed since publication points to its utility to students who have tried to understand race relations in Britain, and I can see how it may be useful in conceptualising a field of race relations. First, it points clearly to the situation of inequality and competition between groups; second, Rex himself points out that he was not attempting a general theory, but attempting to construct a model with limited possibilities; third, whilst not abandoning class analysis, the model goes beyond a formal class approach to racial and ethnic inequality, a point which had long been understood by radical black spokespersons in Britain and the USA (see, for example, Cleaver, 1968; Jackson, 1970, 1972; Newton, 1974; Sivanandan, 1991). Perhaps the strongest aspect of the model, however, is its attempt to delimit or demarcate a space in sociology which is occupied by race relations, and this is more limited than, say, that suggested by Park. Additionally, this sub-area of race relations intertwines with other social relations, such as class or social stratification, but is not limited to them. Rex intended that his model should contribute to further discussion and development and, indeed, he himself in responding to some of his critics appears to withdraw from aspects of his original position. This is particularly so with respect to his sharp distinction between colonial and metropolitan social stratification which critics poited out (Rex, 1983, pp. 163, 167).

Useful as this model may have been in encouraging scholars to look at the colonial and imperial backgrounds to British race relations – which is rarely done – there are a number of drawbacks to the 'race relations situation' model, which makes it less useful than is often implied. In the first place, although Rex intended his model to be limited in scope, his coverage of the colonial and imperial backgrounds tended to be too general and too devoid of historical content. For example, the generalities about post-Columbian Caribbean societies rendered his comments ahistorical and unnecessarily abstract; I doubt whether Caribbean historians would recognise much about the region in Rex's race relations situation. This absence of historical content led Rex to draw too sharp a distinction between the colonies and the metropolitan centres in the model; in seeking to correct this, in his response to critics, Rex contradicted his earlier statement, as indicated above Another of Rex's responses to his critics is that he is a political sociologist, not a political economist, and whilst this is a fair reply, the response does not answer the question his model raises, namely, the nature of the economies in the kinds of societies he places at opposite poles – colonial and metropolitan. After all, there have been major and accessible debates about Caribbean political economy[7] and it would not be unfair to expect a major sociologist to be aware of them, particularly if there is an ambition to construct or contribute to a general model of a set of social relations.

But perhaps the major weakness of the model, particularly in terms of this discussion of race relations in Britain, is its inability to take account of change. The model is static, and therefore of little use in trying to understand the changes that have occurred over the last four or more decades in post-imperial Britain. Nor was it of much use in understanding change in the imperial world. The model's disregard for history aside, it is difficult to understand how change may occur. Despite the obvious weaknesses of Park's optimistic evolutionary 'race relations cycle', at least it has at its centre a perspective of history and of change, which the 'race relations situation' lacks.

I want, however, to pick up a point from Rex's first element, namely, 'a necessary but not sufficient condition of a race relations situation that there should be a situation of severe competition, coercion or repression'. I have suggested elsewhere (Goulbourne, 1997) that it is when groups are in situations of competition over scarce resources, feel threatened by others or wish to maintain a position of dominance, that there may be an appeal to ethnic or racial affinity. In other words, it may be suggested that even where Rex's third condition does not obtain, his first condition, although not sufficient, may be the crucial criterion for the relations between groups to become conflictual and therefore of interest to race or ethnic relations analysts. For example, it is more likely to be the case that one group subjugates another (as a result of competition in, say, war) before the ideology of superiority and inferiority is constructed. So-called scientific racist ideologies of European superiority over other groups of humanity would appear to have been developed some time after subjugation of the Americas, the commencement of the slave trade, and the conquests of Africa and vast tracks of Asia. Indeed, as noted earlier, the heyday of this racist ideology in the late nineteenth century and first half of the twentieth, coincided with the apex and decline of Europe and empire.

### The Mobilisation of Ethnicity

It is appropriate to suggest at this point that it is the mobilisation of ethnic or racial affinity that is becoming of central interest to historians and political sociologists, irrespective of the socio-political and economic contexts in which mobilisation arises. Where Rex's conditions obtain, we are more likely to have this mobilisation, but mobilisation can occur elsewhere with almost equal ease. We might take it for granted that in all human communities there has been at one time or another a mixture of Rex's three elements of a race relations situation, or what Park described as 'relations which are not now conscious or personal, though they have been' so in the past (Park, 1950, p. 83). Although time and the migration of groups may have eroded memories of unequal relationships, these may be relatively easily evoked and may become centrepieces for mobilisation along perceived or actual ethnic or racial lines, which in an increasingly global world order, need not take account of national boundaries.

It is necessary to say what is meant by the mobilisation of ethnic or racial affinity, and to relate this aspect of the discussion to the context of British race and ethnic relations. Ethnic mobilisation involves leaders seeking to transform into political currency those social and natural characteristics generally regarded as defining an ethnic or racial group. The political currency so created is for use in the political marketplace of competition. I take this notion of political currency from the work of Karl Deutsch, who argued that a political system operates, like an economic system, with currencies (Deutsch, 1968, pp. 118–27). Unlike the economic system, political currencies, such as confidence in a government or the vote, are only partly quantifiable. But the state's use of fiscal policy, paper money, gold, credit and taxation are paralleled by the state's asssurance of the individual's security and guarantee of citizenship rights through the use or threat of the use of force. The state, in other words, can depend on what Jeremy Bentham, the founder of utilitarian philosophy in the early nineteenth century, called the citizens' disposition to obey the law, which in his view had been initially established through force.

This notion of political currency is relevant in two ways to the discussion of ethnic or racial mobilisation. First, the mobilisation of ethnicity or racial affinity to achieve ends is a political phenomenon. Whilst the fact of ethnic or racial affinity of itself may be of considerable interest to the anthropologist, for the political sociologist concerned about race and ethnic relations, such affinity becomes of prime interest at the point of mobilisation; that is to say when ethnic affinity is transformed into an interest like other kinds of interests connected to market relations. Marx, Park, and others who believed that the apparently individualised relations of the market would lead to the abolition of ethnic or traditional solidarity did not foresee that groups would be able to use the market so that it responds to collective as well as individual demands, and thereby becomes less than the revolutionary or progressive force they envisaged. Where the market, or capitalism as a whole, has been progressive, it has not been so in the ways envisaged by these and other visionaries. As an overarching system or determinant of change in modern societies, the market has been at once more pliable and accommodating with regard to traditional values than had been expected by the construction of such ideal types as traditionalism and modernity.

None the less, where different groups of people share the same territory, owe loyalty to the same political authority (the state), and participate and compete in the same market, there are already a number of meeting points between them. This is contrary to the social and cultural pluralist theory advanced by Furnivall (1948) and developed by M. G. Smith (1965), where they contend that such groups meet but do not mix or combine. In his argument against diffusionist theories of culture in Africa, Malinowski (1961) suggested that the meeting of European industrial and urban culture and African rural and traditional culture in industrial settings was creating a new culture which could not simply be taken to be 'a migration of elements or traits from one culture to another' (p.18). He argued that dynamic culture-change as a result of culture-contact could not be 'easily invoiced back to place of origin' (p. 21); rather, culture-contact resulted in a 'clash and interplay of the two cultures [and] produce[d] new things' (p. 25). Clearly, here Malinowski under plays what another anthropologist Herskovits (1970) called 'retentions' of cultural traits when speaking of the movement of West Africans to the

Americas. Another way of looking at this, however, is to say that Herskovits' point can hide the significance of the stress that Malinowski placed on culture-change as a result of culture-contact. But, of course, we must recognise that these men had different objectives: one was concerned with change and the other with retention after significant cultural transformation or change had occurred.

Similarly, Frederich Barth's (1969) influential encouragement to fellow anthropologists to concentrate on boundary maintenance between groups when assessing the importance or relevance of ethnicity, may also have shifted attention from Malinowski's point that culture-contact results in culture-change. Malinowski was speaking about a colonial situation in which, as M. G. Smith stressed, the state played a predominant role. The state was also dictatorial. Even so, change occurred. In an open and democratic society such as contemporary Britain where the state refrains from too strong an intervention in the affairs of civil society and the state is in turn constrained by civil society, the potential for culture-change in Malinowski's sense of the term should be greater than in a colonial society. Rex's remarkably static or ahistoric model of a 'race relations situation' cannot account for such potential change as a result of the various meeting points of metropolitan and colonial societies and peoples. Park's notion of a cycle of race relations, despite weaknesses, involved change, even where we are likely to disagree with his goal of assimilation and demonstrate a healthy scepticism about his confidence in a civilising mission.

The second point to be made about ethnic mobilisation as a political currency is that such mobilisation registers an unusual, not an everyday, occurance. After all, neither a person's, or a group's, ethnicity is permanently placed on alert to be asserted against other ethnicities and solidarities. Basic social institutions such as family, household, and kinship groups as well as public institutions such as religion and schools, provide the basis for the natural and public reproduction of the main patterns or characteristics of ethnicity or racial affinity. Ethnic mobilisation invokes images of assertion, outrage, attack, defence, fight, drama and, at one end of the spectrum of mobilisation, the ultimate image of war (Goulbourne, 1997). The ends, therefore, to which ethnic mobilisation may be directed are necessarily varied - sometimes it may be to defend the identity or survival of a group against others, at other times ethnic mobilisation may be the deliberate promotion of an already dominant group over more vulnerable groups. West European colonialism from the sixteenth century outside Europe and Russification in Europe and Asia under the Romanoffs in the nineteenth century and

the Communists after Stalin's ascendency from 1924, are clear examples of dominant groups mobilising their ethnicities to dominate
groups already subordinated.

But ethnic mobilisation is not the exclusive prerogative of either
majority or minority groups who share membership of the modern
nation-state; it is a currency available to any group, although utilised for
different ends. Such utilisation depends on the socio-political and economic situations in which groups find themselves in their relationships
with each other. These relationships may be those suggested by Rex's
typology of a 'race relations situation', but in a world in which ethnicity
is a universal currency these relationships include others which may
appear to be less conflictual at first sight. I have suggested elsewhere
(Goulbourne, 1991a, especially p. 58) that ethnic mobilisation involves
action across a spectrum and is dependent on prevailing circumstances.
At the end of the spectrum where social action demands that community
(ethnic/racial group) should be coterminous with political authority (the
state) we have ethnic nationalism. But at other points along the conti-
nuum the mobilisation of ethnicity becomes of interest to the political
sociologist because ethnicity has been politicised. This utilisation of
ethnicity develops into what Schattschnieder (1960) called the 'mobilisation of bias' in situations of inevitable conflict over ends in a democratic
society where there are conflicting interests.

My suggestion here is that mobilised ethnicity becomes a political
currency in the socio-political marketplace. Additionally, in such circumstances ethnicity or racial affinity is transformed into an interest,
not totally dissimilar to other interests which contend in the market,
namely, class, regional, gender, generational or professional interests.
The anthropologist Clifford Geertz's (1963) definition of ethnicity
conflated racial and ethnic characteristics when he described ethnicity
as 'the congruities of blood, speech, custom and so on'. But the important point about his statement is his contention that these congruities
take precedence over merely 'personal attraction, tactical necessity, common interest or incurred moral obligation' (Geertz, 1963, p. 109).
The point could be pressed further to suggest that the mobilisation of
ethnicity converts Geertz's primordial congruities into a political interest. A typical and recent example of this has been the mobilisation of
Serbian, Croat, Muslim and other ethnicities in the former Yugoslavia.
Another example is the mobilisation of Hutu and Tutsi ethnicities in the
central African states of Burundi and Rwanda. There are, of course,
plenty of other dramatic examples in the post-Cold-War years since
1989 (see, for example, Goulbourne, 1997), or indeed within the UK,

particularly Ulster, for most of the present century. This mobilisation of
ethnicity may be a bid to participate or limit participation in the politics
and decision-making processes of a society in which there are several
competing groups, or groups in a situation of equilibrium, as Park suggested.

But ethnic mobilisation is a two-edged sword: the mobilisation of one
ethnicity is more than likely to stimulate another ethnicity, suggesting
that there are limits to ethnic mobilisation because most societies con-
sist of several groups sharing common allegiance to a single political
authority, the nation-state. Perhaps more importantly for this discussion about race and ethnic relations in multi-racial, multi-ethnic societies, is that ethnic mobilisation has the potential to stunt the dynamic of
culture-contact by directing social action to what Barth called boundary maintenance. Moreover, ethnic mobilisation can push to one side
or even destroy the emergence of a new culture which is likely to be
fragile at its beginning. In such a situation, ethnic or racial solidarity, as
political currency, is likely to become more acceptable because of the
relative ease with which ethnicity can be mobilised and the great difficulty involved in standing against its inexorable logic. As political currency, ethnicity is available to any group, convertible in almost any
circumstance, and has its own justification.

In the British context, the mobilisation of ethnicity as a political currency within the majority autochthonous population led to mobilisation by new minorities in national life. Of course, when compared with
societies in which ethnicity is in a state of constant mobilisation, Britain
is relatively free of this phenomenon. On a spectrum indicating intens-
ity of ethnic mobilisation Britain would be relatively low. None the
less, as we will see in a later chapter, the mobilisation of majority ethnic
solidarity has stimulated new minorities to become aware of themselves as distinct communities and in turn this has led to their active
participation in political affairs.

But at this point I want to turn to the related question of multi-
culturalism, which has become the central ideological principle of British race and ethnic relations, and which is relevant to the discussion
over mobilisation.

The principles and aspirations of multi-culturalism have been variously advanced as providing the way forward for a heterogeneous
post-imperial British society. Multi-culturalism as ideology is now a commonplace and is almost univerally accepted. It was, however, a political decision enunciated by Roy (now Lord) Jenkins as Home Secretary
in Harold Wilson's first Labour government from 1964. In a speech to

the National Committee for Commonwealth Immigrants on 23 May 1966, Jenkins declared that he would 'define integration not as a flattening process of assimilation but as equal opportunity, accompanied by cultural diversity in an atmosphere of mutual tolerance' (Jenkins, 1967, p. 267). The principle embodied in this statement has been reiterated by a variety of public and private sector organisations, all declaring, in one way or another, that the aim of integration into British society is not what obtained until the late 1960s, namely assimilation, but a new pluralism bred of tolerance. In particular, education documents are replete with the statement, but they are also found in documents pertaining to health, housing, policing – in short, in nearly all areas of public life. It was the Swann Committee, however, reporting in 1985 that elaborated Jenkin's statement, and may be taken as the classic formulation of the aspirations for the multi-cultural society in Britain. Swann (1985, p.5) asserted that

> a multi-cultural society such as ours would in fact function most effectively and harmoniously on the basis of pluralism which enables, expects and encourages members of all ethnic groups, both minority and majority, to participate fully in shaping the society as a whole within a framework of commonly accepted values, practices and procedures, whilst also allowing and, where necessary, assisting the ethnic minority communities in maintaining their identities within this common framework.

Multi-cultural Britain would be 'both socially cohesive and culturally diverse' and be a society where individuals can share 'common aims, attributes and values' (p. 7). These goals may be contradictory, but the important point is that the aspiration of the multi-cultural society is for different groups of people to live in peace and mutual respect of their differences. Undoubtedly, there are advantages to multi-culturalism. In the first place, multi-culturalism takes the fact of difference as a given and celebrates it as pluralism. It is not surprising, therefore, that, despite what Alund and Schierup (1991) correctly describe as 'the paradoxes of multi-culturalism', many multi-ethnic or multi-racial societies such as Canada and Australia have adopted multi-culturalism as ideology and policy. Multi-culturalism is a search for tolerance in diversity and it abandons mono-culturalism as a desirable goal for a changing society. It further asserts that all cultures are valuable and should be cherished and be esteemed. The profound drawback, however, of multi-culturalism as both ideology and policy could be that in the long run it results in mobilisation for ethnic boundary maintenance that

Barth spoke of and stifles the potential for dynamic change which can result from the culture-contact that Malinowski spoke about. The following chapters relate important aspects of British society to the ideology of multi-culturalism, but at this point I want to suggest that multi-culturalism as policy may unwittingly function as a palliative for what M. G. Smith called 'differential incorporation' in contemporary, particularly highly complex, societies.

In his earlier formulation of the theory of social and cultural pluralism, Smith drew upon the work of Furnivall and concentrated principally on colonial societies to demonstrate his argument that there are social orders in which groups of people differ in what Malinowski called primary social institutions of language, family structures, customs, religion and so forth. Smith argued that in Caribbean societies people meet through the market, but they do not share this set of common primary institutions. A significant divide exists between the public and the private spheres of social life. In the public realm people relate to rules and regulations set by the state through laws which are applicable to individual agents. A central role is thereby accorded to the state in societies significantly divided by social and cultural pluralism. Following Rex (1987), I have argued (Goulbourne, 1991b) that the adherents of the ideology of multi-culturalism in Britain cannot intend to build the kind of society described by Furnivall and Smith. But given the lack of clarity or care taken in the usage of the concept, it has to be said that there are times when it is difficult to distinguish the aspirations of the multi-culturalists from the description of social and cultural pluralism of the kind described by Smith and Furnivall. This tension is partly expressed in the references to the Swann report discussed above, but in general the problems of pluralism as analysis and pluralism as prescription have not been squarely faced – at least, not in the terms being discussed here.

The vigorous and lively debates in the 1960s that took place in Caribbean studies over Smith's thesis led to his *Corporations and Society* (1974), in which he sought to apply pluralism to a wider range of societies, including the USA, and it is this development that is of particular relevance to the discussion over multi-culturalism in post-imperial Britain. Drawing on the work of others, but particularly Maine and Weber on society as corporation or corporate entities, Smith argued that there are different ways in which groups are incorporated into societies. He outlined three kinds of incorporation: the universal/uniform, the segmental/equivalent and the differential. It is relevant to mention briefly what Smith meant by the concept of differential incorporation, because it has found its way into popular and academic discourses about inequality, usually without any acknowledgement of Smith by academic commentators.

The universal or uniform incorporation of groups involves society conferring the same rights on people of the same racial but different ethnic groups. Thus, in the USA all white Europeans, irrespective of ethnic or national backgrounds, enjoyed the rights to vote, organise, publish, live where they wish and engage in economic activities. In such situations, Smith points out, 'differing ethnic cultures do not entail any differences of formal status in the public domain of political, legal, economic and ancillary activities between ethnic units' (Smith, 1988, p. 195). The distinction between the private and public domains is maintained and it appears that this is what multi-culturalism aspires to in Britain. Multi-culturalism, like universal incorporation 'simultaneously confers equal citizenship and identical legal rights and obligations on individuals' (ibid.). But Smith's point is that in what he called complex pluralities, such as American and British societies, some groups may indeed enjoy uniform or universal incorporation into the social order, but in the same society other groups may simultaneously be incorporated in less favourable and inequitable ways. Thus, whilst white groups which share the same race or colour as dominant groups have been discriminated against, with time they have come to enjoy universal incorporation with the dominant groups. The cases of the Irish in Britain and the USA and the Jews in both these societies illustrate this point. On the other hand, groups of people with black or brown or yellow colours have been differentially or inequitably incorporated into these societies. These points are taken up in the next chapter.

It is important at this point to illustrate further what Smith meant by segmental or differential incorporation. His example is that whilst black Americans may have sometimes had the same *de jure* rights as those conferred on white Americans, these could not be enjoyed by blacks because of the *de facto* situation which prohibited their participation in the mainstream of American life. Blacks were excluded from free, active and equal participation in American life, despite the fact that this contradicted some of the fundamental tenets of American democracy. Similarly, the indigenous Native American population and other groups of people such as the Chinese, Japanese, Mexicans, Polynesians and blacks from elsewhere were segmented from the rest of society by 'differing judicial provisions' (Smith, 1988 p. 196). Expressed another way, they became what Robin Cohen (1987) called 'the new helots', or people who exist beyond the pale of a thriving multi-cultural society. Although not himself employing the concept, the very title of Cohen's recent stimulating work, *Frontiers of Identity: The British and the Others* (1994), suggests some of the new ways in which, in the post-imperial age, differential incorporation may be maintained by strengthening frontiers of identities.


## Conclusion

The question of what sets of social relations properly constitute the field of race relations remains contentious. Indeed, some writers prefer to speak of racialisation and racism and altogether avoid using the term race relations. But this is unlikely to get us far. It is also unlikely that in such an explosive area of social thought and action as relations between groups deemed racial or ethnic, there will be any definition that will be universally acceptable. For example, during the period of primary immigration and early settlement by Asians and Caribbeans in Britain, it appears that some social analysts were impressed by Rex's 'race relations situation' in preference to Park's 'cycle of race relations'. Today, when several isssues concern policy-makers and academics alike, these definitions of the sub-field are inadequate. In this chapter, I have suggested that by focusing on the mobilisation of ethnicity or what is understood to be racial affinity, in a society that incorporates groups of people differentially, we are able to understand better the changing emphases and situations of relations between groups of people who see themselves, and are seen by others, to be different. The mobilisation of ethnicity or racial affinity as a political currency has certainly been a norm of social and political life in post-imperial Britain. Later chapters will take up this point, but in the next chapter it is important briefly to describe some aspects of the general historical and sociological contexts of mobilisation in multi-racial or multi-ethnic Britain by focusing on the imperial and post-imperial backgrounds of these relations.

# 2 Imperial and Post-imperial Backgrounds

## Introduction

The notion of a multi-cultural Britain denotes, as we saw in the last chapter, recognition of the existence of a citizenry composed by people of different colours and celebrating a diversity of cultures. But this has been so for only the last three decades at the very most, and it is not universally embraced. Until mass migration from the Commonwealth Caribbean, the Indian sub-continent and Africa from 1948, Britain was seen as a white country; indeed, in many parts of Britain and the contemporary world, the country is still seen as 'white people's country', reflecting the image of an exclusive imperial order. This perception of Britain is still unambiguously projected by Her Majesty's Government in embassies and high commissions abroad. But even if it is conceded that this perception of British society may have been close to the reality at some point between the Union of England and Scotland in the early eighteenth century and the demise of British imperial power during the second half of the present century, it may be argued that this was not so before nor during the last four or so decades. It is suggested here that it has been the migration flows from the Caribbean, South Asia and Africa, in the years between the late 1940s and the late 1970s, that established the basis for significant change in British society, so that whilst it is predominantly a white European society, it is no longer possible meaningfully to speak of it as being exclusively so.

This chapter discusses aspects of the background or the pre-history of the multi-cultural society in Britain. The outline here also sets the context for discussions in later chapters of the problems of the multi-cultural society and the kinds of ethnic mobilisation that occurred. This took the form, first, of controlling black and brown immigration and redefining British nationality and, second, the emergence of new minority communities and the continuing fight to ensure their universal incorporation into British society.

## Historical Preludes to the Multi-Cultural Society

There can be little doubt that it was large-scale migration from the Caribbean, the Indian sub-continent and Africa which provided the sufficient condition for society in Britain to be widely recognised as multi-cultural. Many aspects, however, of the necessary conditions for a multi-cultural society were already present in Britain before this period. The notion of the multi-cultural society may therefore have important and relevant indigenous historical antecedents, which the success of the English language and cultural dominance combined with the English state had hitherto succeeded in clouding, particularly from outsiders. This pluralism, however, was never entirely lost to Britishers within these islands.

For example, whilst during the days of global imperial power, Island Britain achieved and successfully projected herself as a united economic, political and military force in the world, with decline her constituent parts again became aware of their earlier pre-imperial differences. The articulation of historic British distinctiveness has been variously expressed in the years since the end of World War Two. Modern demands for Scottish autonomy go back a long time, and particularly to the 1880s when such demands led to the establishment of the Scottish Office (Hanham, 1969a, b), but in the last few decades this demand has developed into a cry for total separation of Edinburgh from Westminster, which is not very dissimilar to the independence that was demanded and occurred in colonies in Africa, Asia, the Caribbean and the Pacific. Less vociferous than the Scottish Nationalist Party, Plaid Cymru also has long challenged the continuing relevance or validity of the earlier Union between England and Wales which was forged by the force of arms in the fourteenth century. Recognition of the Welsh language in Wales and the promise of devolution to Scotland by New Labour during and after the 1997 general election,[1] are indications of what Nairn (1981), rather prematurely, called 'the break up of Britain'. Scottish independence would bring to an end the Union of 1707 with England, and the same development in Wales would dissolve the Acts of Union of 1536 and 1542 (see, for example, Fusaro, 1979; Williams, 1982). The longevity of these unions appears not to be lasting security against dissolution. Of course, perhaps the most dramatic challenge to the unity of the British state is the status of Northern Ireland, where Britain is in a no-win situation between the Unionists and the Republican nationalists (see, Boyce, 1993). The first group has the long tradition of loyalty to the United Kingdom and wants to remain part of the United

Kingdom. The nationalists, on the other hand, have long called for a united Ireland.

One of the first modern nation states, Britain, like nearly all nation-states, is a collection of different peoples under a single political authority. The contemporary weakening of this marriage of community and political association affects Britain as it does many other nation-states (Goulbourne, 1991a). But behind these developments in Britain and Ireland may be the memory of an earlier multi-cultural Britain in which what are today mere regions had their own separate political authorities corresponding more closely to the communities of nation groups.

But even during the heyday of unified Britain, there was the urge for communal pluralism to be recognised. In the face of the powerful single authority (that is, the British state), political pluralists argued that the existence of small groups in civil society was a necessary counterbalance to the modern leviathan nation-state, which, in its tendency to centralise, may ride roughshod over the legitimate interests of ordinary citizens represented at local geographical levels and/or through occupational groups. Early in this century, influential pluralists, such as the historian D. H. Cole and the political theorist Harold Laski, saw such groups as positively contributing to democracy. Laski argued that the centralised state is not only incompetent, but also 'morally inadequate', and represents a number of competing interests (Laski, 1921, p. vi). I have argued elsewhere (Goulbourne, 1991b) that there are important links to be made between what is usually described as the tenets of multi-culturalism and those of traditional British and American political pluralist thought, but this is not the place to set out or develop the argument. The point I wish to make here is simply that there has long been an awareness of the fact that the image or perception of Britain as a homogenous social whole has not held sway in all quarters and at all times before the official recognition of the multi-cultural society. The political pluralists' arguments rested on a recognition that civil society was diverse and multiple in interests and needs.[2]

The social basis of such diversity was not only the various classes that had developed in Britain as a result of industrialisation and empire. Before large-scale black and brown entry and settlement, there were a number of groups which were not always equally or universally, to use M. G. Smith's wording, 'incorporated' into society. These included religious groups such as Catholics who were given the vote only in 1820. Similarly, the Jews, who had been in Britain since the Middle Ages, were differentially incorporated into British society, but their religion was no longer a bar from the franchise after the 1820s, and within fifty years of such change Benjamin Disraeli, a Jew converted to Christianity, had become Prime Minister of England and established the pillars of Conservatism for the next century, until the Thatcher revolution in the 1980s. Later in the same century, new groups of Jews fleeing pogroms in Tsarist Russia found homes in Britain, as did German Jews escaping from Hitler's nazi Germany in the 1930s. From the nineteenth century there have been small pockets of Chinese people, and with the reversion of Hong Kong to communist China in July 1997 more Chinese people may be expected to migrate to Britain. In recent times other peoples have also come to Britain. During and immediately after the World War Two, groups of East and Central Europeans from Poland, the Ukraine and Hungary made their homes here, as did Southern Europeans from Italy, Cyprus and Malta. The history of Irish migration to Britain is well known and documented (Holmes, 1988; see also, Woodham-Smith, 1962). Although sharing racial and ethnic characteristics with the British, the Irish have long been discriminated against in British society on the basis of their ethnicity, largely defined by religious adherence to Catholicism. Already in the eighteenth century there was large-scale opposition to Irish workers and Catholics as illustrated by riots in 1724, 1736 and 1763 and calls to burn a Paddy on St Patrick' Day (see George, 1965). But after Oliver Cromwell's subjugation of Ireland in the middle of the seventeenth century, the island slowly came to be seen as part of greater Britain or more part of the British Isles than as a colony in the ways that colonies were to be seen in other parts of the British world.

Moreover, although it has been post-war migration from the Caribbean, the Indian sub-continent and Commonwealth Africa which stands out in the final making of the multi-cultural society in Britain, there was an earlier presence of Africans and Asians in Britain. Indeed, it has been shown that African soldiers came with the Roman legions to occupy Britain (Fryer, 1984; Walvin and Edwards, 1983), and there has been an almost continuous and recognisable African presence in Britain since before the age of the great European explorations of Africa, Asia and the Americas from the early sixteenth century (Shyllon, 1974; Walvin and Edwards, 1983). The plantation economy in the Caribbean provided West Indian planters with wealth to lavish, and many returned to England with their slaves. Similarly, the activities of the East India Company in Bengal, later extending into other parts of declining Moghul India, led to the recognisable presence of South Asians in Britain (Fryer, 1984; Holmes, 1988). The nabobs, many of them lesser sons of the British aristocracy, who had made their fortunes in India, followed the earlier example of the West Indian planters, by taking their servants on return to Britain (Fryer, 1984, pp. 77ff.). In the nineteenth century, Indians, like West Africans and West Indians, also came as seamen to British ports, and some remained (Sherwood, 1991). Outstanding individuals, some of whom were more fortunate than servants and slaves, actively participated in social and political activities of their times, such as the agitation over the abolition of the slave trade and slavery, the founding of Sierra Leone for freed Africans and their British companions, the Chartist Movement, the Crimean War, the two World Wars, and the struggles for political independence in India, Africa and the Caribbean. Some, such as Ignatius Sancho, Ottobah Cugoano and Olaudah Equiano who wrote and stood by their people in the cruel age of the slave trade and slavery, are now relatively familiar names in the historiography being constructed about the prelude to multi-cultural Britain.

The argument, therefore, is not that what is described as Britain's multi-cultural society has been established without foundations in the British past. In the first place, a plurality of indigenous peoples inhabited these islands long before there was an appreciable presence of Africans and Asians. Second, the new minority ethnic communities which sprang up in British industrial cities as a result of the sizeable post-war migration from the Caribbean, Asia and Africa had their precursors in communities in Cardiff, Liverpool, Swansea, London and other parts of the country (see Little, 1947; Richmond, 1955).

I want, however, to suggest that it was the post-World-War-Two migration from those outposts of the empire and the consequent settlement of Caribbeans, Africans and Asians that provided the sufficient condition for the notion of the multi-cultural society to become the compelling ideological force it has been since the late 1960s. As we noted in the last chapter, until this time it was a widespread assumption that newcomers to British shores would be assimilated into the dominant culture, rather than seek to maintain their own cultures. Until the significant entry and settlement of these groups, the incorporation of Jews, Irish, and South, Central and East Europeans were universal or uniform in nature because, with time, the white or European groups came to enjoy the same rights as the indigenous population. African Caribbeans and Asians often had far more in common with the native Britishers than the British shared with several of the European groups. The distinguishing feature was colour, particularly with regard to Caribbean groups. Initially, however, because of racial, as distinct from ethnic, considerations, black and brown communities were incorporated into society on a *de jure* basis but they did not enjoy incorporation into British society on a *de facto* basis. The process of *de facto* universal incorporation is still going on, but as we will see in later chapters, as part of protracted struggles for the realisation of equality.

## Imperial and Colonial Experiences

The wider historical context of black and brown differential socio-political integration and participation in British society, which is unfolding as we approach a new century, is one of imperial expansion, contacts and colonial experience. Although racial differentiation and exclusion are being cast within a larger context of discrimination as a whole, it is important to remember that British race relations have less to do with what M. G. Smith called 'segmented differentiation' (in this instance, the differential treatment of white groups by other white groups), and more to do with differentiation on the basis of colour. This context or background can be explicated by reference to two inter-related but independent historical developments which have been important aspects of British race relations for well over three centuries: the experiences of colonialism, and those experiences of people and institutions in the imperial centre. It may be useful to explain these two factors briefly.

First, the socio-political backgrounds of Britain's new minority ethnic communities must be located partly within the colonial experience. This point is not being proffered as an essential element of race relations theory because, as indicated in Chapter 1, it is not necessary to see these relations as arising, exclusively, as a result of economic inequality and colonial expansion. The colonial past in British race relations is of historical relevance because this past was of considerable importance in shaping and developing Britain's attitudes to racial differentiation. Moreover, as noted earlier, these communities mainly originated in Africa, the Caribbean and South Asia, but whilst they all shared a British colonial past, this past was remarkably varied in practice, giving these groups different experiences of colonialism and of the British. In a similar manner, colonial variation was also to give the British administrative and political elites varied experiences of colonised peoples and would have important influences upon future race relations in the post-imperial metropole. This impact is still deeply marked in race relations matters in Britain. I want to point to a few of the main features of these different colonial pasts, some of which may have a bearing on contemporary race relations in post-imperial Britain.

In Africa, the system of a dual political mandate operated, once the Crown Colony system, and occasionally the protectorate, had been established. The crown colony system was first introduced in Trinidad at the beginning of the nineteenth century, when the island passed finally into the hands of the British as a result of the war with revolutionary France. Crown colony status meant that the colony came under direct control of the Crown through Parliament (see, for example, Sires, 1955; Wight, 1946). Typically, Westminster would send a governor to a colony, and he would be expected to work with an appointed executive council and, for all intent and purposes, this governor was a dictator with only a distant and not infrequently indifferent Westminster Parliament and a Whitehall Secretary of State for the Colonies to curb gubernatorial power. In some places the governor would have to consult elected and appointed members of a legislative council. The governor's annual reports, prepared by a handful of directors of departments (later to become ministers and ministries under post-imperial independent governments) would be submitted to the Secretary of State for the Colonies, but, in normal and sometimes even in extraordinary times, little or no attention would be given to these reports, unless there were some points directly bearing on Britain's own wider interests.

In many respects this was in sharp contrast with earlier colonies which had their own elected assemblies, and enjoyed a measure of autonomy over local affairs, because they were colonies of settlement by Britons, as distinct from colonies of exploitation (see, Beckford, 1972; Best, 1968). In the main, the colonies of the first empire enjoyed such rights because they were regarded as extensions of Britain with British folks. Such were the colonies with their free assemblies in the thirteen British settlements along the Atlantic seaboard in North America, whose leaders rebelled against Britain in 1776, one of their grievances being that as Englishmen who were being taxed they should be represented at Westminster as expressed in their rallying call 'no taxation without representation'. In the Caribbean, the British islands were intended to be settlements for Britons, but since the 1840s the people from Africa, Asia and Europe who made up the population have built on the traditions first introduced by Britain to establish remarkably democratic societies (see, for example, Emmanuel, 1993; Goulbourne, 1988; Stone, 1983, 1985).

In contrast, the territories which became part of the second empire, mainly in Africa and Asia in the nineteenth century, were administered largely under the crown colony system. But, of course, the overall situation was complicated, because of the question of colour, or, expressed another way, the mobilisation of difference of colour or racial difference by the dominant white elites. Some colonies from the period of the first empire, for example Jamaica, became crown colonies; many semi-autonomous or formally independent territories, such as those in West Africa and India, also became crown colonies. There were colonies of continuing settlement, principally in Africa and Australasia, places that became destinations for Britons and Irish colonists (see, Constantine, 1990). In Australia the settlers did not succeed in completely liquidating the indigenous population, but did succeed in establishing complete control over the territory and the people in much the same way as the settlement of North America. In East and Central Africa, a protracted struggle ensued between white settlers and Africans well into the period of decolonisation. Indeed, in Zimbabwe and South Africa, this struggle continued into the last two decades of the twentieth century, because white settlers felt that they could succeed in establishing an exclusive claim to those parts of the continent. The winning of democratic majority rule in Zimbabwe in 1980 and in South Africa in 1994, marked the end of the political take over of the continent by Europeans and the beginning of a new meeting of Africans and Europeans on relatively equal grounds. The new equality is still rather abstract, because whilst Africans exercise political power, economic and financial power remain largely in the hands of Europeans. But because it was political and military power that Europeans used to attain parmountcy, it is likely that Africans will also use political power to redress the economic imbalance that pertains. None the less, it is remarkable that it is still the case that whilst Europeans will be praised for using state power to acquire wealth, when Africans do so a moral finger is quick to point and wag, as a perusal of the British press in the late 1990s will reveal.

In India, after 1818 the British steadily consolidated their hold over the sub-continent. But, following the Mutiny of 1857, direct political control by the crown was firmly established. These events completed the demise of the East India Company, which had long held administrative and significant political power in the declining Moghul empire, but with the might of imperial Britain as guarantor. The events described as a mutiny by the imperial power, were more than just an outburst by Hindu and Muslim soldiers, who had been given cow and pig fats, in violation of tenets of their faiths, to oil their new Enfield rifles. This act of gross insensitivity sparked the events of 1857, but during the fourteen months that they lasted Indians outside the army expressed their grievances against the British and it is not surprising that, whilst imperial historians are wont to see these events as the last strike against European encroachment, Indians are more likely to see them as the first blow for independence. Spear (1970) argues that whilst the Mutiny was a deep shock to the British, 'it was a shock to their complacency rather than to their self-confidence' (p. 145), and they set about establishing an order that the less discerning of them thought would last into the indefinite future. As later in Africa, however, the viceroys sent by Whitehall to oversee the vast Indian empire, recognised the need to have support from the indigenous population. After 1857 the British garnered this support by leaving Indian social institutions alone, securing a degree of acquiescence on the part of the upper classes, and introducing innovation with care. Spears expresses this new policy clearly when he states that there 'was no destruction of the old, but an introduction of the new alongside' (p. 139).

India today is a mosaic of past civilisations, with remnants of several living either side by side or in intricately interwoven layers. It was not surprising, therefore, that perspicacious administrators recognised that they would not be able to change India in all her parts and, indeed, viceroys like Lord Curzon surmised that he and his country men would eventually leave India to responsible and legitimate hands. The British have been prouder of their work in India than of their efforts in any other colony, and they frequently speak of India being the world's largest democracy, as if this is a British achievement. The massive work the British undertook of laying rails, telegraph poles, and building new institutions for governance must be seen as meaningful achievements once the just anger over colonialism is set aside.[3] It was not surprising, therefore, that unlike other British governors of crown colonies across the globe, India's governor had the added title of viceroy, suggesting the crown's special interest. Benjamin Disraeli had seen to it that Queen Victoria had the title of Empress of India, which appear to have suited many in Victorian England and in India.

However, according to Robinson and Gallagher, for 'the official mind of imperialism' in Britain the Indian empire appeared less valuable than the settled colonies in North America, Australasia, South Africa and the West Indies. This was because Victorians saw these settled colonies as an extension of home, they were 'Greater Britain' peopled by English people and their cousins the Welsh, Scots and the Irish, who, at least out in the wider empire, were more part of the British pack than were non-European colonised peoples. Robinson and Gallagher (1965) state that the empire in India 'seemed unnatural, almost improper, like some extra-marital responsibility incurred in youth' (p. 8). Not surprisingly, there was strong opinion against allowing this indiscretion to recur. Although in 1865 a select committee of the House of Commons had recommended that Britain should seek to beat a hasty retreat from West Africa and not be embroiled in the affairs of the region, by the late 1870s Britain was moving, under Disraeli's Tories, towards the final division of Africa. It is not necessary to accept Robinson and Gallagher's thesis that Britain was a reluctant imperialist to understand that sometimes their expansion in India and Africa were acts of blundering. If the colonies in North America had been lost because of the eighteenth-century tendency to let things take their own course and display a generous lack of enthusiasm, then the nineteenth century expansion of empire was sometimes characterised by a series of over-hasty blunders sometimes followed by acts of gross savagery, as in the response to the Indian Mutiny in 1857 and Governor Eyre's barbarity at Morant Bay in Jamaica in 1865 (see Augier, 1966; Dutton, 1967; Heuman, 1994).

But it was Chancellor Otto von Bismarck, the honest broker in European affairs after he had achieved his European ambitions of unifying disparate German states under the Prussian Hohenzollerns and a man always with a plan, who organised the Berlin Conference in 1884 and amicably finalised the carve-up of Africa between West European powers. But the dream of a new British empire from the Cape to Cairo that Cecil Rhodes had sought to realise, involved the British placing the Union Flag at strategic points along the Central and Eastern plateaux of the continent. The colonies of North and Southern Rhodesia (now Zambia and Zimbabwe, respectively), Uganda and Kenya (and after the 1914–18 War in Europe, German Tanganyika, now Tanzania), gave Britain north-bound access through Sudan and Egypt (where influence was shared with the French) to the Mediterranean. And from there, Britain enjoyed naval supremacy, the control of Gibraltar and a diplomatic presence on continental Europe, thereby ensuring security to home base on an island set aside in splendid isolation from the real and imagined problems of continental Europe. Kiernan (1969) rather aptly expressed the point about Britain's global presence and isolation from continental Europe when he wrote that 'Britain often appeared to belong to all the other continents more than to Europe; or appeared to itself, with its growing family of White colonies, a continent of its own' (p. 25).

The philosophy and policy of the dual mandate that the British operated owe much to Lord Lugard, who recognised the need to incorporate the indigenous political authorities in Uganda, and later Nigeria, as appendages to British rule (Lugard, 1922). As the term suggests, the dual mandate meant that two systems of authority existed side by side within the same judicio-political order within a given territory. But these authorities were not equal; the imperial authority was superior and the native authority inferior. Lucy Mair (1965) was of the view that it was a matter 'of course' that 'it is an absurd exaggeration to argue as if European supremacy could not have been maintained without the support of the chiefs' (p. 113). Be this as it may, wh it dual mandatism recognised in Africa, as did the viceroys of India after 1857, was that the imperial authority could not smoothly govern the colonised without support, tacit or otherwise, from the colonised themselves and the system enabled colonialists better to exploit the factors of class and the apparent and real ethnic and regional divisions. Dual mandatism therefore recognised pluralism and sought to incorporate this into the body social and the body politic. Prescribed areas of social and political activities were left to the competence of those who were accepted by the British to be the people's traditional leaders, but this authority was subordinated to the authority of the colonial administration.

British political dualism in Africa and Asia was a recognition of autochthonous political authority, which, notwithstanding Mair, could not complacently and inexpensively be ignored. In the early modern historical era, before the construction of what we know as the nation-state, Nicolo Machiavelli had advised that the most effective way for a would-be modernising prince to hold on to power would be to eliminate all local or native sources of power in a conquered state in order to clear the path for his own undisputed authority. But British dual mandatism did not follow this course. Rather, the British sought to operate through the existing structures and to use them as points of mediation and effective control in an elaborate system of domination – a mode of control that Machiavelli suggested would lead ultimately to the defeat of a new autocratic authority (Machiavelli, 1981; also 1970). With political independence, nationalists went further than Machiavelli envisaged: they were left with a political legacy that they wanted to disown, and this was to establish its own dynamic process of conflict between traditionalists and modernisers, between nation-state builders and those who wished to hold to traditional values and revitalise traditional structures. In India, the modernising Congress party under Jawaharlal Nehru's leadership had a relatively easy time with traditional leaders, perhaps because from 1857 the British had tried to win new supporters amongst the newly Western educated elites. But in Africa this has been more troublesome. From Ghana in the 1950s and 1960s, Uganda from the 1960s to the 1990s, and contemporary post-apartheid South Africa, the problems of the native authority or traditional leaders have bugged modernising nationalists. Whether desirable or not, traditional leaders continue to be a dormant political force in several states, and this social force is sometimes mobilised by ambitious politicians.

Nationalists in the British West Indies did not have to contend with the problems spawned by dual mandatism, because the region lacked autochthonous authoriti. s. In general, these were societies which commenced on a *tabula rasa*, because initial colonisation in the post-Columbian age led to the almost complete annihilation of the Carib and Arawak peoples and, where small groups remained, they have existed largely outside the political process and have had no significant impact on society. In the case of Barbados, the island was uninhabited when the British commenced settlement in the early seventeenth century, establishing one of the first elected assemblies in the Americas, which lasted until independence in 1966. As indicated earlier, in the case of Jamaica, which came under British rule during the last years of Protector Oliver Cromwell in the late 1650s, in 1865 the white planter class voluntarily surrendered its internal autonomy, abolishing the elected Old Assembly in favour of crown or direct rule from Whitehall. This was done in desperation to avoid a coalition of black and brown[4] people against the white plantocracy who controlled the assembly (see, Augier, 1966; Heuman, 1994; Semmel, 1962). Exclusivist white rule was under threat from a coalition and groundswell of oppressed but aspiring black and brown people. The initially non-elected legislative councils established under the crown colony system were slowly reformed to include a small elected element from the early 1880s, leading to internal autonomy in the 1940s and eventually culminating in the 1960s with political independence for most of the islands and Guyana.

Thus, although they had quite different experiences, Britain's colonies in Africa, Asia and the Caribbean came to experience full political independence at roughly the same time, that is, the years after World War Two. This commenced with the independence of India and Pakistan in 1947, took a dramatic leap forward in 1957 with Kwame Nkrumah's achievement of independence for Ghana, followed by the decade of African independence, the 1960s, as Nkrumah had predicted. This was also the decade for West-Indian independence, with Jamaica,[5] Trinidad, Barbados, Guyana and others becoming independent states in that decade, even though the process had commenced much earlier in the late nineteenth century (Sires, 1955). As we have seen, the late nineteenth century was a time when Britain was turning a new imperial page in Africa. It was also a time when Indian nationalism was developing a new phase with the founding of the Indian National Congress in the 1880s. As we will see later, the process of political independence from Britain (from the 1940s) was occurring at the same time that workers, students and intellectuals from the colonies were migrating in significant numbers to the imperial metropole, Britain. Between 1948 and 1976, groups of people from the former British colonial worlds in the Caribbean, Asia and Africa migrated to Britain either as free, autonomous agents or as semi-refugees for whom Britain had taken responsibility in the international community as part of the arrangements of constitutional decolonisation (see, for example, Dummett and Nicol, 1990; Ghai and MacAuslan, 1970).

In this broad story of colonialism, the case of East African Asians stands out as a quite separate situation. The British had encouraged labour from India to migrate to East, Central and Southern Africa (Clarke *et al.*, 1990; Saha, 1970; Tinker, 1974) and there had been earlier migration from the Indian sub-continent to East Africa (Honey, 1982; Twaddle, 1975). But with political independence in Kenya, Uganda, Tanzania and Malawi in the 1960s, there was a problem of where these communities of Asians belonged. This crisis was occurring in an age charged with a nationalism (see, for example, Rothchild, 1973) centred on land, belongingness, the restoration (and in many instances the creation) of African traditions, customs and languages, utilising the vocabulary of Westminster/Whitehall majoritarian democracy. The exclusion of the stranger, the alien or the foreigner, who often became confused with the imperialist, was the issue of the day as part of the process of nation-building in a new age of nationalism. In these circumstances, Britain offered and many in the Asian communities accepted, a rather untenable and cynical solution. This was for Asians to remain living and working in these newly independent nation-states whilst holding the citizenship of the retreating imperial power. Whereas the British government helped with the provision of funds – in Kenya – for Africans to repossess their lands from white settlers, there was no similar sensitivity and care by the imperial power where Asians were concerned. This was a recipe for disaster. As British Asians were later to experience, Britain also had her own post-imperial problems at home and in Europe with which to contend from the 1950s to the end of the century.

In India and the Caribbean the British did not leave this problem. Although the creation of Pakistan separated most Muslims from Hindus and Sikhs, there are today over 100 million Muslim Indians. Sikhs in Punjab and other parts of India feel that they have received less than a fair deal in the Union. None the less, India remains a multi-cultural, multi-national nation-state struggling like most societies with the problems of how best to manage a society in which difference is a major feature and around which people often wish to organise their grievances. Of course, the rise of the right-wing Hindu Bharatiya Janata Party (BJP) in both state and national assemblies and the stalemate national election in 1996, raises the question of whether the Indian Union will continue to survive under the impact of the mobilisation of deep-rooted religious feelings and antagonisms. As we have seen, the Indian sub-continent was not a region of settlement for the British in the way that vast tracts of East, Central and Southern Africa were colonies of settlement during the second empire. One result of this was that when the time came for imperial retreat, there was no problem of European settlers, nor settlers invited by the imperial power, for the indigenous and majority people to handle. The problem of over a million Anglo-Indians has not been a problem over land and autochthony; the country's problems are those faced by a multi-cultural society in terms of plurality of languages, religions and traditions. These are problems compounded by continuing poverty.

Since nearly all groups in the Caribbean were relative newcomers to the region, there could be no authentic claim by any one group against the other on the basis of exclusively belonging to the soil. All groups can claim belongingness, and do. In Guyana and Trinidad, where the South Asian population constitute the majority and the single largest group, respectively, there have been and are likely to be long-running problems between the African/Creole and East Indian descended communities about resources and the public spaces provided for culture and politics, as developments over the last decades have shown (see, Greene, 1974; Ryan, 1972; also Rodney, 1981). But these problems have not been such that any group doubts the legitimacy of their cultural belongingness to these societies and the certainty of their civic and political rights as citizens.

These colonial experiences were not restricted to the realm of politics. After all, with respect to governance, on the whole the British example was not one of democracy as practised at home, but of dictatorship, sometimes benign but none the less autocratic and justified by supposed racial and cultural superiority. But controlling the political life of the colony, the British also exercised considerable influence over many institutions in civil society and thereby ensured for different lengths of time in each colony a degree of acquiescence regarding their presence. Unlike the French and the Portuguese, the British did not require their colonised peoples to become culturally English like the *assimilados* of Angola and Mozambique or the Francophiles in Guinea or Côte d'Ivoire. But education was perhaps the single most significant object that the colonial power imparted to the colonised. From India to Africa and to the Caribbean, people realised that education was important and wanted it for their children. Where in these societies some Muslims resisted Western education, there were other groups for which education provided an opportunity. Education was provided not just by the government, but also by missionaries and other educators, making the imperial experience more than that of state structures and action. The presence of the British changed the course of history in all the colonies, and perhaps nowhere was this more marked than in the field of education.

A brief comparison between the British West Indies and the British Raj in India may be an apt illustration of this point. Whilst the nineteenth century was a period of keen British interest in India, it was a time of declining interest in the well-being of the West Indies colonies, apart from their strategic importance to British naval supremacy. As mentioned, Robinson and Gallagher (1961, Chapter 1) take the view that Britain was reluctant to assume full responsibility over a declining and chaotic Moghul India, but they also noted that by the 1880s Britain had invested about £270m in India, and she was receiving 19% of British exports. With the decline of the sugar industry after the abolition of slavery in 1838 and the Corn Laws of 1844 opening the home market to sugar from the East, the West India economic stake declined in Britain, resulting in the demise of interest in the Caribbean region. This was also true, as Marshall (1985) points out, for British humanitarians whose effort turned away from the West Indies to the East Indies. Thus, while the British did not follow Thomas Babington Macaulay's famous, ambitious and assimilationist Minute of 1835 to make the Indian male an Englishman in taste, disposition and every way but colour, the British did establish universities and colleges with a clear aim of instructing Indians in Western science and literature. This was to be, and was, done through the English language replacing Persian, the official language of Moghul India. Under the influences of the Utilitarian James Mill when he was at India House in London, Governor Bentinck, Macaulay and others, from the 1830s British education came to be seen as the hope for India (Spear, 1970) by aristocratic administrators, who were sometimes, like Macaulay himself, deeply read in the European classics but quite ignorant of India's ancient cultures. But these men were enthused by the humanitarianism of the Abolitionists and other reformers in

England (Kiernan, 1969), and Indians happily embraced the education of the West. This produced not only the fictional Western educated Bengali gentleman whom Rudyard Kipling loved to hate in his novels and unfavourably compared with the martial Northerners, but, more importantly, the new education helped to produce a new elite to challenge the presence of the British as rulers of India.

In sharp contrast, the fate of freed Africans in the West Indies interested just a few Englishmen after 1840, and often only so as to supposedly show how freedom and the African were incompatible (see, for example, Froude, 1888; Sewell, 1861). This led Eric Williams (1964) to comment that the British interest in the West Indies was one of 'froudacity',[6] rather than any genuine interest in the well-being of these colonies. None the less, there was some interest shown in the region by devout missionaries, churchmen and educators so that whereas education during slavery had been denied the slaves, after Emancipation the acquisition of an education became a highly desired goal, and a teaching semi-professional class emerged by the 1880s to contribute to the struggle for self-emancipation and later political independence (Goulbourne, 1988).

The general point here is that in the colonial worlds from which Britain's new minority ethnic groups came, there already were close contacts with, and understandings of, certain aspects of the British. This was so with respect to institutions, schooling, and the broad outlines of British history, literature, sports, architecture and so forth. From the testimonies of those who migrated we know that such knowledge was fragmentary and sometimes misleading (Chamberlian, 1997; Goulbourne, 1980; Thomas-Hope, 1980). It might have been expected, however, that the British would also be familiar with something of the array of peoples and cultures in the empire, or at least parts of the empire. But the imperial world, on which it was said the sun never set, was beyond the reach of ordinary white folks. At the centre of empire, comparatively little was known about the peoples and institutions of the empire, and what was known was based on centuries of myths and propaganda (see, Mackenzie, 1984; Rich, 1986) many of which predated empire (see, for example, Jones, 1965, 1971). The elites had knowledge of some aspects of specific areas in the colonial world, but the British people within these islands, in rather sharp contrast to the colonised, remained comfortably ignorant. This was itself to have important practical implications for the new minorities, as they attempted to settle in the decaying centre of empire. In these circumstances, propaganda, ignorance and prejudice thrived, and migrants were to be at the receiving end of the social and economic processes which are the results of such conditions, as we will see in the next chapter.

The principle and practice of 'divide and rule' which served the administrators of empire, held true not only in the colonies, but also at home in the metropolis, at least in one important sense: citizens came to believe that their state was engaged in civilising missions to barbaric and savage peoples in far off places, and that as part of the great white race they were superior to others. They were unaware that even if Britain's hitherto unrivalled pre-eminence in the world had been earned, as sometimes it had been (Habsbawn, 1973), her position was no longer politically viable nor ideologically tenable in a world Britain herself had, more than many, helped to make. The absence of territorial contiguity did not mean in the post-imperial era that the flow of population would always remain largely one-directional from Britain to the colonies. Migration to Britain from the late 1940s was but a small reversal of the centuries-old and established outflow of people from Britain to the colonies from the age of exploration in the seventeenth century (see Constantine, 1990).

In summary, two broad factors should be taken into account in the political sociology of Britain's minority ethnic communities when considering the colonial and resulting international contexts of their general situation. These are the differential colonial experience and the limited experience of the indigenous British population who were not part of the military, administrative, missionary or business cohorts who traversed the empire. There is a third factor to be taken into account. This is the simple fact that easy communication and cheap travel have helped to maintain close family and communal links between people separated by distance (see Cohen, 1997). And as the first generation of migrants from these countries enter retirement, many have and are returning to the lands of their births for their twilight years. This of itself generates new links and continuing attachments between Britain and the former colonial sites, because children and grandchildren, as well as new in-laws (many from the indigenous population) visit these lands. It was once thought that with the passing away of the immigrant generation the links with the homeland would also die away, but new developments mentioned here are suggesting otherwise.

Taken together, these aspects of the colonial and international dimensions provide a powerful and continuing set of problems, issues and opportunities which impact upon social and political participation of members from these communities in British society. They also provide a broad background against which to discuss aspects of the sociological contexts of Britain's new minorities and the problems faced in the multi-cultural society, which will be outlined briefly in Chapter 4. The remainder of this chapter is concerned with the reverse migration from the colonies to the centre of empire, which was to become part of the general background to the evolution of a multi-cultural society in Britain.

## Colonial Societies and Reverse Migration

Large-scale migration from the West Indies, India and Pakistan started more like a trickle than a sudden rush. The broad details of this movement are well documented and warrant no close discussion here (see, for example, Chamberlian, 1997; Fryer, 1984; Peach, 1968; Roberts and Mills, 1958; Thomas-Hope, 1992). Suffice it to say that the flow commenced with the landing at Tilbury in June, 1948 of the former German pleasure cruiser the *Empire Windrush*, with passengers from Jamaica, followed in October by the *Orbita* docking at Liverpool. Together these vessels landed just over 500 persons, and until 1951 the numbers of Caribbean migrants remained under 1000 each year. But, under the McCarran–Walter Act of 1952, immigration was restricted into the country and this affected the Caribbean islands adversely, because the USA had long been the destination for Caribbean migrants. Jamaica, the largest sender in the English-speaking Caribbean, was restricted by the US policy to 100 persons each year. In these circumstances, Britain became the desired destination for many who wanted to improve their life chances and also saw emigration as one way of achieving these goals. As Roberts and Mills (1958) showed, migration from Jamaica to Britain increased dramatically between 1952 and 1956. Thus, in 1966 people of Jamaican backgrounds accounted for 60 per cent of people from the sub-region, and the 1991 census of population revealed that over 50 per cent of people of Caribbean heritage in Britain were of Jamaican background.

But this should not distract from the fact that Caribbean people in Britain are drawn from a wide range of countries in the region, including Anguilla, Antigua, Barbados, Barbuda, Belize, Dominica, Grenada, Guyana,[7] Montserrat, St Kitts, St Lucia, and Trinidad and Tobago. In 1966 it was estimated that the Caribbean population in Britain (including those born in the UK) was about 450 000 (Deakin, 1970, p. 31). The more accurate 1991 census revealed that 1.6 per cent of the British population described themselves as black. Disaggregated, Owen had the following result: 56.1 per cent or 493 339 persons of all British blacks described themselves to be of Caribbean backgrounds, and 20.3 per cent or 178 401 persons saw themselves to be a mixture of blacks and other groups in the society (Owen, 1994). Over 50 per cent of people with Caribbean backgrounds were born in Britain, and increasingly those of the migrant generation are entering their pensionable years. In this regard they, more than any other minority ethnic group, come close to the age profile of the white population.

As noted earlier, there have long been West Africans in Britain. Like other colonials from India and the Caribbean, West Africans from the Gambia, Sierra Leone, Nigeria and the Gold Coast (now Ghana) came to Britain as sailors and soldiers. Others also came from the Horn of Africa, including Somalia and Ethiopia, and from British East Africa despite the limited opportunities for travel. With post-war opportunities in the 1950s, the number of Africans increased, so that in 1966 there were 43100 from the region, with nearly 8000 children born in the UK (Deakin, 1970, p. 58). Africans with recent backgrounds in the continent accounted for 23.7 per cent or 208,110 of all black people in Britain in 1991 (Owen, 1994). It is when all people of African descent are taken together that they constitute 1.6 per cent of the total minority ethnic population.

Although sizeable migration from the colonial world commenced with Caribbean immigration in 1948, Asians from the Indian sub-continent and Africa became the main source for post-World-War-Two Commonwealth migration to Britain. The break up of colonial India into West and East Pakistan and India in 1947 – the year they also became independent countries within the Commonwealth – occurred just at the point when Britain was being seen as a country of destination for many in this region. Whilst migrants came from all parts of the English-speaking Caribbean to Britain, those who came from the Indian sub-continent were from a limited number of regions. Sikhs from two districts in the Punjab – Jullundur and Hoshiarpur – made up the vast majority of Indians to migrate from the early 1950s to Britain. A small number of Punjabi and Gujarati Hindus also migrated. Both Sikhs and Gujaratis have long traditions of migration to far-flung parts of the British empire and many who had earlier migrated to British East Africa were later to find their way to Britain (see Bhachu, 1986). In West Pakistan, migrants came mainly from the district of Mipur, which had earlier been part of the much neglected areas of Jammu and Kashmir, later to become problematic regions for post-colonial India and Pakistan. From East Pakistan (after 1972 the independent state of Bangladesh), a thousand miles to the east and across India, migrants came mainly from the district of Sylhet, but also from Chittagong.

In 1966 the process of Africanisation in Kenya triggered the large-scale migration of many of the country's South Asians, who had earlier chosen British rather than Kenyan citizenship at the point of independence. Whilst some Kenyan Asians went to India, Canada and other countries that welcomed them, Britain had a special responsibility to provide a home. Much the same pattern was followed in 1976 when British Asians in Malawi found it necessary to take up their British citizenship option by finding homes in Britain. In Tanzania too, the South-Asian-descended population fell by half to 40 000 by the 1980s, not so much because of Africanisation but because of the socialist centralising policies outlined in the 1967 Arusha Declaration. Many Asians, and others, who owned properties and housing estates found their assets nationalised. But by far the most dramatic exodus of Asians from East Africa was from Uganda in 1972,[8] as a result of large-scale expulsion of Asians, citizens and non-citizens alike, by the dictator Idi Amin (see Dummett and Nichol, 1990; Mamdani, 1973; Twaddle, 1975).

Altogether, people with a recent or historical background in the Indian sub-continent make up the greater proportion of the new minority ethnic population in Britain (Owen, 1994). This is in sharp contrast to the earlier years of migration. Indeed, for the first eighteen years of post-war migration, it was estimated that Jamaicans alone constituted the single largest group of new minority ethnic communities (Deakin, 1970, p. 58). The 1962 Commonwealth Immigration Act aimed at curbing black and brown migration to Britain, but initially it had the effect of stimulating a race to 'beat the ban', and migration from both the sub-continent and the Caribbean increased significantly (Peach, 1968, especially chapter 5). By the late 1960s, however, Peach records a steady flow of Caribbean people leaving Britain, and this has continued into the 1990s (Peach, 1991). This decrease of the Caribbean population coincided with the increase of Asian communities from East Africa, as indicated above.

Primary immigration into Britain has been effectively stopped, and the reunion of families, particularly Asian families, has taken place slowly. Relatively few refugees and asylum seekers find homes in Britain, and there is a progressive tightening of the law (Cohen, 1994, especially chapter 6; S. Goulbourne, 1997). With the deeper integration of the European Union (EU), there are good reasons to expect more continental Europeans wanting to make Britain their home, just as there might be more Britons wanting to live in other EU countries. But the British population is no longer the relatively homogenous, mono-coloured and mono-cultural society that is perceived to have existed before sizeable immigration of Caribbeans, Asians and Africans. John Beddoes would certainly not recognise the Britain of today when compared with the Britain of the 1880s that he sought to describe in terms of races, who were all Europeans and were ethnically rather than racially differentiated. Indeed, the mix of peoples of different colours and cultures that presently makes up the British people has changed significantly over the last fifty years.

But the bare facts of migration and numbers do not adequately convey the meaning of change that Britain has undergone during the last five decades or so. After all, both the percentage and the actual numbers of new minority ethnic groups, or, more properly described, people of African and Asian backgrounds, are not in themselves significant. We sometimes speak as if these groups constitute a homogenous whole as a result of their experiences of British colonialism and racial discrimination, but their experiences as discrete communities are likely to be far more important in determining perceptions as well as social and political behaviour. The 1991 census of population established the recognition of these groups' specificities, by offering a range of categories from which individuals could indicate what they considered to be their ethnic group. These are now generally taken into account in most matters relating to minority ethnic groups.

This is particularly so with respect to the socio-cultural backgrounds of these groups. As indicated earlier, people from the Commonwealth Caribbean came from societies created on a *tabula rasa*, and were therefore among the first modern societies in which individualism, the rule of law and capitalist market relations obtained. Only in a few places, such as Guyana, have a small number of Native Americans survived the post-Columbian invasion of the Americas, but their survival had little or no relevance for the kinds of societies which emerged. Indeed, these societies were hardly societies to begin with, because slave holders from Europe and slaves from Africa stood in sharp opposition to each other, and shared only the production of commodities for the European market (Sheridan, 1974; Williams, 1964). They tended to resemble the social orders or disorders of frontiers, where only the bare or crude rudiments of society were present (see, for example, Patterson, 1967; Smith, 1965). With time, slaves and masters came to share certain values, but there was always the fundamental antagonism between them, based on the master/slave relationship. Post-slavery society in the region, however, gave way to the development of what had already begun in slavery, that is, Creole society. This involved the emergence in some countries of a landholding rural population that Frucht (1967) described as 'neither peasant nor proletarian'. In islands with largely uncultivated mountainous interiors such as Jamaica, there developed after 1838 a substantial rural smallholding class in contradistinction to the urban population (Cumper, 1956; Eisner, 1961). In Creole society all the groups that migrated there contribute something from their once discrete cultures, and therefore all groups are taken legitimately to belong to the society. The hub of Creole societies in the Commonwealth Caribbean has been established by British and African cultures, but since independence South Asians have increasingly contributed and participated in that culture. This does not, however, mean that there are no problems in the meeting, conflict and adjustments of cultures taking place today in societies such as Guyana and Tinidad (see Premdas, 1995).

The societies, therefore, from which Caribbean migrants came to Britain were highly stratified social orders in which colour gradations were important, but no longer the entire or even the key determinant of a person's social status. Wealth and education had become more important social variables than colour or race for a place in the Creole societies of the sub-region. Political independence in the 1960s would change much in the social structure and allow for rapid social mobility, which had been stifled under British rule. M. G. Smith's (1965) portrayal of these societies as socially and culturally plural societies, in much the same manner as Furnivall (1948) had found in the Dutch East Indies, was mentioned in Chapter 1. It is relevant to make the point here that the theory has been convincingly challenged by several sociologists (Braithwaite, 1953; Smith, 1962) and historians (Brathwaite, 1978). Studies in the 1950s, the height of Caribbean migration to Britain, suggested that most migrants came with some skills, leading Deakin (1970) to say, rather grudgingly, that whilst a skilled person in Jamaica may not have had the same degree of skill as the UK person, none the less, 'on the whole those who migrated were successful in their own societies' (p. 35). In general, many migrants came with creditable skills and nearly all paid their own way in the hope of improving their lives and the life chances of their families. Like South Asians, Caribbean migrants were not therefore the dispossessed that some leading British experts appeared to think they were (see, for example, Rex, 1983, p. xvi and Chapter 7).

If Caribbean societies were generally social orders established on a *tabula rasa*, and over the period of close on four centuries developed modern societies remarkably free of the constraints of traditionalism, then the societies in South Asia and Africa from which people came to the United Kingdom were typically traditional societies. The countries in the sub-continent from which migrants came to Britain, including Bangladesh, India, Pakistan and Sri Lanka, are societies with traditions and customs stretching back in time to the centuries before the beginning of the Christian era. Although knowledge of West and East African pre-modern societies is less extensive than knowledge of Asian societies, contemporary African societies attest the longevity of African traditions (see, for example, Fage and Oliver, 1970). The notion of traditionalism denotes societies in which values, social structures and practices enjoy the sanction of convention, custom and longevity, such that over time these become acceptable justifications in themselves for different forms of social action (see, for example, Weber, 1947; Durkheim, 1933).

With Partition, the Indian Punjab had to cope with over four million refugees from the newly created West Punjab, now in Pakistan (see Rai, 1986). The Punjab allocated to India also had small land-holdings and the absence of primogeniture led to greater fragmentation in a densely populated area. In 1857 the Sikhs had supported the British during the Hindu and Muslim Mutiny or rebellion, and for this the keshadhari[9] Sikhs received favoured-group status in the British Raj (see, for example, Nayar and Singh, 1984). The proud warrior traditions of some castes were adroitly exploited for the reformed army in India, and the agricultural skills of others deployed on the fertile lands of the region after the British had established necessary irrigation schemes (see, for example, Nayar, 1966; Singh, 1966).[10] Not surprisingly, the Sikhs who migrated to Britain were mainly from the rural areas, where there was an unfavourable ratio of population to landholdings. With the majority of South Asians, religious and social norms go together, and *keshadhari* Sikhs strongly hold to the 'Five Ks' of Sikhism as essential elements of the definition they have of themselves. These include, leaving the hair and beard (*Kesh*) uncut, wearing a comb (*Kangha*), a pair of shorts (*Kachha*), a steel bangle on the wrist (*Kara*) and carrying a sword (*Kirpan*). The ten Gurus of Sikhism – from the saintly founder Guru Nanak in the fifteenth century to the warrior and last Guru Gorbind Singh in the eighteenth century – sought to abolish caste, but it is still highly relevant to their followers (see Kapur, 1986). It would appear that chain migration from particular areas and occupational specialisations (see, Ballard, 1994) may have reproduced caste differentiation.

Pakistani migrants also tended to have been farmers, as well as some middle-class professionals and entrepreneurs (see Shaw, 1994; Werbner, 1994). Like the Sikhs, Muslims make no sharp distinction between the secular and the religious worlds. They would seek to maintain the pillars of Islam: profession of faith, daily prayers, alms-giving, fasting during Ramadan and pilgrimage to Mecca; the eating of pork and the drinking of alcohol were also prohibited amongst the faithful. Hindus from India tended to be craftsmen and members of the agricultural castes who were hard pressed for land in Gujarat, but many were also educated with professional occupations. British Asians from East Africa tended to be, in the main, skilled and professional people from the groups which had migrated earlier to that region of the empire. On the whole, they had become more used to British ways and were better educated, but still holding fast to their traditions largely because East African societies, dominated by British settlers, demanded these of them. In the socially and culturally plural societies of East Africa, each individual was European, Asian or African – and in that order (see Twaddle, 1975)

The movement of peoples from very different societies within the empire remains dynamic. In the age of high technology, cheap travel and the awareness of folk and community, people are able to keep in close contact with each other, as noted earlier. What may be described as 'diasporic relations' and 'diasporic politics' have therefore emerged as major features of contemporary societies and are to be regarded as part of the international context of race relations. It is now possible for groups to maintain close links across considerable spatial distance, even when they are located deep within other cultural centres. Cheap and abundantly available means of mass communication by telephone, facsimile, the internet, and travel, are directly accessible to individuals. The more impersonal television, radio and newspaper media bring instant reports of news and items of interest to a world community increasingly aware of global events. Thus, communities in Britain with backgrounds in Africa, Asia and the Caribbean have maintained close and living links with the homelands of their parents in closely knitted ways which were not before available to communities of immigrants or even European colonisers. Travel to and from the Indian sub-continent, Africa and the Caribbean is a common feature of the contemporary world, providing challenges and opportunities for culture-contact that were undreamt of not so many decades ago during the imperial age.

Moreover, there have also been a number of political considerations which have helped to maintain such close links between Britain's new minority ethnic groups and the politics of their homelands. Some of Britain's new minority ethnic communities have experienced minority status in their homelands and, therefore, have sought to help those who remained at home and continue the struggles against oppression and sometimes the struggle for autonomy (Tatla, 1994). Such have been the situations with the Sikhs in India and Tamils in Sri Lanka. In Pakistan and India, there have been various generalised and specific struggles demanding the loyalty and support of communities in Britain and the diasporic politics of these countries continue to throw up real problems for these communities. With respect to Caribbean communities, the New Jewel revolution in Grenada in 1979 and the American invasion in 1984, the situation of division and conflict between Africans and East Indians in Guyana from the 1960s, and a series of natural disasters such as hurricanes in the region, have acted to ensure close links between communities in Britain and those 'back home'.

## Conclusion

As suggested in the last chapter, M. G. Smith's notion of differential incorporation is relevant to an understanding of British race relations. In the colonies, the British differentially incorporated groups of people into the social structures and political systems found, modified and sometimes established more or less from scratch. The essential dividing factor was the colour or race of both the colonised and the coloniser. Class and status depended on race and colour and, to a lesser degree, wealth and education. As we will see in later chapters, this kind of racial and social differentiation carried over into the management and control of ethnic pluralism in post-imperial Britain. None the less, in the face of an overwhelming majoritarian society, these differences did not always hinder unity of purpose on the part of those who did not enjoy what Smith called universal or uniform incorporation. Indeed, the new minorities were often to find a basis for political action, particularly in their responses to ethnic mobilisation in sections of the majority society. It is now relevant, therefore, to explore further some salient aspects of the political context of the multi-cultural society.

# 3   The Political Context

## Introduction

The discussion so far suggests that the political dimension of a society is of considerable relevance to the sociological understanding of race relations and this is as true for multi-cultural Britain today as it was for the imperial order considered in the last chapter. Issues or problems of race and ethnic relations are discussed and solutions sought in a variety of institutions of civil society, but the resolution of such problems is generally pursued within the political system. Of course, sometimes these problems are deliberately avoided, often because a political system may not have the capacity or will to address them, or their avoidance may serve powerful interests. As we noted in Chapter 2, the attitude of the imperial British state towards the multiplicity of peoples throughout the empire was important in shaping the patterns of race relations that developed. But in post-imperial Britain, the unitary state has not discouraged these groups' adaptive political capabilities. Thus, whilst society may be described as multi-cultural, the state remains the traditionally unified construction it became from the seventeenth century. To be sure, in the late 1970s there were talks of devolution of state power to Celtic Britain, and in October 1997 the Blair government conducted two referenda in Scotland and Wales to gain support for such devolution. But essentially the British state's unitary structure is significantly mediated by the globalisation of capital and an increasingly strong European Union. In these circumstances the best option for new minorities has been to articulate their views of public affairs through existing political institutions. Within the existing complex of political organisations, the party political system remains the single most relevant institution in integrating new members of the electorate and offering opportunities for active participation in deliberations over public affairs. However, in focusing upon the processes of political life it is also necessary to consider non-party forms of political participation.

The discussion in this chapter therefore revolves around two closely related factors: first, the general political response to the entry and settlement of black and brown people in the country; and second, the ways in which these new minorities have sought to become active participants in the political life of post-imperial Britain.

## The General Political Response

Almost from the start of large-scale migration to Britain in the 1940s, black and brown entry and settlement have been a focus of political attention. Cabinet papers released for the early years of migration reveal that Clement Attlee's government as early as 1950 were concerned with West Indians coming into the country, and discussions commenced about how to influence their patterns of work and settlement as well as to curtail their future entry into the country (Carter *et al.*, 1987; Layton-Henry, 1987; also, Dean, 1987). These concerns emerged within the Labour leadership only two years after the passing of the 1948 British Nationality Act, which had sought to clarify the notion of a common British citizenship for all members of the empire and dominions. But the Act was one of political exigency that the Attlee government devised to control the emergent nationalism of the white Dominions (see Goulbourne, 1991, Chapter 5). The Home Secretary, Chuter Ede, explained to the cabinet that Canada's unilateral move to establish her own citizenship, posed the

> danger that one or more of the Dominions may in the future be disposed to drop the common status altogether and give way to demands from within for completely separate nationhood. (Cabinet Papers, August 1946, p.1)

The attempt was of course ultimately futile. Nationalism swept not only the white Dominions but much more dramatically it spread like wildfire in the brown and black colonies and this led to the construction of separate citizenships for the new nation-states that emerged in Africa, Asia and the Caribbean. Just as decolonisation was leading to the construction of new national identities in those parts of the world, the same process was influencing the war-torn and decaying imperial centre to strive for a redefinition in an emergent post-imperial order. New minorities were to provide the sharp focus against which redefinition of island or lesser Britain would be moulded. In particular, new minorities were to become the snare in the politics of immigration and citizenship. Much has been written about these matters from the legal point of view (for example, Evans, 1983; Macdonald, 1977), as well as from the standpoint of the nation's political life (for example, Layton-Henry, 1992; Messina, 1989; Sewell, 1993), making it unnecessary to repeat the details. However, from the point of view of the argument being advanced here about the enterprise of redefining the British, it may be worth briefly mentioning a few points about these developments.

The problems associated with decolonisation and post-imperial restructuring became enmeshed with the process of migration. The concerns of cabinet members in the early 1950s about the entry of West Indians into the country turned, by the end of the decade, to a rallying call within the Conservative party for an end to black and brown immigration. Debate in Parliament over the issue was to continue, resulting in the 1962 Commonwealth Immigration Act. This Act marked the first dramatic and overt political intervention in the process of immigration from the black and brown Commonwealth and established, or at least signalled, the terms on which a declining imperial power would henceforth come to arrangements with emerging nation-states in Africa, Asia and the Caribbean about the movement of people across national boundaries. Significant immigration has long ceased, with relatively few individuals joining their families and Britain gaining the reputation of being an unlikely recipient European Union state of asylum seekers (see, Cohen, 1994; S. Goulbourne, 1997). None the less, even if the fact of immigration is dormant most of the time, it has been utilised to effect rapid majority ethnic mobilisation, particularly at election times, by some members of the Conservative party. The ease with which this majoritarian ethnic mobilisation can be effected suggests that the majority indigenous British people have been uncomfortable with their country's post-imperial identity and there are significant elements in this population who continue to see black and brown citizens as an hindrance to the emergence of a new identity. Thus, although post-imperial Britain is becoming more clearly defined as a European country with a relatively moderate future as one of several members of a large political union, an uncertainty lingers for politicians to exploit in their pursuit of office.

The political potential of the immigration question has been closely bound up with the attempt to redefine nationhood through citizenship. In considering legislation over citizenship, Ede and his colleagues wanted to create

> some form of citizenship which would be the gateway through which the status of British subject would be conferred upon the inhabitants of the United Kingdom and . . . upon the inhabitants of the colonies.
>
> (Cabinet Papers, July 1946, p. 4)

This notion of an inclusive citizenship not only collapsed in the face of vibrant nationalism, but it also gave way to a narrowly defined British citizenship. The 1971 Immigration Act had commenced this process of –developing an exclusive understanding of British citizenship–a project that stood in sharp contrast to the inclusive intentions of the 1948 Act. The 1971 Act outlined several categories of British citizens, including a British Dependent Territories citizen, a British National (Overseas), a –British Overseas citizen, a British protected person and a British subject. These statuses are matters of much controversy among immigration and anti-discrimination lawyers, but for the purpose at hand the most important aspect of the Act was the distinction made between 'patrials' and 'non-patrials' with differential rights conferred on British citizens. The –exclusiveness on ethnic or racial grounds was most forcefully expressed by this infamous provision. This was not unfairly understood to be Britain's way of maintaining close links with kith and kin in those parts of the former empire which had been peopled by them. For millions of people in the former empire, particularly those areas which had been colonies of settlement–Australasia, Canada, South Africa and the then rebel colony of Southern Rhodesia, now Zimbabwe–British citizenship and free entry into Britain were available because a grandfather had been born in this country. At the same time, the Act made some British citizens non-patrials. Non-patrial citizens had no automatic right of entry into the country, but sometimes they were precisely the people who needed to emigrate to Britain because, in the main, Asians in East and Central Africa were the people immediately and significantly affected by this aspect of the legislation. Those who had opted for British citizenship at the point of political independence in these parts of the empire found themselves without rights of entry into Britain. The patrial and non-patrial principles of the legislation sanctioned the distinction Enoch Powell had made from 1968 between people who belonged to Britain and those who did not. At the Conservative party conference the year after the Act was passed Powell confidently reasserted his point thus

> when the East African countries became independent there was no suggestion, let alone undertaking, in Parliament or outside, that those inhabitants who remained citizens of the United Kingdom and Colonies would have right of entry into this country . . . the practice of international law . . . applies in our case only to those who belong to the United Kingdom and not to other Commonwealth citizens, whether classified as citizens of the United Kingdom and Colonies or not. (Conservative Party, 1972, p. 72)

The process of redefining British ethnic nationhood through citizen-ship legislation came to a close with the 1981 British Nationality Act. The measure continued the principle of differential rights first begun in the 1971 Act by abolishing the ancient Anglo-Saxon tradition of *jus soli*, that is, citizenship deriving from the place of a person's birth, and implementing the principle of citizenship by descent, that is, the Contin-ental European practice of *jus sanguinis*. This was to bring Britain in line, it was claimed, with European partners in the then Community as they moved towards deeper integration within the European Union un-der the Maastrict Treaty. Children of Commonwealth citizens resident in the UK do not become British citizens by virtue of being born in the country. Such individuals can apply for citizenship after ten years' con-tinuous residence in the country and the children born outside the UK to registered citizens are also regarded as British citizens, but these two rules came as amendments to the original Bill (see Layton-Henry, 1992). The Act reinforced the distinction between British Overseas subjects, who do not have rights of entry and residence in Britain, and United Kingdom citizens, who do have these rights.

But it was not only the matter of immigration into Britain which led to political response and legislation by the central state. The settlement of new minorities also triggered right-wing responses, further forcing the state to take action. The most dramatic of these events were the white riots of 1958 in Notting Hill, Nottingham and other British cities against the entry and settlement of people from the Caribbean islands (see Pilk-ington, 1988). Of course, these events were not unique or new. They were parts of a recognisable pattern of objection to initial black entry and settlement in these islands since at least the first Elizabethan age in the late seventeenth century. An Act of Good Queen Bess in 1596 made it clear that

> there are lately divers blackamoores brought into the realm, of which kind of people there are already here too manie considering how God hath blessed this lande with great increase of people of our owne nation as anie contrie in the world, whereof manie for want of service and meanse to sett them in work fall in idleness and to great extremytie that those kinde of people shall be sent forth of the lande.
>
> (Shyllon, 1974, p. x)

The intent and spirit of this statement are very clearly understood in contemporary Britain, particularly with respect to such matters as housing, employment and social services, and, of course, the very pres-ence of black and brown people. Almost four centuries after the Good

Queen's measure, in 1919, there were riots in Liverpool and Bute Town in Cardiff, against black seamen, who had settled in British ports and established families with their partners from the indigenous population. These disturbances led to the repatriation of blacks by the imperial state in the 1920s (Cohen and May, 1975; Phillips, 1974). When in 1968 the then Conservative MP for Wolverhampton, J. Enoch Powell, began a new career as a prophet of doom warning that the entry and settlement of black and brown people in Britain would result in the running of 'rivers of blood' on British streets, many workers marched in his support (see Foot, 1969). Again, in 1971, at the height of the Ugandan Asian crisis, dock workers marched in London in an attempt to dissuade Edward Heath's Conservative government from living up to their international obligations to provide a home for the British refugees. More generally, the objections to the presence of black and brown people in Britain have been expressed by extreme right-wingers within the Conservative party, such as the Monday Club, as well as extra-parliamentary groups, such as the National Front. These groups advocate a policy of repatriation for all British citizens who are not white. But whilst the views of these groups have significantly influenced politics and specific policies about immigration and nationality, they do not represent the views and practices of the majority population and therefore have not been able to find party representation in Parliament. They have, however, won seats in local government elections, particularly in areas of concentrated settlement by Asians, such as Tower Hamlets. Moreover, individuals on the right of the British political spectrum have had a significant influence on decision-making with respect to new minorities, particularly in the changes to immigration and citizenship laws. But these general responses must be situated within the more specific context of party political competition for office.

## The Political Parties and New Minorities

It is not surprising that the crucial political responses to the black and brown presence in post-war Britain have been those of the political parties, particularly the two main parties, the Conservatives and Labour, but also the Liberal party and later the Liberal Democrats. Political parties aggregate votes and interests in order to form governments and in so doing they serve the important functions of introducing and integrating new members of an electorate into a democratic political system and, where necessary, they may even introduce new voters to the political culture. As organisations based on popular support, parties necessarily respond to changing events and the feelings of their supporters, but they also influence and sometimes form public opinion. They are perhaps more likely to perform these functions in the British situation where competition historically has been between two main rivals, and where party loyalty has been strong. The Conservatives, Labour and Liberal Democrats have, therefore, been in a unique position to channel, manipulate and influence their supporters in public debates over highly charged issues about minority ethnic groups, as well as providing the institutional means whereby these groups participate in national and local politics.

In general, the conclusion drawn by most commentators on new minority ethnic groups and politics in Britain is that for the better part of two decades, from the late 1950s to the early 1960s, the Conservative and Labour parties succeeded in maintaining a neutrality about race relations. The view is that the parties refused to make immigration and the black presence a political issue for party political gain (see Sewell, 1993, pp. 22–3). The parties also refrained from addressing many of the problems the new communities faced, until 1965 when the first Race Relations Act was passed, as we will see in Chapter 5. The period has therefore been seen as one of benign neglect on the part of the parties and governments, because they appeared to have thought that to discuss openly problems of race relations was to be less than gentlemanly. Indeed, these years have been generally seen as a kind of open, *laissez-faire* period, or liberal hour, in British race relations. This view is valid in so far as the parties did not seek to exploit the situation by mobilising racial animosity in the majority population, but instead chose to let white asperity remain relatively dormant. The view, however, has to be modified to take account of the early concerns of politicians and government members and leaders about the entry and settlement of black and brown people as Carter *et al.* (1987) and Layton-Henry (1987) have described. The period may not have been as liberal or *laissez-faire* as was thought in the 1960s, because the state had long kept a close eye on such matters as number of immigrants entering the country, areas of work and residence, and points of potential conflict such as social care provisions, housing and policing. The first response of the state to the black and brown presence was carefully to watch the situation but take as little action as possible. The liberalism of the time, therefore, was displayed in the relative passivity of the state, not an absence of vigilance nor ignorance of the situation.

The white riots in Notting Hill changed this by giving courage to those in the Conservative party who wanted to see action taken to stop further immigration. The result was the 1962 Commonwealth Immigration Act, which placed a check on primary immigration by requiring immigrants to have work vouchers, but also allowing some dependants to join families already in the country. It was, however, the dramatic election of the Conservative candidate, Peter Griffiths, who Harold Wilson was later to describe as a parliamentary 'leper', in Birmingham on a platform opposing black and brown immigration against a front-bench Labour politician, Patrick Gordon-Walker, which sounded the death knell for benign neglect or the supposed 'liberal hour'. After 1964, real and imagined problems of immigration would become regular features in national elections, with the Conservatives taking the lead to introduce or reinforce strong immigration controls and forcing Labour to defend supposedly more liberal policies. In office, however, both parties have tended to behave in much the same way in this area of national life. The notable exception is that Labour, as we shall see in Chapter 5, introduced three Race Relations Acts during their tenures in office in 1964–70 and again in 1974–9. The Conservatives, on the other hand, have consistently refused to take any major or decisive action to modify the law to take into account new developments. This passive approach to race relations was particularly strong during the party's long period in office from Margaret Thatcher's victory in 1979 to the defeat of John Major's government in May 1997. Although the issues of immigration and citizenship have been extensively covered in the literature and I have already suggested their relevance to this discussion, it may be worth returning to them to illustrate further the similarities and differences between the parties' responses to the presence of black and brown people, before turning to the question of these groups' participation within the parties.

The 1962 Commonwealth Immigration Act marked a watershed in British race relations. In opposition the Labour party opposed the measure, but once in office from 1964 their leaders changed their tune. At the height of the debate around the 1962 measure, the party called for an end to racial discrimination and the equal integration of the new minorities into British society. In the House of Commons, Labour opposed the Conservatives who linked immigration with rising crime, argued that immigrants brought new diseases into the country and that they made undue demands on the social services in local authorities (Labour Party, 1962). In 1965, the annual conference at Blackpool was assured by the leadership that Labour would 'tighten up the regulations governing entry with a view to preventing evasion of controls' (Labour Party, 1965, p. 79) that they had earlier opposed. Labour in office did not seek to reverse these controls, but rather sought to build the party's policies on them. This tough stand in office has probably been intended to be an answer to the charge that as a party they were 'soft' on immigration, and in the 1990s 'soft' on asylum seekers. From the mid-1960s to today, Labour's leadership have been careful to stress that the party supports monitored control hand in hand with the promotion of good race relations. This two-pronged perspective has long been elevated to a kind of bi-partisan motto about something loosely called 'good race relations'. Not to have control is not to have good race relations; allow many black and brown people into Britain and there will be poor race relations. This formulation appears to pick upon one of the assumptions first clearly articulated by J. Enoch Powell in his 'rivers of blood' speech in Birmingham in 1968: that is, the presence of black and brown people will inevitably result in much spilling of British blood on British soil. This conjures images of the savagery meted out to natives in different parts of the empire. It was as if Powell saw such savagery reversed in a visitation by ex-colonial peoples, or as if he had a nightmare of the kind of social and psychic cleansing George Sorel (1967) envisaged in syndicalism, and Frantz Fanon (1968, 1970) saw as necessary for the individual as well as communities to become mentally free from European colonial domination.

In contrast to Labour, the Conservatives perceived questions about entry, settlement and integration of black and brown minorities in relatively simpler terms. Since the debates about control of immigration in the early 1960s, the question of black and brown immigration and settlement have been about control followed by a bland refusal to legislate to improve race relations in the country. The party's caption on the picture of a young black man in 1979 which stated 'Labour says he is black, Conservatives say he is British' may be the best expression of the party's approach to the integration of new minorities into the party. Whilst the Conservatives have taken few steps actively to promote good race relations through legislation, they have none the less been active in attempting to redefine the notion of the British nation so that as few as possible non-white peoples are included. Thus, the 1971 Immigration Act made it necessary for individuals who were British from birth to register as citizens or lose what they thought was an inalienable right that they enjoyed. Again, in 1981 the Conservatives placed on the statute book the British Nationality Act to define still more closely the meaning of British status. Most commentators on these developments have remarked upon how exclusionary nationality and immigration laws have been counterposed with the three race relations acts from

1965 to 1981, and they have pointed to the underlying principle as being that more immigration would be inimical to good race relations within Britain. This perspective of developments was to have a profound effect on race relations legislation.

It might be suggested, however, that three additional points should be borne in mind about the attempt to redefine British national identity through citizenship and immigration laws. First, the fact that immigration and settlement of former colonial peoples from Africa, Asia and the Caribbean were taking place on an unprecedented scale within a relatively short period of time, helped white Britishers to redefine their own specific national identity in a rapidly changing post-World-War-Two world in which Britain was no longer the global superpower she had been during the eighteenth and nineteenth centuries. Had there not been the presence of former colonised peoples on metropolitan soil, the issue may not have been as focused as it became in the decades of the 1960s, to the 1980s. It is usual to point to the benefits that immigrants brought to the economy, but this catalytic function of their presence is generally ignored.

Second, the attempt to redefine and come to grips with a national British identity in the decades of final decline mirrored the construction of national identities in the new nation-states which were emerging out of the former empire. There is a tendency to see the imperial power as having a relatively clear sense of its own national identity, going out into the wider world and retreating back into its own boundaries intact, as if nothing had happened in the intervening centuries. But even if British national identity were a settled matter before the acquisition of empire, the contact with the wider world and the experience of domination would be expected to modify conceptions of the nation and the state. It may, therefore, be suggested that the British nation-state at the centre of the empire re-discovered nationalism, or sought to take up from where it left off during the formation of such an identity in pre-imperial days. This was an historic enterprise not entirely dissimilar to that in the new nation-states which were emerging from a dying imperial order. In other words, de-colonisation in the colonies implied de-imperialisation in the imperial centre; they were two sides of the same coin. The problems of integration of Anglo-Indians, Muslims, Hindus, Christians and others in India, Asians and Africans in post-colonial East Africa, and Africans, Asians, Caribbeans and indigenous Europeans in Britain may not be as different as they first appeared, and when we point to differences we too often ignore some important similarities. At the very least, the political contexts of these different situations share certain common features, particularly the need to redefine, or define for the first time, national identities. It is interesting to note that in the distinguished literature on political development, few political analysts concerned themselves with this aspect of development. Samuel Huntington's (1968) work on the emergence of Turkey as the Ottoman Empire crumbled, is a notable exception, and it may be suggested that, although unlike Turkey, (Ireland apart) Britain had no physical boundaries with her empire, making the experience of loss less traumatic. But she too faced the need to find herself in a post-imperial age.

The third point to be made about the process of de-colonisation and de-imperialisation is that it is still unfolding as we approach the twenty-first century and is likely to penetrate deep into that new age. In Britain, new minorities from the former colonial world are therefore faced with the double task of constructing new post-colonial as well as post-imperial identities. Through a quirk of history (migration) these new minorities do not directly experience post-colonialism. At the same time, partly because of their initially hostile reception into a Britain herself uncertain about her post-imperial future, these new minorities are not exclusively British in their own perceptions of belongingness. This does not mean that they are necessarily caught up in the *angst* of what some sociologists have described as being 'between two cultures' (see, for example, Watson, 1977). What is happening is much more complex than this. The *angst* that new minorities experience has to do with the tensions necessarily involved in the incipient change of cultures, what Malinowski called culture-change as a result of culture-contact. After all, far more culture-contact is freely occurring between ordinary indigenous white Europeans, Africans of all description and Asians than ever took place under the empire. Post-imperial Britain is a democracy with a range of possibilities, whereas the imperial order was essentially a dictatorship which had an interest in keeping people apart.

Race relations in Britain may therefore be said to be situated within, or interspersed with, the tensions created at a time when people from differentially shared historical experiences are forging new forms of identities in a world in which belongingness to the nation-state is no longer the significant identifier it was. Whereas in the past politicians and managers of state institutions had enough power to censor or close off some of these pressure points, or at least manipulate political situations for their own purposes, today this is not so easily done. Indeed, it may be that this increasingly complex situation of post-imperial society in Britain has been forcing the pace towards an apparently greater tolerance of difference. Legislation and the activities of organisations directly concerned with race relations provide ways through which potentially disruptive social and political forces can be largely managed and sometimes channelled towards desirable ends within the social and political structures. Perhaps in the long run the active participation by voters and politicians from minority ethnic groups will prove to be the most effective of these means. It may, however, be best to discuss these forms of participation within the parties as part of the response of minorities themselves to the political situation in Britain. After all, the initiative to engage closely with political institutions came from minority communities, not the reverse.

## Political Responses by New Minorities

These general comments provide a basis for a closer assessment of how the parties have been channels for the active participation of new minorities in the political life of the nation. Three closely related strands in the political participation of Britain's new minority ethnic groups in the nation's political life informed events to this point: first, self-organisation within communities around specific issues; second, participation as voters in local and national elections; and, third, the emergence of politicians from these communities seeking a base within the mainstream of established political parties. People from the Caribbean, India, Pakistan and parts of Africa enjoyed voting rights under the law in Britain and did not need to be formally enfranchised in order to participate in the electoral and political systems in the country. Moreover, Commonwealth citizens who have not formally changed their status whilst resident in Britain are able to vote. Even so, it took concerted effort on the part of Asians and African-Caribbean politicians to realise the legitimate and active participation of members of their respective communities in the nation's political affairs. In the mid-1990s this was still a developing political situation, because whilst in the Labour party at least one front-bench speaker came from the minority ethnic communities, none had been a member of national government. This is unlike the situation in France where there have been African and Caribbean members of administrations by virtue of membership of the French nation and the incorporation of Réunion, Martinique and Guadeloupe into the unitary French political system (see Hintjens, 1995). In the years leading up to Tony Blair's victory of New Labour in 1997, it was widely expected in the minority ethnic communities in Britain that there would be at least two members from the new minority ethnic communities in a new administration.[1]

But members from these communities have been active in the established political parties, and are therefore being integrated into the complex mainstream of political life. However, in the main the process of integration remains rather one-sided. Voters and aspirant politicians from African-Caribbean and Asian communities have maintained a remarkable loyalty to the Labour Party. To be sure, the former Liberal Party and their successors – the Social and Liberal Democratic Party and now the Liberal Democratic Party – have enjoyed support from minority ethnic communities both as voters and would-be politicians, but overwhelmingly support has been for Labour as those interested in electoral behaviour have pointed out for the election years since 1974, when for the first time voters in the minority ethnic communities came to the attention of the political parties (see Anwar, 1994).

Similarly, there are now several aspirant black and brown politicians in the Conservative Party, as the lists of the 1987, 1992 and 1997 general election candidates revealed. For example, the names of the ten candidates for the 1997 election from Asian and African-Caribbean communities suggest strong participation in the party by Asians: Javed Arain (Derby South), Dr Kabir Choudhury (Bethnal Green and Stepney), Nirj Deva MP (Brentford and Isleworth), Bashir Khanbai (Norwich South), Mark Kotecha (Liverpool Walton), Derek Laud (Tottenham), Mohammed Riaz (Bradford West), Geeta Sidhu (Blackburn), Shailesh Vara (Birmingham Ladywood) and Councillor Nadhim Zahawi (Erith and Thamesmead). None were elected, and even Nerj Deva lost his seat as part of the historic Labour victory at the polls throughout the country in the elections held on 1 May 1997. The tour of Bangladesh, India and Pakistan by John Major and businessmen in early January 1997, followed by his keynote speech at the Commonwealth Institute on the commemoration of India and Pakistan's fiftieth anniversary of independence were correctly seen as attempts to attract more Asian voters to the Conservatives (Conservative Party, 1997). These developments suggest a significant change in Conservative politics: it appears that leaders at least wish to draw more directly than hitherto on the resources of the Asian communities, rather than constantly harp on about the dangers of immigration and the threat to British culture and identity that former spokespersons such as Enoch Powell and Margaret Thatcher mobilised from the 1960s to the 1980s. For example, Major's speech stressed that his party is inclusive, and stood for all sections of the nation, including new minorities, and whilst he preferred the concept of cosmopolitanism to multi-culturalism to describe British society, his speech marked him off from aspects of his Thatcherite legacy. This was picked up by the new Leader, William Hague, in late 1997.

But the Conservatives do not enjoy the overwhelming support that Labour now runs the danger of taking for granted. While there was a decline in Asian voters' support for Labour between the elections of 1987 and 1992, over 70 per cent still voted Labour in 1992 (Anwar, 1994). Support from the African-Caribbean population remained around 98 per cent in 1992 (ibid.) This kind of support for one party has, none the less, had some rewards for aspirant politicians from the minority ethnic communities. For example, the Labour party, pressured by its unofficial 'Black Sections' in the 1980s (see Shukra, 1990), succumbed to demands to nominate black and brown candidates for winnable seats in the inner-city areas of the country such as Leicester and some parts of London. This resulted in 1987 in the election of four MPs from the African-Caribbean and Asian communities for Labour: Diane Abbot in Hackney, Paul Boateng in Brent, Bernie Grant in Tottenham, and Keith Vaz in Leicester East. In the 1992 general elections these members were re-elected to the Commons and joined by Piara Khabra, whilst Nirj Deva became the first post-War Asian member of the House on the Conservative side. John Taylor in Cheltenham was defeated by the combined efforts of Tory rebels and the Liberal Democrats who had not so subtly played the race card by asking supporters to vote for 'a local man'. Dr Ashok Kumar who had won Langborough in Yorkshire in a by-election in November 1991 for Labour was defeated in the 1992 general elections by the Conservative candidate he had defeated in 1991. In the 1997 general election[9] Labour fielded nine and the Liberal Democrats fifteen candidates from minority ethnic communities, and, as noted, the Conservatives ten individuals from the new minority ethnic communities, mostly from the Asian communities. All the Labour candidates were elected, but none of the black and brown candidates in the Conservative and Liberal Democrat parties were successful. But the candidates selected by the Liberal Democrats suggested that political participation by members from communities other than African-Caribbean and Asian is now taking off, because two were of Chinese and one of Iraqi backgrounds.

Although the interest in black and brown political participation tends to centre around current involvement in elections and the parties, it must not be forgotten that individuals from African, Caribbean and Asian backgrounds have long been engaged with British politics. In the latter part of the nineteenth century Lord Sinha of Raipur sat in the House of Lords, and later in the century and during the first two decades of the present century, Dadabhai Naoroji, Sir Mancherjee Bhownagree and Shapuriji Saklatvala were members of the House of

Commons for the Conservative, Labour and Communist parties. In the post-World-War-Two period, Lords Constantine, Pitt, Chitnis, and Desai and Baroness Flather have been individuals from the new minority ethnic communities. Whilst Flather, a former Conservative councillor and mayor in Maidenhead was the first woman from these communities to sit in the Lords, Lord Taylor of Warwick (the former John Taylor) was the first person from the Caribbean communities to sit on the Conservative side in that place.

The general elections of 1987 were significant in being the first time that black and brown candidates succeeded in being elected to the House of Commons in the post-World-War-Two years, but this should not overshadow the successes of individuals from minority ethnic communites in local government. In the 1980s, the key decade of Thatcherism which asserted a strong majority ethnic nationalism, Britain also witnessed the burgeoning of black and brown electoral participation in local government in cities across the country. In a number of these cities we saw black and brown mayors but, more significantly, elected councillors appeared from these communities (see Anwar, 1994). Haringay, Brent and Lambeth councils elected Bernie Grant, Merle Amory and Linda Bellos as leaders, and Herman Ousley was to become chief executive of Lambeth. In late 1996 one leading observer[3] of black and brown participation in local electoral politics estimated that there were about 400 Asian and African Caribbean elected councillors throughout the country.[4]

Within minority ethnic communities, self-organisation as a response to difficulties found in the land of settlement as well as the desire to establish on a fairly regular basis shared aspirations and common grounds for discussion and fellowship, were quick to appear soon after arrival in Britain. A number of types of self-help organisations emerged vociferously voicing protest over specific issues in education, housing, employment, immigration, nationality laws, and so forth. Such activities nearly always involved working with different groups, sometimes with the trades unions and other groups from the majority society, and sometimes community groups acted independently of each other. For example, important aspects of the context in which the Race Relations Act 1976 was passed was, as Sooben (1990, Chapter 6) has pointed out, were the highly publicised strike by Asian workers at the Mansfield Hosiery Mills in 1972, the 1974 dramatic disputes between Asian workers and employers at Imperial Typewriters in Leicester, and the widespread militancy of Caribbean youths against police brutality in major British cities, particularly from the late 1960s to the 1980s (see, for example, Humphry, 1972; Solomos, 1988).

Although these were the most salient and broadly covered events in the media, there were several other interlinked developments from the early 1970s which helped to create an atmosphere or the context for change. These included the formation of protest groups, particularly by black youths who had either been brought up in the UK or were born here to the immigrant generation. In 1970 the Black Panther Movement and the Black Unity and Freedom Party were formed in London with branches in other parts of the country such as Manchester. In various parts of London and other major cities where Caribbean people had settled, a number of radical groups also sprang up. In the black communities of London and elsewhere, perhaps the single most dramatic event of these years was the trial of the Mangrove Nine in Notting Hill (see Keith, 1990, 1993) where the police came into direct confrontation with young and articulate black youths who saw the militant activities of the Black Panthers in Oakland, California led by Huey Newton, Bobby Seale and Eldridge Cleaver as their models. Some of these groups organised around major issues of the day such as the 1971 Immigration Act, internment in Ulster and the Industrial Relations Act of Edward Heath's Conservative government. Others pursued knowledge about Africa, the Caribbean and black people in other parts of the world. In 1971–2 a Select Committee of the House reported on the poor relations between the police and the black community (see Solomos, 1988). Whilst some groups addressed the issues involved, others were more concerned with the depressing situation of black children in schools detailed in Bernard Coard's (1971) book and the Select Committee's report in 1972, as well as that from the Department of Education in 1974 on the education of immigrant children. These groups espoused Pan-Africanism, African liberation on the continent as well as in the diaspora, and called for radical change along class as well as racial lines in Britain and elsewhere. Most saw black people in Britain as members of the working classes, but there were some, for example the South East London People's Organisation based in New Cross, South London, who saw colour or racial affinity to be the most relevant consideration in the life chances of black people generally.

Dramatic international events in these years brought the Asian communities into considerable public view, leading to the formation in 1973 of the Standing Conference of Asian Organisations. These events included the war of liberation for Bangladesh (then East Pakistan), involving India and Pakistan in 1971 and the departure of Pakistan from the Commonwealth in 1973. Throughout much of 1972 the media carried numerous accounts of Idi Amin's Uganda, where he had taken power from the elected President Milton Obote and soon expelled the Asian population (Twaddle, 1975). In Britain, Enoch Powell urged the government not to accept the Ugandan Asians, but over 20 000 of them were accommodated in camps in different parts of the country (see Mamdani, 1973). At the same time, Martin Webster, leader of the National Front, made a good showing and saved his deposit in West Bromwich's by-election. The industrial militancy of Asian women was also taking place. But racial attacks against Asians were also increasing and this was dramatised by the fatal stabbing of eighteen-year-old Gurdip Singh Chaggar at a bus stop in Southall.

Taking the period from the 1980s, two dramatic and quite spontaneous events in the new minority communities have been of particular importance in having their voices heard by the wider community and local and national governments. These were the Rushdie affair, which started in 1988 and is continuing well into the 1990s, and earlier the Brixton disturbances of 1981. In 1988 Penguin published Salman Rushdie's *The Satanic Verses*, and within months there was a widespread national and international campaign led by militant Muslims in British cities such as Bradford and Ayotollah Khomeni's Iran against both the publisher and the author. Muslims were outraged by Penguin's publication of what some faithfuls saw as blasphemy against their religion, and against the author for writing what some saw as unacceptable utterances from a person born and brought up within a Muslim family and culture. The demand grew for the publishers and author to withdraw the book and for the author to apologise to adherents of the faith. When the book was not withdrawn the Ayotollah opened the last year of the decade with a *fatwa*, the call for the faithful to kill Rushdie as an act of vindication of Islam. In Bradford there was a dramatic burning of *The Satanic Verses* by Muslims, and in general many British Muslims availed themselves of the occasion to articulate their grievances against their perceived and actual treatment within a society which at one level postulates that it is secular, and at another level is deeply Christian in traditions, institutions and social practices. It is sometimes said that these features of British society may inadvertently exclude or hurt faithful or devout Muslims. In general, their demand on British society was for the law of blasphemy to be applied to Islam as well as to the Church of England, whose teachings the law protects.

Whilst Muslims have not gained what they want from the Rushdie affair, they have obviously gained much from the exposure of their hurt and subordinate position in Britain. Their status has been the subject of much discussion, the problems they face have been aired, and their case has been seen to present a real challenge for the principal tenets of British multi-culturalism, that is, toleration and celebration of difference. The events occasioned a series of seminars organised by the Commission for Racial Equality (CRE) to discuss the issue within the context of the ideology of the multi-cultural society (CRE, 1990a). The Commission has also worked with the national Action Committee on Islamic Affairs as well as other religious bodi:s 'to gather information about cases where people might have suffered discrimination on religious grounds' (CRE, 1996, p. 20). But the annual report of the Commission for 1995 stated that 'we were unable to find many examples of religious discrimination that were not already covered by the provisions of the Race Relations Act on indirect discrimination' (ibid.) None the less, Muslim organisations continue to organise to protect their faith in a society they believe to be hostile to them. Towards the end of the 1990s the influence of the anti-Rushdie agitation is still very much alive and Rushdie himself continued the life of an enforced recluse who dares not exercise his rights as a citizen of a free society. It is a paradox that perhaps the most well-known British person from a Muslim background is forced to lead such a private life in the multi-cultural society whose key virtue is toleration.

The second dramatic series of events which I wish to mention here is the earlier 1981 disturbances in Brixton, South London. These events also challenged many of the assumptions about fairness and justice for all in multi-cultural Britain, but in a manner that was perhaps more attuned to traditions of intrusion into the body politic. Whilst the Rushdie affair evoked images of religious intolerance of the kind experienced in the Europe of the Reformation and the Inquisition, the Brixton disturbances had echoes of more recent historical intrusion into the political system by popular movements during the last two centuries, when the frontiers of democracy were expanding beyond earlier narrow confines. It is therefore possible to see the Rushdie affair as being by far the more radical, and therefore more disturbing of these two sets of events within the British socio-political tradition of popular action. Whilst Brixton drew upon more recent British and Caribbean democratic traditions of popular protest, the Rushdie affair brought back onto the political agenda questions and forms of popular action that had been assumed to have no place in Europe of the post-Enlightenment era.

Sometimes referred to as 'the riots', the Brixton disturbances occurred on the weekend of 10–12 April 1981 and in November Lord Scarman who was appointed by the Home Secretary, William (now Lord) Whitelaw to investigate them reported that the events 'had not

previously been seen in this century in Britain . . . demonstrating to
millions . . . the fragile basis of the Queen's peace' (Scarman, 1981, p. 1).
The Brixton events triggered off similar disturbances in major cities
such as Bristol, Liverpool, Manchester, Birmingham, Wolverhampton
and Smethwick. The issues behind these events centred around the
poor relations between local police forces and the African-Caribbean
communities. The authorities had taken to saturation policing in black
communities and pouncing on any act which appeared to be outside
the law. In Brixton they had taken this a bridge too far. Community,
church and other leaders had been warning about this from at least 1972
when the Joshua Francis Defence Committee was formed by a group
of concerned individuals and groups such as the Association of Jamaicans, the Croydon Collective, the Black Panther Movement, the Black
Unity and Freedom Party and others around the case of a respected,
devout churchman, who had been viciously beaten by the police on his
way from work to home. In the eyes of the community this marked the
transition from police brutality against young black males to intimida-
tion of any black male who dared to walk the streets beyond certain
hours. By 1981 the presence of the police in the Brixton neighbourhood of
Coldharbour Lane, Railton Road, Somerlayton Road, and Shakespeare
Road to the south of the town was perceived to pose an ever-present
threat to the well being of the community as a whole.

The impact of these disturbances was far-reaching. They highlighted
the deplorable depths to which community–police relations had sunk
in inner cities up and down the country where African-Caribbean
people had settled. In Southall, with a high concentration of Asians,
there was the clear and unmistakable view that the police were inordin-
ately inactive in protecting Asian citizens from racist attacks by white
youths such as the skinheads. Thus, whilst in the African-Caribbean
communities the police were over-active or over zealous in going about
their duties, in Asian communities the opposite attitude was adopted.

These apparently innocent stances reflected differential imperial ste-
reotypes of African-Caribbeans and Asians. African-Caribbeans, particularly Jamaicans, were supposed to be factious in their attitudes to
authority. This reputation may have arisen as a result of the frequent defeat of British forces by the Maroons of Jamaica in the eighteenth century,
the constant fear of white Jamaicans that they would suffer a similar fate to
white Haitians following the successful Haitian Revolution under
Toussaint L'Ouverture (James, 1963) at the beginning of the nineteenth
century, and the memory of Paul Bogle's rebellion at Morant Bay in
1865. Of course, these events do not adequately explain the lingering

reputation for defiance that African-Caribbeans are either supposed to suffer or enjoy. South Asians were not passive recipients of European intrusion, but they none the less had a reputation for being non-confrontational, exclusive and accommodating. The two examples from British sociology that probably best illustrate this point are to be found in the work of John Rex and Geoff Dench. Arguably the most influential of the genre, Rex strongly asserted that West Indian associational groups are essentially 'confrontational and aggressive' and they tend to deviate from the norm of aggregate socio-political behaviour (Rex, 1979, chapter 8). On the other hand, Asians were collaborative and non-confrontational with regard to authority (ibid.) Dench made much the same assertions about Caribbean and Asian groups in British society and suggested that the non-confrontational approach of Asian groups is to be preferred to Caribbean forms of open protest and insistence on participation or incorporation on the same terms as the majority population (Dench, 1986). When, however, events such as those surrounding the Rushdie affair and incidents of Asian youths in the 1990s protesting on the streets as Caribbean youths had done in the 1970s, these authors have been conspicuous by their silence.

The Brixton disturbances led to public attention being turned onto the activities of the police and the nature of policing in a multi-cultural society. Brixton led to the recognition that the police needed to be more accountable to the communities they ostensibly serve, and the events raised questions about possible complacency about the fairness of British justice for all. The system as a whole required critical appraisal and change. After Brixton and the Scarman report, police forces in various parts of the country began to be more cautious and sought to build closer links with communities. They sought to hear and understand what communities might have to say about how they are actually served by the force, and the police addressed some of the problems which the authorities should have dealt with in the first place. For example, after Brixton they have sought to attract more Asians and African-Caribbeans into the force, but partly because of their poor reputation in minority ethnic communities there is still a strong reluctance by individuals from these groups to seek a career with the police.

More generally, after Brixton, society became more aware of the activities of the police and have wanted to make them more accountable for their actions to the specific communities they serve, rather than being satisfied with bland statements about democratic accountability through the Home Office. The response to Brixton by the police force throughout the country may have had something to do with the relatively low response to subsequent protests against the police in Tottenham where PC Keith Blakemore was killed in autumn 1985, and rioting in Handsworth, Birmingham. In the 1990s there have been, from time to time, comparatively low-key disturbances in a number of inner-city areas such as in Leeds, Birmingham and Bradford, but on none of these occasions have the cause or causes of the rioters caught the imagination of the public or their sympathy as occurred in Brixton in 1981. It might be hypothesised that at least part of the reason for this may have been the quick response of the force in the early 1980s and a recovery of a degree of the traditional support they enjoyed with the British public.

But self-organisation by African-Caribbean and Asian communities took forms other than spontaneous protests on the streets against the authorities, as with African-Caribbeans or against the establishment, as with Muslims. These communities have made their voices heard about injustices in the professions which affect their lives, and there have also been more relatively stable organisations to articulate grievances to decision-makers and those who implement policy. In the medical and legal professions groups have been formed to articulate the interests of black and brown members; in the semi-professions, such as school teaching and the caring occupations there have been similar bodies formed to articulate protest and promote mutual interests. Perhaps the most successful of these bodies has been the Society of Black Lawyers with membership from both sides of the profession. They have successfully challenged the exclusivity of the occupation and gained places in chambers and firms where earlier there had been exclusion of African-Caribbean and Asian lawyers. Similar stories would be true for the teaching and probation services, and many other occupations, but more work in this area is required before we can have the requisite appreciation of black and brown participation in the professions and the semi-professions.[5]

However, before engaging in spontaneous protests and before organising within and around occupations, minority ethnic groups formed other kinds of organisations which were largely based on widely shared experience, values and needs. Sometimes these organisations sought to address directly homeland issues and other times these organisations addressed general problems faced in this country. For example, the Association of Pakistani Organisations in the 1960s sought to provide an umbrella body to strengthen a wide range of such organisations throughout the country where Pakistanis had settled (John, 1969; also, Anwar, 1996; Werbner, 1994). In 1938 the Indian Workers Association (IWA) was founded in Coventry and at first concerned itself with supporting the struggle for independence in India. With independence and large-scale migration to Britain, the various associations also became concerned with problems of settlement and what leaders saw as working-class issues in Britain. As nationalism in the sub-continent fragmented or threatened to dismember parts of Pakistan and India, particularly the disputes between India and Pakistan over Kashmir, the Kashmiris' own aspirations, and the break away of East Pakistan to form Bangladesh in 1971, the IWAs also fragmented. Two major factions, both claiming to be the true IWA, emerged to claim the loyalty of their followers (see Josephedes, 1990). As noted, when it became increasingly important to organise around specific concerns arising from settlement in Britain from the 1970s, the Federation of Asian Organisations emerged with the aim of providing a central voice for all Asian groups.

In the meantime, as the Asian population has settled down to life in Britain a more complex and varied array of organisations has emerged. Having made a significant mark on the economy, particularly in the small-business sector, several Asian organisations have sprung up to represent their business interests. For example, in most major cities there are Asian business associations which seek to promote products and the interests of their members, share experience, and establish useful and practical links with other relevant bodies in the local communities. In response to new needs, small promotional groups have also sprung up in these communities, such as the radical Southall Black Sisters Collective, which challenges some long-standing assumptions about gender relations in Asian communities and their supposed passivity and tendency to be accommodating.

Very similar developments have taken place in the African-Caribbean communities, particularly in London and Birmingham where the vast majority have settled. In some respects it may be said that black organisations have been in Britain since the first attempts in the seventeenth century to encourage former slaves to return to West Africa and the founding of Sierra Leone. In the early twentieth century, Sylvester Williams, W. E. B. DuBois, and others organised the first Pan-African Congress in London, with the most important Fifth Congress taking place in Manchester in 1945. This Congress was significant for at least two reasons: first, it marked the taking over of the movement from diasporic leaders, such as George Padmore and W. E. B. DuBois, and the emergence of Africans from the continent, particularly Kwame Nkrumah of the then Gold Coast (later Ghana); second, a number of African and Caribbean settlers in Britain also attended the meeting, so that the proceedings were no longer restricted to diasporic intellectuals who had started the movement at the turn of the century. Earlier, in 1931, middle-class settlers, led by Dr Harold Moody, had started the League of Coloured Peoples in South London, and although there are not many direct continuities, these bodies provided the backdrop to the burgeoning of smaller organisations from the late 1950s and early 1960s in Caribbean communities.

The first and most durable of these organisations have been the island associations and the West Indian Standing Conference (WISC) founded in 1958 in the aftermaths of the Notting Hill riots. Migrants from each of the Caribbean islands established organisations to provide places where people with the same experiences could meet for companionship and mutual assistance. They also provided the opportunity for giving support to the decolonisation process taking place at the time throughout the region. There was a time when it appeared that these organisations – the Association of Jamaicans, Association of Barbadians, and so forth – would atrophy as the migrant generation became inactive, but the persistence of cultural values and close affinity to the islands would appear to provide sufficient energy to maintain these groups. This may be less the case with WISC, although it has displayed remarkable resilience and has survived despite changes, many of which appeared to make the organisation less relevant than the new ones. WISC, like a number of organisations in the Asian communities, has been an umbrella body which seeks to bring together individuals, but particularly groups of like mind and purpose.

It was noted earlier that from the 1960s several new organisations emerged. These were cross-national in character and strongly influenced by developments in the USA, such as the Civil Rights Movement, the Black Panther movement, and radical Pan-Africanism as well as the struggles against Portuguese colonialism in Angola, Mozambique and Guinea-Bissau. The struggles against apartheid in South Africa and opposition to the war in Vietnam also strongly influenced these new groups in their ideological outlooks, styles, rhetoric and vocabulary. In the late 1960s the United Coloured Peoples' Alliance (UCPA) was founded by the Nigerian playwright, Obi Egbuna (see Egbuna, 1971). The group's demise spawned both the Black Panther Movement and the Black Unity and Freedom Party mentioned above, groups which themselves were birthplaces for Alrick Cambridge's *The Black Liberator* and Darcus Howe and Linton Kwesi Johnson's *Race Today* journals, which sought to raise radical political awareness in the black communities (see Hall *et al.*, 1978). Radical bookshops and publishers, such as New Beacon Publishers in North London and Bogle L'Ouverture Publishers in West London, gained much strength from being based in communities, and in turn these communities were strengthened by the presence of publishers at the centre of discussions about Third-World issues, development and change.

In both the Asian and Caribbean communities, perhaps the most re-silient and widespread community organisations have been religious bodies – churches, mosques, temples and gurdwaras. It is well known that from ancient days migrants from the Indian sub-continent carried their religions with them wherever they went in Asia, Africa, the Carib-bean and more recently Europe. Indeed, for many Asians ethnicity is defined by their religion, and therefore religion plays a vitally import-ant role in the respective communities of Hindus, Moslems, Sikhs, Bud-dhists and Jains (Banks, 1994). The organisation around these faiths, including regular meetings at designated places, provide not only spir-itual succour, but also welfare and other kinds of mutual support and assistance. For example, a typical Sikh gurdwara will not only be a place of devotion and worship. A vitally important characteristic of that faith is the institution of the *langar*, or kitchen, which is usually open to all, irrespective of whether the individual is an adherent of Sikhism. For the faithful the gurdwara is a complex of worship, companionship, and sup-port for all members of the family and community.

Similarly, in Caribbean communities what are called black-led churches have provided mutual support for their members, their families and the community at large. After slavery in 1838, the non-conformist denominations, such as the Baptists, and later the Pentecostals, have been at the forefront of providing support for the people of the Carib-bean in their search for spiritual and physical well-being. It was natural, therefore, that Caribbean migrants to Britain would look to the churches for spiritual guidance and support. As with other British insti-tutions, however, migrants found that the traditional churches in Brit-ain were less than welcoming, and their hostility drove Caribbean Christians to found their own places of worship. These now provide the Christian faith as a whole with one of their most dynamic growth areas (see, for example, Charman, 1979; Gerloff, 1992). Not unlike Asian reli-gions or indeed radical Christian communities, the black-led churches have provided spiritual as well as material support for members, their families and the wider Caribbean community irrespective of racial or ethnic differences. Unlike other communities, however, and true to a strong Caribbean tradition, the black-led churches have in the main refrained from active participation in, or even general comment on, matters political. They have restricted themselves to the day-to-day material and spiritual needs of their members, some of whom are from other cultural or ethnic backgrounds.

## Conclusion

This chapter has been concerned with aspects of the political dimension of British race relations. It has not been concerned with giving a comprehensive description of political life with respect to minority ethnic groups and the majority population and institutions, but principally to point out that whilst in the social sphere of British life pluralism exists, in the political sphere there is a remarkable singularity. This distance between the social and the political is not essentially different from what obtained in the British imperial world, where the total system was kept together by the political which although itself of a dual nature, was none the less singular in so far as the British authority was highly centralised and paramount. The active participation of minorities in the three major political parties augurs well for the future of what many see as a multi-cultural Britain. Unfortunately, however, this relatively positive prospect may not be so evident in other areas of national life. It is necessary, therefore, to turn to some problems faced by the multi-cultural society.

# 4 Practical Problems of the Multi-cultural Society

## Introduction

The concept of a multi-cultural society in post-imperial Britain entails, as we have seen, more than toleration of cultural pluralism. The ideology embraces notions of fairness and equality, and the proponents of multi-culturalism presumably do not intend that celebration of difference should be used to justify inequality as the promotion of difference in Jim Crow America and apartheid South Africa was used to establish grossly unjust social orders. There are, however, considerable problems to be confronted in the endeavour to build a fair and equal multi-cultural society in Britain. Those issues which I considered to be of a theoretical nature were discussed in Chapter 1, but it is now necessary to look closer at some of the practical problems which have had to be, and are being, confronted in the effort to make the multi-cultural society a reality in the lives of people from both majority and minority communities. In drawing a general outline of these problems I wish to suggest that some problems have been long-standing or historical, whilst others are of relatively recent origins. Both old and new problems reflect the increasingly complex incorporation or integration of new minority ethnic groups into British society. The historical problems have been characterised by struggles to achieve equality of opportunity in employment, fairness in the criminal justice system, equal access to good housing and obtaining a satisfactory education. Increasingly, however, the problems of health, social and community services, and representation of new minorities in the media have become important areas of concern for policy-makers, providers of services, community organisations and politicians, as new minorities become more easily identified as parts of the British social and political fabrics. It is not necessary to attempt a description of all the problems minority ethnic groups, researchers and policy-makers have been concerned with in these areas over the past three decades or more, because not only has a voluminous literature developed around most problem areas, but there has also been a high degree of specialisation in race relations research since the 1970s.

The purpose of this chapter, therefore, is not to offer an exhaustive or comprehensive account of the practical problems faced by the multi-cultural society, but to illustrate the kinds of problems British society purports to address in the multi-cultural post-imperial age.

## Some Persistent Problems

The persistent problems concerning the attainment of a just and equal multi-cultural society surfaced in Britain in the early years of entry and settlement of new minority ethnic groups. These problems, however, were not new to these groups. Problems of housing, employment, education, the criminal justice system and so forth were already present in the colonial parts of the British world from whence the new minorities came. In post-imperial Britain it is not unusual for some politicians to invoke feats of apparent heroism and conquest (See, for example, Thatcher, 1988), but to place a distance between the social problems in the colonies and the imperial authority. Education, which the imperial authorities did tackle, was education for some, rarely if ever for all.[1] The persistence of the problems mentioned here may therefore be seen as problems within an overarching British world. They are persistent problems also because, whilst they have been variously discussed, and remedies suggested and often tried, they remain with us in the last years of the century and are likely to be with us well into the next. Each of these has a vital impact on the individual's as well as the community's life. Without a modicum of certainty and security in each of these areas the individual cannot be regarded as being in a position to enjoy and take on responsibilities commensurate with membership of society or citizenship. In the multi-cultural society a failure of this kind, patterned on racial, ethnic or colour lines, strongly suggests that difference is a basis for unfavourable differential not equitable treatment.

As mentioned in Chapter 2, the colonies were characterised by clear racial, ethnic or colour bars enforced by the colonial state and what provisions there were were generally restricted in distribution to the few; there was little by way of social services for the majority of the population. At political independence, the majority population usually aspire to some of the services and utilities enjoyed by the colonial elites, mainly white settlers, missionaries, administrators and businessmen and their families. Of course, the narrow tax base of most post-colonial societies rarely yields reforming politicians enough money to provide their electorates with the services and utilities the elite strata of the colonial order may have taken for granted. Such provisions as were on offer came from philanthropic individuals, the churches and communities themselves. The emergence and development of trade unions in the colonies occurred later than in Britain and it meant that, unlike in Britain, this kind of modern organisation was not available to provide a modicum of assistance to needy members. In these circumstances other forms of collective assistance developed through family, village and religious networks. The migrant generation of African-Caribbeans and Asians had to depend on these resources during the early years of entry and settlement.

In Britain, on the other hand, not only were philanthropic efforts more advanced and trade unionism more developed, but from early in the present century the state had undertaken to provide a social net for the most vulnerable and needy. Initially, this added to, more than replaced, provisions by church, parish and other bodies. It is not surprising, therefore, that some of the first questions asked by politicians during the early years of immigration and settlement by African-Caribbeans and Asians were whether they had the wherewithal to sustain themselves or would call upon the resources provided for white British people. The questions were posed particularly with respect to Caribbeans, because they were the first to arrive in significant numbers. Thus, for example, as Carter *et al.* (1987, pp. 338–9) found, in 1954 a government questionnaire to labour exchanges wanted to have answers to whether it was true that 'coloured' people are workshy, are poor workers and unsuitable to work available in the country. A working party appointed to look into the conditions of 'coloured' immigration reported in 1955 that 'coloured' workers would be 'rather more liable than white people to become a charge on National Assistance' (ibid., p. 339) because 'coloured' people would be unsuitable to the rigours of work and employers would therefore be less willing to employ them. Government concerns about the newcomers in the 1950s and the 1960s were punctuated by the increased pressure black people were presumed to have placed or be about to place on already scarce resources.

I want to comment briefly on some of these intractable historical problems in housing, education and employment. There has, of course, been a range of other persistent or historical problems faced by new minority ethnic communities apart from those in these three important areas. For example, one of the most persistently problematic areas of life for black people has been the criminal justice system, including the police, the courts, the probation service and prisons, and these have been thoroughly documented (see, for example, Humphry, 1972; Humphry and John, 1971; Keith, 1993; NACRO, 1989; Scarman, 1982; Solomos, 1988). Another example is that of violence against black and brown people: they are far more likely to be victims of physical attacks on the streets or in their homes than are white people (see, for example, Home Office, 1992; Virdee, 1995), and no less an authority than Prime Minister John Major, was willing to state publicly that 'black households are twice as likely to be burgled as white households' (Major, 1997, p. 6).

For much of the period since the beginning of post-war migration, housing and employment were perhaps the most important problem areas in the lives of new immigrants, and were subjects of constant comment by officials, the media and the government who were concerned to allay public fears about immigrants taking jobs and making demands on limited housing. Without somewhere to live and a job to earn a living, other problems of life must appear minor. There was a tendency, therefore, in early and later reports on the conditions of immigrants to concentrate on problems in these two areas. For example, W. Daniel's 1968 Political and Economic Planning (PEP) Report, entitled *Racial Discrimination in England*, focused attention on housing and employment in the immigrant communities. This report is believed to have exerted a strong influence the framers of the Race Relations Act 1968 to make it illegal for institutions to discriminate on grounds of a person's race in these areas of national life. Almost a decade later, in 1977, when the PEP published their new findings in *Racial Disadvantage in Britain* the author, David Smith, was able to draw upon a number of specialist PEP reports on employment and housing in new minority ethnic communities.[2] The PEP's successor, the Policy Studies Institute (PSI) carried on this periodic investigation of the state of minority ethnic Britain in key areas of housing and employment and these were documented in Colin Brown's *Black and White Britain* (1984). The 1991 census provided nation-wide data on these and other aspects of new minority ethnic communities, and a number of commentators, including the PSI,[3] have drawn on these to produce much useful and relevant material about minority ethnic Britain (see, for example, Coleman and Salt, 1996; Owen, 1994).

In the main, the PEP and PSI reports, corroborated by the research of others, provided relevant data about the less than equal conditions of African-Caribbeans and Asians in housing and employment. For example, housing tenure and quality – which generated widespread interest because of their significance as indicators of other aspects of family and community life – revealed the unfavourable living conditions of new minority ethnic communities in relation to the majority community over the period. Unsurprisingly, in 1977 Smith found a strong correlation between owner-occupation and good-quality housing in 'the general population' (Smith, 1977, Chapter 9); as might have been expected, affluent people tended to own their own homes and the richer they were the better were the quality of their homes. With respect, however, to the new minorities 'none of these connections holds good, and it seems that owner-occupation performs a completely different function' (ibid., p. 210), that is, in these communities ownership of homes did not go hand in hand with good quality.

Drawing on the 1971 census, Smith showed that 50 per cent of Caribbean homes, like 'the general population', were privately owned, but for Asians this was an impressive 76 per cent. Similarly, the figures for properties rented from local councils accounted for 4 per cent of Asians, 26 per cent in Caribbean communities and 28 per cent in the indigenous white population; the private rented sector of the housing market recorded a similar picture: 19 per cent Asian; 24 per cent Caribbeans; and 22 per cent indigenous whites. Smith argued that because new minorities tended to be less affluent than whites, had less well paid jobs, were relatively new to the British housing market and had larger families to support, they were doing remarkably well. Given too that many from the sub-continent (Anwar, 1979) and the Caribbean (Chamberlian, 1997; Thomas-Hope, 1992) expected to return to the lands of their births, these high figures are revealing about the deep roots the new communities were establishing in Britain.

Earlier, it had been shown that in Brixton, in the London Borough of Lambeth, where West Indians had concentrated, they were making do with far less than the white population who enjoyed the support of the local authority (Deakin, 1970, pp. 148 ff.). The work of Rex and Moore (1967) in Handsworth, Birmingham, had suggested that newcomers from the former colonies were excluded from council accomodation through the criteria used to allocate housing. African-Caribbeans and Asians had to call on their own resources, because public housing was unavailable to any newcomer within specific local authorities which required a period of residence within the authority. Nor were mortgages and bank loans available. Self-help through the partnership system[4] and loans with high repayment rates from individual entrepreneurs provided the wherewithal to many Caribbean people to buy their own homes. Asians, whose migration started and continued later, suffered the same deprivations but also drew on family and communal resources to purchase their homes. These communities are still predominantly located in the inner cities, which have experienced environmental, social and economic decline since World War Two.

The PSI report in 1984 revealed much the same patterns of house-ownership and home quality as Smith had shown earlier (Brown, 1984, Chapter v). These, as well as the patterns of renting from council and private owners, appear to be continuing in the 1990s. Drawing on the 1991 census, Owen's work provides many examples of these patterns. The data revealed that 48.1 per cent of African-Caribbeans live in owner-occupied houses, 35.7 per cent live in local authority properties, 9.7 per cent in housing associations, and 5.6 per cent in private rentals. For the category of Black-Africans these figures tended to be higher, with the exception of the owner-occupied category where it was only 28.0 per cent. Black-Others, or black people of mixed backgrounds, reflected correspondingly low owner-occupation and higher reliance on local authorities and housing associations. Whites consistently compared well with 66.6 per cent owner-occupation, 21.4 per cent in local authority properties, 3.0 per cent in housing associations and 7.0 per cent in private rentals. South Asians maintained a consistently high owner-occupier status at 77.1 per cent, 11.1 per cent in local authority housing, 2.5 per cent in housing association, and 7.6 per cent in the private rental sector. Other-Asians, including the Chinese, Vietnamese and Asians of mixed backgrounds displayed an expectedly high owner-occupier pattern at 53.9 per cent, low dependence on local authorities and housing associations, but relatively strong dependence on the private rental sector at 24.5 per cent.

The quality of housing continued to reveal the disadvantage of new minorities when compared with white people. Over the years the PEP/PSI reports have detailed these conditions and the 1991 census provided data in the same terms.[5] These included type (detached, semi-detached, terraced); age of property; the number of rooms in households; the density of room occupation; and amenities available to households. In each of these categories the new minority ethnic communities consistently scored significantly worse than the majority white population. But there appeared to be a correlation between quality of housing and longevity of settlement, with Caribbean people enjoying less density of household and room density than Asians, and Caribbeans being more able to gain access to local authority property. It may be only a matter of time before some Asians too become more strongly represented in council housing, because they will increasingly become eligible for such accommodation.

Drawing on census data for Greater London and the West Midlands, where 60 per cent of new minorities lived, Deakin suggested that the single most useful 'indicator of housing conditions is housing density measured by the number of persons per room' (Deakin, 1970, p. 67). The data revealed that whereas overall there were 0.6 persons per room in the white population, the figure for new minority ethnic communities was around 1.0 per room and there was little variation between the different immigrant groups from South Asia,[6] the Caribbean and Cyprus. More specifically, whereas only about 12 per cent of whites lived more than one to a room, the density for new minorities ranged from 50 per cent to 60 per cent (ibid., p 68). In London over 70 per cent of these families shared dwellings, as compared to 22 per cent of white households. Such density of residence had chronic consequences for the amenities people shared. The 1971 census showed that in the densely populated South East, Caribbean and Asian households were five times as likely to share dwellings than were whites (Smith, 1977, p. 231). A decade later, Brown (1984, pp. 73–8) showed a slight improvement, but in general the situation remained much the same. Owen (1993, p. 9) has shown that the earlier unfavourable density of room occupation had generally improved over time, but the distance between minority and majority ethnic communities has continued into the 1990s. In the white population, households with more than one person to a room amounted to 1.8 per cent, whereas in the minority communities the figure was 13.1 per cent for all groups taken together. Disaggregated by specific minority groups, the figures revealed Bangladeshi households to be the most densely occupied at 47.1 per cent of households with more than one person per room. With only 4.7 per cent of Caribbean households having more than one person to a room, this group came closest to the situation in the white population. This suggests that despite exclusion, protest does bring about a degree of equality.[7]

Other factors have also worked against improvement in housing for new minority ethnic communities. What was called 'white flight' in American cities during the 1960s and 1970s, also occurred in Britain, where many whites retreated from inner cities to new towns and more salubrious surroundings. Sometimes there was objection to black and brown families following white families to these new areas with better living conditions, as Wrench found in his study of new towns (Wrench et al., 1993). One response to hostility and discrimination in the housing market has been the development of parts of cities being almost exclusively or strongly brown or black in population, and this seems likely to continue as the white population's desire for suburban or rural life continues to drive what is being called 'urban sprawl' beyond the historic towns and cities (see, for example, Stillwell *et al.*, 1992). Since most cities, towns and villages in the country are either exclusively or predominantly white, there is no reason why a few areas, such as Brixton and Southall in London, should not be similarly black or brown. The point, however, is that this kind of development reflects not only the desire of groups of people to be together, but the development also reflects a broader exclusion by the majority population which results in residential pluralism (see S. Smith, 1989). This kind of development must have more in common with the principles of social and cultural pluralism which Furnivall and Smith described, than with the egalitarian tenets of multi-culturalism, as discussed earlier.

Employment may be more basic to the sustenance of life in any society than is housing. Where, however, people have travelled great distances to find work to improve their life chances, employment may initially take on an even greater meaning than it has for people who have experienced stable employment. This can and often did lead immigrants to compromise the quality of residence for the opportunity to work. Moreover, the very manner in which minorities from the Caribbean and the Indian sub-continent were incorporated into British society made employment a primary consideration for them. The single most important – but not the sole – reason for migrating in the first place from the Caribbean and the Indian sub-continent was to find jobs which, where available in their original societies, were too few and competitive, often low-paying and intermittent. The promise of industrial, predictable and relatively well-paid work in war-torn Britain was a powerful incentive to migrate temporarily. But large-scale migration is rarely, if ever, temporary or wholly reversible, and employment soon became a problem not only for the immigrant generation but a much more acute one for subsequent generations born and bred in Britain and with a more discriminating view of employment opportunities than their parents had.

As noted earlier, the British government was concerned, from the beginning of large-scale migration, about the prospects and capacity for employment of the new immigrants, and this concern soon became generalised. But far from them not being able to adapt to whatever employment prospects there were, like immigrants generally, West Indians and Asians were quick to grasp whatever opportunity came their way. Thus, speaking of the male immigrant work force in Greater London and the West Midlands, Deakin (1970, Chapter 4) drew on the 1961 and 1966 census data to show that only Cypriot immigrants were highly concentrated in selected occupations, with 33.9 per cent of them in the service industries. Indians (18.1 per cent) and West Africans (17.5 per cent) were also highly represented in professional, technical and artistic work. A further 17.9 per cent of Indians and 20.8 per cent of West Africans were concentrated in clerical work. On the other hand, there was a spread of Indians, Pakistanis, Jamaicans and other Caribbean groups in semi-skilled and unskilled engineering and allied occupations. Caribbeans were over-represented in the transport, communication and woodworking industries. The figures for women workers from these communities during the same period revealed that there were few Caribbean women in clerical positions, and although there was already a decline in their participation in nursing, it was still the employment of greatest concentration for them. Caribbean women, however, were also well represented in engineering (factory or industrial) work. In contrast, two in three Cypriot women worked in the London clothing industry. Whilst between 1961 and 1966 the percentage of men in white-collar jobs increased in Britain, for the immigrant population it decreased, but for females there was an increase (ibid., pp. 79–80).

Occupational differentials were carefully considered in 1977 by Smith, who compared the labour force across occupations, for Asians, West Indians and whites (Smith, 1977, Chapter 3). He found the occupational status of these groups skewed in favour of white men engaged in skilled occupations, such as the professions and management, and black and brown men in unskilled occupations. The gap between white and Pakistani men was the widest, followed by Caribbeans and Indians, with African-Indians closest to whites.[8] Overall, whilst all groups had managed to make in-roads into the skilled occupations, it was found that 'minority groups have penetrated comparatively little into non-manual jobs' (ibid., p. 73), particularly the higher echelons of the professions and management. When East African Asian males were partly exempted, males from all black and brown communities 'tended to be doing markedly inferior jobs compared with white men' (ibid., pp. 74–5). With respect to women, the sample was said to be too small for detailed breakdown, but job levels were considered to be 'distinctly lower than for white women, though the differences are less striking than they were in the case of men' (ibid., p. 77). Thus, of the 29 per cent of working women engaged in semi-skilled and unskilled manual work, 47 per cent of them were West Indians, 58 per cent Indian and 48 per cent African-Asians; the figure for Pakistani women was thought to be higher than for other groups.

Brown (1984) organised his report in a manner that took into account the changes in emphases and concerns, but also provided figures along the lines set out from the 1960s about occupational levels. In general, he concluded, 'the job levels of whites are much higher than those of Asians and West Indians' (ibid., p. 157). It was found that 83 per cent of Caribbean males, 73 per cent of Asian males and 58 per cent white males were engaged in manual labour. More men from the minority ethnic communities were doing unskilled and semi-skilled work than were white men. Pakistanis and Bangladeshis were found to be the sub-groups most highly represented in the lowest job levels, but, again, they themselves were found to be differently represented, with the latter having the highest proportion of semi-and un-skilled relative percentages. Women were less sharply distinguished from whites in the labour force. The percentage of Asian women in professional and managerial work was almost as high as white women; and whilst the percentage of white women in unskilled work was higher than for Asian and black women, this was accounted for by reference to the higher proportion of white women in part-time employment (ibid., p. 158). As in the 1960s, the distribution of workers according to ethnic categories continued, with whites and Caribbeans displaying much the same strong patterns in construction and the service industries; Asians and Caribbeans with strong representation in manufacturing industries; Asians particularly strong in the textile industry; and Caribbeans continuing to be fairly well represented in transport and communications. In these respects, the patterns for women were seen to be broadly similar.

These fairly detailed examples of indigenous majority and new minority ethnic groups illustrate the wide differentials between these communities. In general, minority ethnic workers earned less than their white counterparts, lived in less healthy homes and in less clean environments. Considerable data have been gathered by a wide range of researchers in community and campaigning organisations, academic and policy researchers and others which show wide disparities between new minorities and the majority communities in almost every area of national life in multi-cultural Britain.[9] The bodies to which workers and members of specific occupations look to redress aspects of such disparities did not themselves achieve a great deal more by way of advancing the ideals of multi-culturalism. Perhaps the most relevant example here is that of the industrial unions. But as late as the mid-1980s Brown found that whilst 47 per cent of employees were union members, 56 per cent of Caribbean and Asian workers had joined (Brown, 1984, pp. 169 ff.). Disaggregated by gender, the figures were even more revealing: only 34 per cent of white female workers were members of unions, but 38 per cent of Asian and 57 per cent of Caribbean women were union members. The differentials between men revealed a similar but not such a sharp divergence between the groups: 57 per cent white, 59 per cent Asian and 64 per cent Caribbean men were members of unions. Even so, something like 11 per cent of white males reported that they held posts in unions, whilst the same was true for only 4 per cent of both Asian and Caribbean men;[10] the figures for females were even less, with 6 per cent for white women and 3 per cent for women from the two minority groups under consideration.

Moreover, the trade union principle that the last to be taken on a job should be the first to leave in hard times, cruelly applied to immigrant workers when recession set in from the 1970s, and particularly in the 1980s. This negatively complemented the practices of discrimination utilised by employers with respect to black and brown Britons over the period. Discrimination in employment has been documented by too many researchers, including the PEP/PSI reports, and academics to warrant repetition here. Suffice it to say that the evidence has been such that legislation against it became necessary. The overall consequence of this has been that during hard times minority ethnic groups have been over-represented in the unemployment queues and statistics. For example, the PSI report revealed that whilst in 1974 unemployment was at around 4 per cent for all males, in 1982 when the economy was in deep recession unemployment among white males stood at 13 per cent but at 24 per cent for Caribbean men; the percentage for white women was 10 per cent and 16 per cent for Caribbean women. Unemployment for both men and women in the Asian communities stood at 20 per cent. By the 1980s, unemployment was affecting not only young males but also older males in the Caribbean community. Lord Scarman's report into the Brixton disturbances in 1981 recognised that unemployment was high amongst all school leavers in Lambeth, but higher in the black community. Whilst in that year the Brixton Employment Office record showed an overall 13 per cent unemployment, in May it was 25.4 per cent for the minority ethnic communities and for Caribbean youths there was an estimated 55 per cent unemployment record (Scarman, 1982, p. 10). From the 1991 census, Owen (1994) found that African-Caribbean males (African, Caribbean and people of mixed backgrounds) were two and a half times as likely to be unemployed as were white males; overall, however, Pakistani, Bangladeshi and African males had amongst the highest levels of unemployment.[11]

As crucial as residence and employment are, it is the education system that has been most vital in the endeavour to realise the ideals of the multi-cultural society. As noted in the discussion about the theoretical problems of the new pluralism, multi-culturalism has been largely defined in Britain by the debates which have taken place in education. Two aspects of the debate are of particular practical relevance to the notion of a multi-cultural British society: the provision of, and access to, an adequate education for life in modern society; and, second, the strong view of many pedagogues that education should reflect the multi-cultural character of the country. There is, however, a third dimension which does not sufficiently feature in the debate over education and multi-culturalism. This is the question of education preparing individuals for employment in a highly competitive society.[12] The competitive society aside, however, it has long been taken for granted that education in and of itself is a vital aspect of national life in effecting upward social mobility (see, for example, Heath and McMahon, 1996), maintaining social peace and democratic institutions, stimulating economic development and generally enriching the life of the individual and their family.

These points were taken up in the two most comprehensive and perhaps the most important public statements about education for a post-imperial society during the period – the Rampton Report of 1981 and the Swann Report of 1985. The Rampton Report on West Indian children in British schools, stressed that 'a good education' should encourage every child to develop individually and enable them to possess the knowledge and skills 'to the limits of his or her age, aptitude and ability' (Rampton, 1981, p. 19), as well as transmit knowledge and values across generations. Education, Rampton stressed, should provide 'an equal opportunity of playing a full and active part in adult social and working life' (ibid.). The report pointed out that education is important in promoting desirable change and good race relations, in the belief that knowledge is likely to reduce prejudice. The underlying but questionable assumption here is that the more knowledge people have about each other the less they are likely to discriminate against each other. The Swann Committee's report of 1985 argued that the role of education is

> to equip a pupil with knowledge and understanding in place of ignorance and to develop his or her ability to formulate views and attitudes to assess and judge situations on the basis of this knowledge. In thus encouraging a child to think critically and to make increasingly rational judgements, education should seek to counter any mistaken impressions or inaccurate hearsay evidence which he or she may have acquired within the family, peer group or, more broadly, from the local community or the media. (Swann, 1985, p. 13)

In using education to combat prejudice, it was not intended that education should seek to replace negative with positive prejudices by presenting the child with any particular view as the correct one to hold. The two reports highlighted the pivotal position of the school and schooling in contemporary British society for both majority and minority populations. Rampton and Swann suggested that the school was the critical site where children may receive the kind of 'good education' Rampton spoke about and which includes preparing individuals for equal and active participation in the life of the overall society.

Although very many immigrants from the Caribbean and Asia thought that they would soon return to the lands of their births, the 1960s saw them settling down to work and life in Britain. Many had also sent for their spouses and children. Inevitably, families were partially reunited and new families started, sometimes with partners from communities other than their own (see Berrington, 1996). In the course of the 1960s, the school increasingly became a site of grave concern for many immigrant families, as the workplace and the housing market had earlier been. In the late 1960s Caribbean parents began to feel that their children were not being equipped with the 'good education' they needed for adulthood and the competitive market, and, therefore, far from improving on the lowly occupational positions of their parents, these children were destined to form a depressed lumpen proletariat with a future on the rim of society. The debate about this was triggered in the late 1960s when the North London Branch of the West Indian Standing Conference organised at London University a weekend seminar on the question of West Indian education in Britain. At the seminar Bernard Coard,[13] then a school teacher and educational researcher, presented a paper which raised questions about the many West Indian children who were being sent to what were then designated as 'educationally sub-normal schools'. In 1971 this was published by John LaRose's New Beacon Publishers as *How the West Indian Child is made Educationally Sub-normal in the British School System*, and stimulated widespread debates throughout Caribbean communities in Britain. The debate over this work marked the beginning of the alternative schools organised by small groups in Caribbean communities. These 'schools' sought to provide a balance to the mainstream schools and taught African history, the histories of the African diaspora, and the 'three Rs' (of reading, writing and arithmetic), which were felt to be absent from classrooms attended by children of Caribbean backgrounds.[14]

Almost a decade was to pass, however, before the agitation and organisation by Caribbean groups and parents around the question of the deplorable education their children were receiving was to have an impact on public policy. In 1977, the House of Commons' Select Committee on Race Relations and Immigration heard the concerns of Caribbean parents about the deplorable educational performance of their children, and a committee of inquiry into the education of children of ethnic minority groups was established. The brief of the committee was to inquire 'into the causes of the under-achievement of children of West Indian origin in maintained schools and the remedial action required' (Rampton, 1981, p. 1), but within the wider framework of education provisions for children from all minority and majority ethnic groups in England. As noted in the last chapter, in 1972 and 1974 there were two reports on the education of children from new minority communities. Thus, although much talked about and of deep concern to educationalists, parents and community spokespersons, it was not until the 1970s and 1980s that the education of children of Caribbean families loomed sufficiently large or became of such salience as to be placed on the public agenda (see, for example, Tomlinson, 1983).

The political dynamics surrounding the work of the Rampton Committee, therefore, reflected wider developments in the country and the state's attitude to race relations. Established under James Callaghan's Labour government, the committee's membership was completed after the 1979 general election which brought Margaret Thatcher and the Conservatives to office. The new government was willing to continue what Labour had started, but the final report of the committee under Lord Swann in 1985 was largely ignored, and its many findings and recommendations did not have the positive reception many educationalists and concerned individuals hoped for and the Conservative government's monumental 1986 Education Reform Act was more influenced by right-wing writers on education than by Swann. The committee submitted an interim report in 1981 under the first chairman, Anthony Rampton, and a final report in 1985, under Lord Swann, both of which were severely criticised from all sides when they were published. Like most public inquiries, they are today invaluable sources for educationalists, contemporary historians, and social scientists interested in education and race relations.

The reports deal with two central problems: the poor quality of education that children of Caribbean parents were receiving in schools, or the low performance of children of Caribbean backgrounds; and the question of what kind of education might be relevant for all children in a multi-cultural Britain. In dealing with these questions both Rampton and Swann took on board several related questions of teacher training, the religious heterogeneity of Britain, problems of language and teaching of mother tongue, the role of teachers, parents, community organisations, and central and local governments. Over three hundred knowledgeable individuals submitted evidence to the committee, as did over thirty education authorities, forty-four higher education institutions, and scores of community and professional groups. Members of the committee attended several meetings organised by community groups throughout England over a four-year period from 1980, and they drew upon the literature available on a range of issues in the field.

Although heatedly contested and debated, the findings were clear enough and did not surprise educationalists, parents and other concerned individuals. The interim Rampton Report found that children of Caribbean parents were indeed under-performing and sought to explain why this was so, particularly in light of impressive levels of achievements by children of Asian backgrounds, who were the equal of native white pupils or their superiors in public examinations and university entrance results.[15] Although racism was highlighted as the chief cause of the low educational achievements of children of Caribbean parents, several other factors were considered. These included the interference of Caribbean Creole with language development, the higher proportion of mothers from this community at work as compared to other groups, the high incidence of fathers in night work, poor housing and sub-standard pre-school facilities, the absence of toys and playtime for children, and the readiness by adults to use corporal punishment in disciplining their children. The committee concluded that whilst Creole was not a hindrance to these children's performance, schools should nonetheless build on the child's knowledge of Creole, reflecting the view of some educationalists who felt that part of the handicap of Caribbean children in British schools arose from the status of Creole as a language. But parents – in the spirit of a strong Commonwealth Caribbean tradition – were of the view that Standard English was what they sent their children to school to learn and associated education with that form of English. Recognising that in Britain, unlike the Caribbean that people left in the 1950s, homes have to play an active role in a child's education, the committee stressed that parents should play a more active part in the education of their children, and made specific recommendations to this effect.

The responses to the interim report, set out and addressed in the final report, highlighted the accusation of racism where teachers sought to show that they were colour blind and, therefore, not racist. But both reports are sensitive to the teacher's perspective and stress the obvious point that not all teachers were racist and that there were some good practices in the classroom which should be emulated. Even so, the final report had to reassert the view that racism was a key consideration in the British school system. In particular, work on teacher expectation, the stereotyping of children and the resultant treatment of children of Caribbean backgrounds were found to be negative, whilst positive with respect to children of Asian backgrounds. Moreover, Caribbean children were said to be difficult to control and lacked concentration in the classroom, where Asian children were seen to be highly attentive and co-operative (Swann, 1985, pp. 22–37).

The committee recommended that whilst schools cannot be expected to take the whole burden of changing society, they were 'uniquely well placed to take a lead role' (ibid., p. 767) in this endeavour. They were of the view that this diversity should be reflected in the school curriculum and other provisions. Second, specific measures should be taken to tackle racism at every level in the school. Third, the multi-cultural aspect of the curriculum must not be tacked on to existing programmes, but must permeate the whole structure and provisions of schools. Such change could not be left to local education authorities, but needed central government action. The committee's recommendations cover education authorities, inspectors of schools, teacher training, public examination boards, and the Department of Education itself. It was reasoned that the curriculum in state-maintained schools should not undertake the teaching of mother tongue languages, but local authorities could help communities provide for this need by making premises available and offering grants and other resources to community providers. Pre-school provisions should be available for teaching English as a second language, and all teachers in schools with high intakes of minority ethnic groups should be encouraged to be in a position to 'cater for linguistic needs of pupils' (ibid., p. 771). In these ways it was expected that education could indeed become the means whereby Britain may build a more just and equal multi-cultural society; the adequate education for individuals from both majority and minority communities would necessarily be multi-cultural in nature. This was emphasised in the title of the report – *Education for All* – which has been described as a landmark in the emergence and definition of a multi-cultural Britain (Verma, 1989).

Of course, education is intricately linked to employment and, as Rampton asserted, one of the functions of education is to prepare the individual for full participation in the life of the nation, including participation in the employment market. Like migrants elsewhere, the immigrant generation in these communities was prepared to accept more or less whatever employment opportunities came their way, and frequently this meant that the skills they had were not used. Most went into entirely new areas of employment and learnt new skills. Indeed, this generation which came mainly from rural areas with agricultural skills, settled in urban centres and became employed in industrial work. This was as true for people from the rural Punjab as it was for Jamaicans. Given that immigrants had come to Britain to fill gaps in the labour market during the 1950s and 1960s, most found jobs although this involved undergoing changes in occupation and status. This downward social mobility was often accompanied by severe discrimination by both employers and fellow employees. With more formal education than their parents, subsequent generations of people of Caribbean and Asian backgrounds have experienced more than the usual difficulties in securing employment because of their colour and cultural backgrounds. Unfortunately, in the Caribbean communities this has led to some young people seeing education as a waste of time. Accordingly, many appear to be abandoning the high status accorded education in the Caribbean of their parents, where education was the main means of upward social mobility (see, for example, Gordon, 1963; Goulbourne, 1988; Williams, 1950).

As noted above, central to the debate over multi-culturalism and education has been whether its provision and content should reproduce and promote the cultural pluralism of contemporary British society. Even where it is agreed that this is a desirable public good, there is much controversy over how this might be implemented within a context of equality and fairness to all. This problem has been sharply articulated in two ways from the late 1980s. First, the problem has been raised in terms of whether children from Muslim families should not be given the opportunity to attend schools entirely devoted to their faith. Second, the difficulty of realising the ideals of the multi-cultural society through the agency of education has been raised by white parents about schools with a high proportion of children of minority ethnic, particularly Asian, backgrounds. There are, however, some white parents who see the mix and combination in the class room and the playground as cultural opportunity, not disadvantage, for their children.

The pressure for Muslim schools began during the period that Rampton and Swann were sitting in the first years of the 1980s, but it was after the 1988 Education Reform Act that many Muslims intensified the demand for their own schools to be established from public funds. They argued that since there were Church of England, Catholic and

Jewish schools, there was good reason for there to be Muslim schools supported from the public purse like schools in other faith communities. The Swann committee rejected the plea for separate schools for children from new minority ethnic groups, because it appeared to members of the committee that the promotion of such schools would be inimical to the underlying philosophy of providing an education for all children in Britain. Perhaps the committee hoped that education would help to provide a set of common values across particularistic communal boundaries in a pluralist society. Given the philosophical perspective of tolerance that members brought to the committee's deliberation, their views were that separate schools may 'exacerbate', not resolve, some of the problems of minorities in British society. However, in an attempt to overcome some of the necessary problems of a society embracing the ideology of multi-culturalism, the report called for greater attention to be given to the pastoral needs of Muslim pupils, for more teachers from minority ethnic groups to be employed and for proper provisions to be made within schools so that girls, (whose parents did not want their daughters to mix with boys) could have separate lessons in physical education and games.

The opposition by some white parents to their children attending schools with a majority of children of Asian backgrounds in inner-city areas may be seen as much the same kind of demand as that for separate schools for Muslims. This demand hits the headlines periodically in cities with high densities of new minority ethnic population, such as Bradford, but also in less dense areas. Perhaps, however, the most well known of such cases was in Drewsbury, Lincolnshire, where white parents in the late 1980s argued that because their children attended a school with a majority of children of Asian backgrounds, white children were being denied a traditional English education. The parents then demanded that their children be sent to another school. When the local education authority was not forthcoming, parents took to keeping their children at home and eventually defied the authorities by holding classes at a local pub for their children (see, for example, Tomlinson, 1989).[16]

For a long time the government held out against demands from both white parents and Muslim communities for their own choice of schools. But by the mid-1990s this position appeared less and less tenable, given the government's policy of encouraging schools to opt out of local government control and strengthen self-management of schools in accordance with parental and teacher preferences. In the phoney war between the political parties in the year or so leading to the 1997 general election, the Conservatives and Labour competed over who could convince the electorate that they would give greater choice to parents and schools. It is not unlikely, therefore, that in the near future there may be a number of Muslim schools alongside other religious schools with financial support from the public purse, and it will be wondered what the fuss and opposition to them was about.

These demands for separate schools transform old or historical problems into new problems. The demands are very much part of the urge to define or redefine collective identities in a rapidly changing world, so that whilst the broad liberal principles of Swann were enunciated in such a manner as to embrace new minorities into a recognisable mainstream British educational and therefore social structure, we find that the grounds have moved and from different directions the boundaries of the multi-cultural society have suddenly changed. Old problems spawn new ones or transform them in bewildering ways that defy the tenets of liberal social and political thought. In the first place, minorities and reformers wanted a better deal for their children, but this demand gave rise to new problems within the majority population. Particular groups which have been left behind in the restructured economy of the last decade or more, have not only lost their certainty, but some have come to feel that they are the victims of social forces beyond their control, and somehow newcomers and their children are the cause. The result is a series of conflicts between what appears to be justifiable positions or causes, or a series of conflicts of rights.

## New Problems of the Multi-cultural Society

Alongside these historical problems and the new lines of departures they have taken, there are several quite new problems which now face the multi-cultural society. As people have settled down to life in Britain with their families, and these families have themselves gone on to reproduce themselves, it was inevitable that new problems would arise, requiring resolution in the public arena. If, for example, problems of housing were typical of the period of entry in the 1950s, and problems of education and the criminal justice system faced the first generation of Caribbean children born and/or brought up in the UK, then it would be fair to say that the new problems from the late 1980s have centred largely around questions of health and social welfare. Whilst education and the criminal justice system are problems which focused on youth, the new issues are more distributed across generations and gender, with the elderly and the disabled requiring attention which is often outside the competence of the family which traditionally, in both Asian and Caribbean communities, provided the necessary material assistance and moral support.

Perhaps the central view that is emerging in the growing body of critical literature on race, health and social care in Britain is that the health and social welfare systems are inherently biased against the interests of new minority ethnic groups. There are at least two variants of this general position. Fiona Williams (1996) argues that historically the very provision of welfare was exclusionary. She suggests that the limits placed on eligibility to such provision – based on residence, nationality and citizenship – involved principles which conditioned today's welfare state and the location of new minority ethnic groups within the planning and delivery of such provisions. Under the 1834 Poor Law, relief had to be sought in the person's parish of birth and this provision inevitably disadvantageously affected needy Irish immigrants in the last century. There was no provision of pension for a person who was not a resident and of British nationality for twenty years under the 1908 Pensions Act. A non-British resident of five years made a full contribution to the health scheme under the 1911 National Insurance Act, but was entitled to only seven-ninths of benefits. Relief to people out of work was denied to black seamen in the years immediately after World War One.

Williams suggests that these developments in the early decades of the twentieth century were intricately linked to the emergence of a new British nationalism. Reforms introducing old age pensions, national insurance, school meals for those in need, help for mothers and their babies, and public housing were intended to improve the lot of the working people and were in line with changes in countries in mainland Europe, such as Britain's main competitor, Germany. For Williams, it was not coincidental that these reforms appeared at much the same time as the 1905 Aliens Act to curb Jewish immigration from East Europe. Intending immigrants who could not support themselves were to be kept out, and those who could not support themselves after twelve months were to be deported, as were black ex-soldiers and seamen in 1919 following the race riots against them in Liverpool, Cardiff and South Tyneside. Williams makes the further point that racism and community care came together in the eugenics movement in the early part of the century. She argues that

> It is also at this intersection, and especially in policies for segregation and incarceration, that it is possible to see the complex interplay of

the social relations of class, gender, race, disability, age and sexuality and the influence of these upon the construction of social problems.

(Williams, 1996, p. 21).

Under the influence of the Eugenics Society, founded in 1907, the state passed the Mental Deficiency Act in 1913 which provided sweeping powers to incarcerate and isolate people who were considered to be mentally or physically deficient, or whose behaviour appeared different from what was considered normal. The poor, some women bearing children out of wedlock, the physically disabled and aliens were deemed to pose threats to society, and therefore society needed protection from them, rather than the reverse. Williams concluded that new minorities from the Commonwealth in the 1950s and the 1960s came to a welfare system already possessing a 'rich and complex legacy' of exclusion and racism (ibid., p. 23). This observation may be not entirely unrelated to the relative absence of welfare provisions in the colonies for which Britain was responsible.

The second variant of the view that the British welfare system was not established to cater for the needs of new minority ethnic groups stresses that the system is oriented to meeting the needs of a white population and is resistant to necessary or radical change. Waqar Ahmad, editor of an excellent Open University Press series on problems of race, health and care, argues that issues of health concerning Britain's African-Caribbean and Asian communities had been racialised to ensure oppression of the colonised during the imperial age. In his view the colonial relationship has continued in the sphere of health and social care matters in Britain. Following Frantz Fanon's (1968, 1970) analysis of the colonised, Ahmad argues that the relationship was complicated by the colonised themselves, particularly medical practitioners who complied with the colonisers. The 'frontline' role of medicine in colonial policy has an even earlier root in slavery when rebellious slaves were diagnosed as people with mental problems. Ahmad convincingly argues, therefore, that health and care in race relations in Britain is a politicised field, and he correctly argues, like Gunnar Myrdal as we shall see in a later chapter, that 'good' scientists are those who recognise this fact as an essential element 'of their enterprise' (Ahmad, 1993, p. 31).

The points made by Williams and Ahmad establish a framework for understanding many of the problems of health and social care in race relations. Like other commentators, they depict a general situation in which Britain's new minority ethnic communities receive less than their just share from the system (see, for example, Johnson and Songster, 1995; National Health Service (NHS), 1996). There is little doubt that historically the provisions of health and social services were arranged on an exclusionary basis in Britain, and within this there was already a racial element. On the other hand, minority groups from the former colonial world already had the experience of exclusion in the relationship of ordination and subordination that obtained. Again, we see the dualist nature of the imperial/colonial situation and this dualism remains part of the wider experience of British citizens who also have a consciousness from beyond the shores of these islands, but whose sojourn has not taken them outside the world bounded by colonialism/imperialism and their aftermaths.

There have been several areas of medicine that have been of particular concern to African-Caribbean and Asian communities. For example, there is the view that Asian women are prone to suffer from depression and from time to time the Press carry items of news about this (Watters, 1996, p. 107). It would appear that Caribbean men are more likely than men in the indigenous population to suffer high rates of depression. Individuals of Caribbean backgrounds are also prone to hypertension, high incidence of diabetes and strokes, and women may be more likely to suffer disability earlier than white women (LeFranc, 1997).

It is not surprising, therefore, that there is deep concern over the high incidence of African-Caribbean men being diagnosed as mentally ill, particularly as schizophrenic. Sashidharan and Francis (1993) argue that 'the alignment of mental illness and ethnicity or race is indicative of underlying political ideologies rather than the product of empirical findings' (p. 96). This appears to be the view of the Caribbean community, because so-called mental illness has become a rallying point for community mobilisation against institutional bias. After all, significantly more African-Caribbeans are likely to be compulsory admitted to an institution under the Mental Health Act 1993 than other groups (see Watters, 1996, pp. 105–6). This development confirms Williams' view that the context for racial segregation was set with the Eugenics movement from the start of the century and whilst many providers and medics might deny this, it would appear that their actual behaviour reaffirms the prevalence of this perspective. The point is not that there may not be a connection or connections between ethnicity and mental illness, but that the relationship between psychiatry and black patients has been intertwined with pseudo-science and racist ideologies from the imperial age. Sashidharan and Francis argue, correctly, that the simple fact of blackness cannot be enough to establish mental illness, yet a person's skin colour appears to be taken by professionals as a determinant of illness.

One of the first major concerns amongst minority ethnic communities was over blood disorders. African-Caribbean groups highlighted the high probability of sickle-cell anaemia in their population, following the concern amongst African-Americans about the disease during the course of the radical Black Power movement in the late 1960s. The concern spread within the African diaspora and in Britain, communities began to organise around the issue. It was soon found that another blood condition, thalassaemia, predominantly affected minorities from the Indian sub-continent and Southern Europe. Both thalassaemia and sickle-cell anaemia are disorders of the blood passed on to children by parents, and can have disastrous results if not detected early and treated. Whilst there is no accurate knowledge of the number of people who suffer from these disorders, it was estimated in the mid-1980s that there were about 5000 sickle-cell sufferers in Britain. It has been said that the number of people who suffer from haemophilia and cystic fibrosis is much the same as those who suffer from sickle-cell anaemia, but the latter group does not receive the same attention as the former (Anionwu, 1993, p. 80). Indeed, it took much community action to draw the attention of the health authorities to the disorder of sickle-cell anaemia and much of the improvement in necessary provision for sufferers is due to community action. The UK Thalassaemia Society, which was established in 1976, publicised the conditions of the Cypriot community, and a number of centres emerged to give advice, particularly to those getting married. The Sickle-Cell Society and the Thalassaemia Society campaign for greater public awareness and for the health and social services to provide more support to the communities adversely affected by these conditions.

With respect to social care provisions, there are several specific areas of concern to new ethnic minority communities. Of particular importance are children in care and fostering, and care for the elderly.[17] From the 1980s, a number of social carers from minority ethnic communities have themselves highlighted the desirability for black and brown children to be brought up with black and brown families, but one of the several problems involved has been that not enough of these families either come forward as volunteers or are considered suitable for these children by the relevant services. As in other areas of social care, radical reasoning appears to be that the interests of clients are best served when delivered by members from their own natural communities rather than by members from the majority white population.[18] In a society described as multi-cultural, this kind of reasoning is a powerful consideration for social policy, but it can also allow broad and generalised principles to become paramount over the individual child's immediate material and spiritual welfare and well-being.

The generation of migrants from the Caribbean and India have been steadily entering their twilight years (Owen, 1994, 1996; Warnes, 1992, 1996) and consequently new problems are emerging. For example, as Ahmad (1996), Atkin and Rollings (1996) and Blakemore and Boneham (1994) have variously shown there is considerable dependence on the traditional family in both Asian and African-Caribbean communities to take care of their elderly. The policy of 'care in the community' has heightened this expectation. But family obligations amongst these groups in Britain cannot be taken to be what they may have been in the Caribbean or the sub-continent. For example, unlike the experience of there being more elderly women in the indigenous population, in both African-Caribbean and Asian communities, men over 65 years out number women, reflecting the pattern of early migration. In the case of Caribbean elderly men, it is now becoming clear that many are isolated and lead lonely lives as a result of physical and social distances from their wider families elsewhere throughout the African diaspora in the West. The extended family and household to which such elderly men could be expected to turn in the Caribbean have not yet developed in the United Kingdom. These circumstances create problems which were absent in the years of migration and settlement, and are being variously addressed by professional carers and voluntary groups in relevant communities (see, for example, Ahmad, 1996, Chapter 11; Blakemore and Boneham, 1994), but the problems will continue well beyond this century.

## Conclusion

The issues mentioned here do not exhaust the new nor the old practical problems of the multi-cultural society in post-imperial Britain. The discussion in this chapter was intended to indicate what some of these problems have been and continue to be as we approach the end of the first half-century of large-scale entry and settlement by people from Africa, Asia and the Caribbean. Multi-culturalism as policy and ideology has not succeeded in abolishing differential incorporation, because new minority ethnic groups suffer disproportionately from the ills of society and we will begin the next century and millennium with an accumulation of race relations problems. But when compared to the colonial degradation and imperial pomp with which the century opened, the poverty of multi-culturalism in post-imperial Britain might appear to be less of a failure than we now think.

# 5  Outlawing Racial Discrimination

## Introduction

The state's attitude to relations between groups of people distinguished by racial or ethnic characteristics is of enormous importance to the ways in which the problems emanating from such relations are tackled within the various institutions of the state itself and in civil society generally. We have already seen how the plurality of attitudes of the imperial state, as represented in different colonies, was important in shaping the patterns of race relations. In post-imperial Britain, the state's policies regarding new minorities are equally important in setting the context for the development of what is widely regarded as 'good' race relations between minorities and the majority and between minorities themselves. For much of the second half of the twentieth century a significant aspect of the struggle to advance social justice in Britain has therefore taken the form of a protracted fight against racial discrimination in public life. One aspect of this has been the concerted effort to convert abstract or formal rights into practical, realisable rights for the enjoyment of black and brown citizens on the same social and economic bases as any white fellow or sister citizen. Legislation in 1965, 1968 and 1976 sought to grapple with the problem of racial discrimination, and to a significant degree has succeeded in not only outlawing but also limiting the legitimacy of such discrimination in the public arena. This willingness to legislate is a significant departure from the active use of the law in the imperial age to sanction formal differential treatment of people who came under British jurisdiction. There has therefore been a serious attempt to establish structures which would make incorporation of new minorities universal in the sense that all citizens should *de facto* as well as *de jure* be endowed with equal rights and opportunities irrespective of racial or ethnic differentiation.

This chapter is a general discussion of the arrangements instituted by the state to accomplish such legal and practical uniformity or equality of Britain's multi-ethnic, multi-racial or multi-cultural population and society. The discussion focuses on two aspects of this attempt to universalise rights and obligations in post-imperial Britain. First, the legal sanctions against discrimination on the grounds of what is regarded as a person's race, ethnicity, colour and national origins are outlined here. Second, the discussion turns to a brief consideration of some limitations of the law in effectuating universal incorporation into British multi-cultural society.

## Outlawing Racial Discrimination

The 1976 Race Relations Act (hereafter RAA 1976) has been the basic law against racial discrimination in Britain during the last decades of the twentieth century. This measure, which superseded the 1965 and 1968 Race Relations Acts, became law in November 1976, and generally took effect in June 1977.[1] The first of these measures had made it illegal to bar a person because of their colour from entry to hotels, swimming pools and similar places of general public use. A Race Relations Board was established to conduct investigations into discrimination in these areas, but the Board had no power to demand relevant documents or call for witnesses. The Attorney-General's agreement had to be secured to prosecute in cases involving incitement of racial hatred, the only criminal offence under the Act. The Act was very limited in scope, and strongly reflected a view that promotional and educational work would be important in limiting racial discrimination in Britain. The Race Relations Act 1968 extended the law by making it illegal to discriminate on racial grounds in the vital areas of housing and employment, because the PEP report in that year on racial discrimination in these areas impressed the government with the need to take legal action.

Despite its limitations, the Race Relations Act of 1965 was significant, because it was a political recognition that racism was an undesirable aspect of British life, and demonstrated a willingness to use the law in the fight against racial discrimination. It was a weak measure, barely touching the vital aspects of social, economic and educational life, and, from the vantage point of the last years of the century, the politicians and lawmakers of the 1960s must appear to have been even more pusillanimous than they probably were. After all, from the 1950s the staunch anti-colonialist and anti-racist Labour MP Fenner Brockway had repeatedly failed to secure Parliament's support for a bill against racial discrimination in the country. When the measure came, it was not only limited in scope and application, but it was also what some commentators have seen as a high price for the drastic measures the Labour government of Harold Wilson was willing to introduce against the immigration of black and brown Commonwealth citizens into Britain. Commenting on immigration and race relations laws over the period from 1962, one anti-discrimination lawyer argued that the

> price for the Race Relations Act 1968 was the Commonwealth Immigration Acts 1962 and 1968 and the price for the Race Relations Act 1976 was the Immigration Act of 1971 and the British Nationality Act 1981. (Hepple, 1992, p. 28)

This tying together of race relations and tight immigration control has been a major feature of discussion and legislation in the decades since the mid-1960s, when they were seen to be intricately linked with respect to policy (see, for example, Labour Party 1962, 1972). In their comprehensive study of British nationality laws, Dummett and Nicol (1990) recognised this and made much the same point as Hepple when they stressed that the

> scope and powers of the Race Relations Act 1965 are in sharp contrast to the widely drawn immigration legislation, with its large discretion for quite junior officials, extensive bureaucracy, and its list of criminal offences. (p. 193)

The fact, however, that Parliament was willing – even if grudgingly – to legislate against racial discrimination was a step in the right direction. Extensions of the law in 1968 and 1976 suggest that Parliament regarded legislation against racial discrimination as an area of activity to be at least intermittently reviewed and provided for this in the RRA 1976, which has been the single most influential piece of legislation that has stamped the image of the law on relations between people with different pigmentations in Britain. The 1965 and 1968 measures may be rightly regarded as a prelude to the 1976 initiative on the part of Home Secretary Roy Jenkins and his adviser Anthony Lester. Although the law has undergone some minor modifications, and there have been some attempts to introduce appropriate changes as provided for under the Act, in the main the measure, as passed in 1976, remains the basic law governing British race relations. Given the pivotal position of this measure, it is worth mentioning its main features, some weaknesses as highlighted by supporters and critics, and the role of the body with responsibility for overseeing the enforcement of the law, as well as promoting good race relations in the country – the Commission for Racial Equality (CRE).

The RRA 1976 made it illegal to discriminate on the basis of 'colour, race, nationality or ethnic or national origins', or to segregate people 'on racial grounds'. In a significant departure from the 1965 and 1968 Acts, the RRA 1976 provisions applied to a wide range of activities in British life. In the words of the veteran anti-discrimination campaigner and lawyer, Geoffrey Bindman, the Act is 'probably the most comprehensive in Europe' and he noted that 'there are no matching provisions prohibiting discrimination on racial grounds' in the European Union. (Bindman, 1996, p. 170) As we will see later, the CRE has accordingly suggested that the protection provided by the RRA 1976 could usefully be extended to the European Union.

The law has a wide berth, outlawing very many acts of racial discrimination in relations between employees and employers, and in employment agencies; in the provision and delivery of vocational training; within trade unions and other organisations 'whose members carry on a particular profession or trade' (section 11); in schools and other educational institutions; in planning agencies; in local authorities; in the provision of goods, facilities, disposal and management of premises and other services; dwellings; in advertisements; in partnerships, law firms, and other professional bodies; and in sports and competition. It also became unlawful for individuals exercising authority to instruct others to discriminate, or for pressure to be applied on others to discriminate. Either the individual or the corporate body can be found guilty of racial discrimination under the Act.

Important distinctions between direct and indirect discrimination, and a distinction between discrimination and victimisation, are made in the RRA 1976. An act of direct discrimination occurs when person $x$ treats person $y$ less favourably than $x$ would treat others on the grounds of $y$'s race. Discrimination on racial grounds requires two things to be reasonably shown: first, that person $y$ was, or was likely to be, treated by person $x$ less favourably than another person in the same circumstances; and, second, that 'racial grounds' constituted the reason for the differential treatment. The law does not require that there should be proof of an intention on the part of the discriminator to discriminate. In other words, the proof of discrimination is an objective, not a subjective, one; that is, if the action of the respondent is discriminatory, then the provisions of the law apply. The law does provide, however, that in racial discrimination cases the court or the tribunal hearing the case is obliged to take into account all aspects of the circumstances to determine the motives of the accused. But it would appear that case law has somewhat muddied the situation, because the CRE have recommended that whilst the Lords have made the legal position clear, Parliament should make a direct statement about the meaning of the phrase 'on racial grounds' or give an illustration of their intention so there should be no dependence on case law. In *James* v. *Eastleigh Borough Council* [1990] IRLR 288, the House of Lords made clear that a person has acted unlawfully if their action resulted in another person being treated differently on grounds of race. The Lords also decided, however, in *Perera* v. *Civil Service Commission* [1993] IRLR 166 that if several criteria are used and only one of them disadvantages persons from minority ethnic groups, then the discrimination is not unlawful, even if it is not possible to show that the particular criterion is justifiable.

The RRA 1976 states that an act of indirect racial discrimination occurs when treatment of different racial groups is formally equal, but the treatment has a discriminatory effect on a particular racial group. This is not an easy concept to grasp when it is applied to the law. As we noted in Chapter 1, the concept was first introduced in the USA by the academic Charles Hamilton and the political activist Stokeley Carmichael (1968) during the civil rights agitation of the 1960s. Hamilton and Carmichael (now Kwame Toure) argued that although there is the tendency to focus upon individual acts of racism against black Americans, the problem was essentially one of racial discrimination on an institutional basis and this was more likely to be experienced indirectly rather than directly by an individual. The US Supreme Court's decision in *Griggs* v. *Duke Power Co.* in 1971 established this point in American law. Chief Justice Berger supported the Equal Employment Opportunity Commission (EEOC) in their contention that the law against discrimination in employment had intended to address the consequences, not the intention, of action taken by individuals and corporate bodies (Ringer, 1983, Chapter 10). At first, Anthony Lester, who drafted the Bill, and the Home Secretary Roy Jenkins, whose initiative it was, had no thought of including this construction of racial discrimination, but a visit to the US in 1975 convinced them of the wisdom of doing so (Lester, 1994, p. 227; see also Sooben, 1990, Chapter 4).

The Act, then, requires that the following factors are present in a given situation for there to be a *prima facie* case of indirect racial discrimination: first, the condition or requirement for a job, a promotion or service applies equally to all or any racial group; second, this requirement or condition is such that only a very small proportion of the victim's racial group could qualify or meet it; third, the condition or requirement is such that a particular individual from the group discriminated against cannot meet it; and, finally, where the person who discriminates cannot justify the condition or requirement set out for the job, promotion or service to be universally applicable to people of all racial groups.

The framers of the RRA 1976 envisaged a situation in which individuals who sought redress under the law could become victims of the persons or institutions they alleged discriminated against them or others. The law therefore sought to protect such individuals by making it illegal to victimise a person who seeks protection under the Act, a person giving information or evidence in the case of another person who is seeking redress or protection under the Act, and, third, a person who is involved in any way in relation to the discriminator or any other person having to answer under the Act. Consistent with the spirit of the Act, victimisation is defined as involving the notion of the individual being treated less favourably than others on racial grounds.

A number of cases have been brought before the courts around these issues, and since judges interpret the law, much attention has been given to judicial decisions about the provisions of the Act. The case law that has developed around the RRA 1976 has, however, turned mainly on indirect discrimination, because it is in this area of public life that discrimination is likely to be actively, but covertly, practised. This suggests that the law, as an instrument for change, has been vindicated because the kinds of direct discrimination evident in most areas of British life up to the 1970s are now less apparent.[2] The law partly restrains would-be racial discriminators, because at least they are having to think about the legal consequences of their action in significant areas of the public sphere. Anti-discrimination lawyers and others are of the view that the law does not go far enough, and have called for reform to strengthen it in particular areas. Before turning to this point, however, it is important briefly to describe some of the relevant exemptions under the RRA 1976 and the organisational framework provided for enforcing the legislation.

The RRA 1976 specifies areas where to discriminate on racial grounds is not against the law of the land. These exemptions are, however, generally less commented upon than are the other aspects of the Act. There may be several reasons for this. It is possible that the framers of the legislation struck the right balance between discrimination in the public and private spheres of British life, or the law may have helped to drive discrimination underground or behind closed doors; perhaps too there is a mistaken assumption that the law is universally applicable to all situations of racial discrimination and therefore would-be discriminators think about the likely consequences of their actions in more utilitarian terms. It is probable that the relative success of the law and its availability have encouraged such perceptions. Whatever the case, it may be useful to mention some of the main exceptions sanctioned by the law.

First, in the key area of employment, which was described in the last chapter, it has not been illegal to discriminate in favour of employing a person 'where being of a particular racial group is a genuine occupational qualification for the job', and where this situation requires promotion, transfer or training (section 5 (1) (a) and (b)). This important exemption is generally referred to as the GOQ (genuine occupational qualification) provision, and the Act offers four examples of situations in which this kind of discrimination would not be considered illegal. The first is where 'dramatic performance or other entertainment in a capacity for which a person of that racial group is required for reasons of authenticity' (Home Office, 1977, p. 9). In a publication explaining the Act soon after it became law, the Home Office gave an example of this GOQ as being 'the portrayal of a well-known historical figure in a play' (ibid.). The second example is where 'participation as an artist's or photographic model' such as visual imagery for authenticity is deemed necessary, that is, as the Home Office guide suggested, 'where a photographer requires as a model a person whose appearance is associated with a particular ethnic or national origin' (ibid.). The third example of where the GOQ principle may apply is the food industry where particular settings and persons are required for authenticity; the Home Office example of such a situation was that of the employment of a waiter in a Chinese restaurant. The fourth example of where the GOQ principle may apply to employment is where 'the holder of the job provides persons of that racial group with personal services promoting their welfare, and those services can most effectively be provided by a person of that racial group' (Section 5 (2) (d)). Perhaps the clearest example of this situation is where, as the Home Office suggested, 'a particular racial group might respond best to help offered by a social worker who belongs to the same racial group' (ibid., p. 10). As the migrant generation of Caribbean and Asian men and women increasingly entered their twilight years in the 1980s and 1990s, the meaning of this provision became clearer because of their specific needs. Consequently, a number of welfare jobs were advertised specifically in terms provided under the law for treating difference as a legitimate concern of social policy.

In addition to the GOQs there are other forms of discrimination in employment that are not unlawful. First, it is not unlawful for a British employer to discriminate against seamen, who applied for employment outside Britain or are recruited from outside Britain, or were brought to Britain from another country.[3] Second, it is not unlawful for an employer to discriminate against an employee where the employee is not a UK resident, where the employee will benefit from the discrimination, and where the employment will give the employee training which the employer believes the employee will use outside Britain. Finally, if employment is in a private household, the employer may discriminate on the grounds of colour, race, ethnicity and national origins. Here it appears that the framers of the law were keen to distinguish between the public and private domains of life discussed in Chapter 1.

This relates to a second set of exemptions which reinforces the public/private spheres of social life. Under the general prohibition against discrimination in the provision of goods, facilities, services and premises, it is not illegal to discriminate in household and family arrangements. Second, individuals may discriminate in the letting of small dwellings where the premises are occupied by the owner's relatives, provided there are less than six persons, plus the owner and members of his or her household, for whom such dwellings are available. Third, it is not unlawful for an association with less than twenty-five members to discriminate on racial grounds. Nor is it unlawful to discriminate favourably 'in affording persons of a particular racial group access to facilities or services to meet the special needs of persons of that group in regard to their education, training or welfare, or any ancillary benefits' (section 35). Not surprisingly, action 'done for the purpose of safeguarding national security', that is, broad exemptions indicating executive discretion, are not covered by the law against discrimination on racial grounds. Through an Order of Council the Secretary of State can take action which may discriminate on grounds of race, but the CRE have been eager to have these exemptions changed (CRE, 1991).

Whilst some of these exemptions are benign, others are intended to be sensitive to what policy-makers and politicians appear to have believed the white majority voting public will or will not tolerate. On the first of these points, it may be noted that although Lester and Jenkins were strongly influenced by US practice, they resisted going the whole American way of legislating for positive action, that is, where the law is used to try to redress past, historical discrimination. This approach to public policy has not generally been accepted in Britain. The idea has been frequently used in public discourse about race relations and it has also been subjected to much criticism. John Edwards, for example, has suggested that past, historic injustices to whole groups of people cannot be justifiably redressed in the present because not all members of a past denied group stand in equal need in the present. He is certainly correct to stress that the notions of positive discrimination and equality of opportunity have been loosely used in Britain, unlike in the USA where the courts have deliberated and refined the meaning of 'positive action' or 'positive discrimination'. But his insistence that justice 'is not the whole of morality' (Edwards, 1987, p. 2) is an *ad hominem* argument because it rather too carefully ignores, first, the practical concerns of those who are involved with correcting present inequalities and, second, Edwards seems to be unaware of the fact that we do not have to support fully the nineteenth-century French phisosopher and Utopian socialist, Proudhon, who contended that all property is theft to recognise that some present socio-economic structures may be a continuation of the immorality and injustices of the past. Moreover, it has not been the contention of those who fight for justice to have more than what is justly their's, but rather that from their present unequal positions they wish to be treated equally in the present. The benign aspects of the RRA 1976 do not go beyond this position.

Indeed, the framers of the legislation appear to have been very sensitive to the delicate balance between what they thought to be tolerance, and revolt on the part of the majority white indigenous population, and this was no doubt important in gaining all-party support in the Commons. In any event, in a majoritarian democracy politics do occur under such constraints. Thus, the Act is premised on a distinction between the public and the private spheres of British life: it is mainly in the private sphere that it is not unlawful to discriminate on racial grounds, leaving the Englishman's castle sacrosanct, and safe from the eye and arm of the law. In the public realm of competition, however, the law seeks to ensure that the application of impersonal rules obtains. But the distinction between public and private is not always clear-cut, as Lord Scarman's insightful Foreword to Edwards' book on the question indicates; against Edwards' arguments Scarman rightly suggests that

> perfect justice and a perfect fulfilment of moral obligations may have to wait upon the success of policies and principles which move towards each without immediately achieving either of them . . . to reject policies and principles because of their dangers will, I believe, result in total defeat and endless discontent.    (Edwards, 1987, p. x)

The RRA 1976 established what were expected to be relatively adequate remedies and structures to oversee the enforcement and review of the law. First, unlike under earlier legislation, individuals can themselves seek redress against discrimination and victimisation through the courts (in England and Wales), through the Sheriff's office (in Scotland), as well as through tribunals. Second, the Race Relations Board and the Community Relations Commissions, which had been set up under the 1965 and 1968 Acts, were abolished and a new Commission for Racial Equality established. It was expected that there would be no less than eight and no more than fifteen commissioners, some on full-time and others on part-time appointments all drawn from different areas of national life. These commissioners and the officials of the CRE are not civil servants, but they are appointed by the Home Secretary, who also appoints one of the commissioners to be Chair of the Commission.[4] The responsibilities of the Commission are clearly set out in Part VII of the Act as being '(a) to work towards the elimination of discrimination; (b) to promote equality of opportunity, and good relations, between persons of different racial groups generally; (c) to keep under review the working of this Act and, when they are so required by the Secretary of State or otherwise think it necessary, draw up and submit to the Secretary of State proposals for amending it'. This mission statement is to be found in most, if not all, publications by the Commission.

The CRE's brief is, therefore, a wide one: on the one hand, it embraces law enforcement under the Act, and on the other hand, it has the responsibility of promoting racial equality through public awareness and exemplary practice. There have been suggestions that these functions should be separated, but the CRE appears to be comfortable with the situation, and under Herman Ouseley the promotional side of their work has become quite significant and visible. The Home Secretary can ask the CRE to instigate formal investigations or the Commission can themselves decide to initiate such investigations into any situation with which they are concerned. The Commission are, however, required clearly to state the terms of reference for an investigation of individuals or groups, and a person being investigated has the right to legal representation. Unlike its predecessor, the Race Relations Board, the Commission has the power to request relevant information such as documents and oral evidence, and is empowered to issue non-discriminatory notices which will be taken into account by a court deciding on a specific charge under the Act. Assistance may be given by the Commission to individuals seeking redress under the Act, and to organisations 'concerned with equality of opportunity and good race relations', a function previously carried out by the Race Relations Commission under the 1968 Act. The CRE may also issue codes of good practice as guidelines for employers and others whose activities come within the purview of the legislation. In 1985 and again in 1991 the Commission called upon the government to extend the areas in which they may issue such codes.

This skeletal description of the provisions of the law is useful, but does not necessarily convey what influence or impact they may have on the lives of victims of racial discrimination and on the course and texture of British life. It is therefore necessary and useful to give some more direct illustrations of the work of the CRE, as an indication of how the commissioners and their staff seek to ensure adherence to the law and have some impact on reducing discrimination and inequality in British society. In this respect, a close look at the Commission's 1994 annual report may serve as a fair illustration of their work in the 1990s under Herman Ouseley, who approached his work as Chairman in a vigorous and campaigning style. The annual report is, of course, presented to the Secretary of State for the Home Department, and in 1994 the incumbent was Michael Howard, himself from an East European immigrant family but under whose stewardship the Home Office became extremely hostile towards applicants for asylum (see, for example, N. Cohen, 1997) and individuals wishing to join their families in Britain, and displayed an attitude bordering on indifference about race relations. The report is divided into an extended introduction by the Chairman, followed by brief statements about complaints under the Act, developments in the law, racial harassment and violence, problems of assuring equality, working to make Britain a just society for all, a summary of the Commission's work for the year and appropriate appendices dealing with expenditure, aid to a range of projects, and other activities.

In his report the Chairman stressed the need for the Commission to be seen as a campaigning as well as a law enforcement body, which actively seeks to establish partnerships with racial equality councils, law centres, advice centres, local governments and employers in the public as well as the private sectors, to promote good race relations. The Commission had established a seven-point action plan for the year, which involved giving priority to aiding individuals and groups with complaints under the Act, publicising formal investigations conducted by the Commission so as to encourage others to take appropriate action themselves against racial discrimination, tackling institutional racism, harassment and violence, the problems of youth, promoting public awareness of CRE programmes and establishing working partnerships with a variety of bodies in public life. Under each of these, several cases and instances were reported to show what the Commission have done over the year to enforce the law and promote good race relations.

In particular, it may be instructive to look closer at how the Commission addressed complaints about racial discrimination. In 1994 the Commission received 1937 applications for assistance, of which 47 were outside the scope of the Commission's brief; of the remainder, 1314 were about employment and 576 about non-employment situations, with 116 settled on terms, 15 dismissed and 21 successful upon a hearing. There were a further 31 cases won by other agencies supported by the Commission (CRE, 1995, Table 1, p. 8). In general, the numbers of total applications increased between 1978 and 1994, although not on a year-by-year basis, and the report showed that the numbers dismissed also decreased over the period. The Commission stressed that many of the cases ended in respondents recognising that there was a need to improve policy and practice (ibid.).

Specific acts of discrimination in public life were highlighted, giving a sense of urgency and purpose to the report. Overall, the 1994 report conveys the sense of a Commission concerned about the big and the small things affecting the lives of individuals, irrespective of their racial backgrounds. For example, in his introduction the Chairman deliberately stressed that the Commission

> have a duty and responsibility under the law to assist *anyone* in Britain who has been discriminated against on racial grounds (which include grounds of nationality and ethnic origin), and not, as one myth would have it, only black and Asian complainants. (CRE, 1995, p. 4)

Perhaps because Ouseley is himself a black person with considerable experience of administration and commitment to good race relations, and is also the first person from the minority ethnic communities to be appointed to this important post, he was keen to ensure that Commission reports and publications conveyed a strong view to readers that they were engaged in a common enterprise of making Britain a more equal and fair society for new as well as old minority ethnic and majority ethnic groups. He recognised that the media did not like this, but stressed that their hostility would not deter the Commission from so interpreting their brief to make Britain a more fair and equal society for all. In particular, some spokespersons from the Irish communities in London and elsewhere had for sometime been asking the CRE to champion their cause as a minority ethnic group. Earlier, Michael Day, whom Ouseley succeeded, had reported in his chairman's introduction to the 1991 annual report that

> the demands on our resources continue to increase. Over the past two years we have been involved in lengthy consultations with representatives of the Irish community. They have presented a powerful

case that in all our work of a general nature we should take the Irish dimension into account.   (CRE, 1992, p. 10)

Day also stated that of the 1655 complaints received in 1991 only 20 were from the Irish communities, and suggested that this may have been because 'many Irish people do not see the Race Relations Act or the Commission as relevant to their circumstances' (ibid.). The increase in demand appears to have continued into the 1990s and in 1996 it was being frequently reported in the media that the Commission was involved in discussion over alleged acts of discrimination between Welsh and English and discrimination on racial grounds against British (white and brown) employees of Japanese companies operating in Britain. As Britain becomes increasingly integrated into the global economy and more firms re-locate themselves here, it is possible that the Commission will also increasingly be seen as an obvious champion of groups and individuals who experience racial discrimination on the basis of their race or their ethnic backgrounds, and this will involve minorities as well as majorities.

## Promoting Good Race Relations

The framers of the RRA 1976 recognised the value of achieving 'good race relations' through promotional work, and made this one of the main responsibilities of the Commission. The Community Relations Councils (CRCs) were also established in the same spirit. These replaced the largely voluntary National Committee for Commonwealth Immigrants (NCCI) which had been established under the 1965 Act. In turn, in the early 1990s the CRCs were replaced by the Race Equality Councils (RECs), following a 1987 review of the relationship between the CRE and the CRCs. As Gay and Young (1988), who conducted the review, have pointed out, these community based bodies have their origins in the 'liaison committees' which sprung up spontaneously in London and elsewhere where black and brown Commonwealth immigrants settled from the late 1940s. In some instances some of these bodies may have had their origins in pre-World-War-Two organisations established to help seamen from the colonies at the port cities. These liaison committees were concerned with the welfare needs of the new immigrants, who, as we saw in Chapter 4, did not always qualify for state assistance. From the 1950s some local authorities established liaison officers, thereby providing another arm of the community relations movement. According to Gay and Young these bodies out of which the CRCs were formed under the 1968 Act 'may thus be fairly said to have begun as white people's organisations, geared to the welfare of black people' (ibid., p. 16), but there were exceptions. In the early days of migration, conciliation and harmonious relations between 'the races' formed the basis of these groups. These remain the chief aims and objectives of the RECs in the communities in which they are based.

The RRA 1976 marked, however, a shift in emphasis from conciliation to the achievement of equality in race relations, reflecting Roy Jenkins' notion of a multi-cultural society in which there would be no attempt to achieve integration through assimilation, but through promoting mutual tolerance within diversity. Moreover, as noted in the last chapter, the first half of the 1970s was characterised by militancy on the part of black youths and Asian women workers, concerned about change, not reconciliation or harmony. The Act reflected this mood for change and required local authorities to take active steps to promote equality of opportunity, thereby providing a firmer basis for the CRCs and their successors, the RECs, to work closely with the CRE at national level and with local government. Whilst the RECs are not under any legal obligation to oversee the enforcement of the RRA 1976, the CRE is. The Commission's brief is not therefore merely that of the RECs writ large. In 1992 the CRE entered what they called a 'partnership' with the over eighty RECs, but the partnership was never an easy one. In the first place, it appears that some RECs continued to see the CRE as a kind of national voice representing their interests. There was a tendency too for some to see the CRE as an unequal partner because the Commission's funds are more certain. The 'partnership' between the CRE and the RECs, which followed the 1987 evaluation, itself required a fresh examination in early 1996, and the outcome of this review is awaited.

It would appear that many REC officials believed that the exercise will lead to the CRE distancing themselves from the RECs, and subsequently the usual mistrust between these bodies would continue. What is clear, however, is that the tension between voluntary effort at the local level and any streamlining of the RECs in line with the CRE may not be reconcilable. It may well be that the centrally funded CRE and the multiple-funded and voluntary RECs will have to continue to lead an uncomfortable co-existence in their not unrelated fight against racial discrimination at local and national levels. If the CRE were, however, to play a more prominent role in the RECs, then there is the possibility of a para-statal institution destroying the autonomy, creativity and flexibility of a voluntary movement.

## The Limitations of the Law

Despite the achievements of the CRE, as reflected in their annual reports and the national media, and the fact that individuals and groups look to them for help, as we approach century's end and the completion of the first fifty years of significant large-scale settlement in Britain of black and brown communities with backgrounds in Africa, Asia and the Caribbean, it is pertinent to ask whether the RRA 1976 has been a success, a failure, or, more realistically, fallen somewhere between the two stools. In any event, as the CRE have suggested, this important piece of legislation has to be reviewed fundamentally to take into account societal change. In 1997 the Act had been in operation for twenty-one years, and if only for this reason it demands a fundamental review such as the CRE have tried to initiate. Speaking of the Conservatives in 1991, Michael Day said that a government 'which continues to pledge itself unreservedly to the cause of equal opportunities should have no difficulty in attending' to necessary changes in the law (CRE, 1991, p. 6). Of course, this statement should apply more forcefully to a government formed by Labour which has consistently enjoyed the overwhelming support of voters in minority ethnic communities and the party that has long been committed to equality for all.

An assessment of the Act's success or failure requires setting it alongside other specific legislation concerned with equality in British society in the 1970s. One of these situations was the division between Catholics and Protestants in Ulster, where 'The Troubles' broke out in 1968 and went on until the cease-fire in 1994.[5] The RRA 1976 was not intended to, and did not, apply to Northern Ireland. There, the Fair Employment Act of 1976 outlawed discrimination on grounds of religious affiliation, thereby directly addressing the conflict between Catholics (over a united Ireland) and Protestants (over continued membership in the United Kingdom). Thus, it has been possible for acts of racial discrimination to be not unlawful in Northern Ireland, whilst they would be unlawful in Britain; and for religious discrimination to be illegal in Northern Ireland, but not unlawful in Britain. Lester saw this apparently cruel irony when in 1994 he stated that these were 'incoherent constitutional arrangements' (Lester, 1994, p. 235), and called for the 'principle of equality' to be applied universally to all forms of unjustifiable inequalities.

In December 1992, the Secretary of State for Northern Ireland, Sir Patrick Mayhew, issued through the Central Community Relations Unit in the Northern Ireland Office, a consultative document entitled *Race Relations in Northern Ireland*, and this formed the basis for discussion over the form that legislation about race relations in the province should take. The paper surveyed UK legislation – such as the Prevention of Incitement of Hatred Act (Northern Ireland) 1970, the Public Order (Northern Ireland) Order 1987, the Fair Employment (Northern Ireland) Act 1989, the Sex Discrimination (Northern Ireland) Orders 1976 and 1988, and the Equal Pay Act (Northern Ireland) 1970 – so as to be able to outline legal protection of the individual against exclusion and discrimination in Ulster. The document also outlined the UK's obligations under European Union and international law, as they apply to the province, such as the United Nations' International Covenant on Civil and Political Rights (which seeks to protect the individual against discrimination and violation of equal rights before the law), and the European Convention on Human Rights (which seeks to protect the individual's rights to life, social, political and economic liberty, freedom from arbitrary arrest, family privacy, freedom of conscience and peaceful assembly). The main question that the public was asked to consider and about which to express their views was whether the government should extend the RRA 1976, the Equal Opportunities Act (EOA) 1975, or the Fair Employment Act 1976, to include racial discrimination in Northern Ireland. The government's own view, however, was that these Acts may be inappropriate for the specific situation of Ulster, where the new minority ethnic population was believed to be only around 10 000, and that there may be a case for setting up a new agency to oversee, enforce and promote good race relations in the province.

However, as Lord (Anthony) Lester, who drafted both the Equal Opportunities Act and the Race Relations Act 1976 wrote in 1994, the drafting of these measures was strictly kept apart, and efforts were made to 'distance' the measures from each other. As Sooben's (1990, Chapter 4) work on the origins of the Act has shown, although Roy Jenkins consistently stressed that he intended to treat race and sex discrimination legislation together, political imperatives kept them as separate measures. Lester (1994) stated that the distancing between these measures

> was unfortunate because it meant that the statutory anti-discrimination codes were piece-meal and fragmented, rather than a coherent set of principles and procedures throughout the United Kingdom.
>
> (p. 226)

Subsequent developments would appear to have vindicated Lester's view that the measures against discrimination on the basis of gender, race and religion should have been thought through and drafted together on the basis of 'a coherent set of principles'. This wish, however, is counter to a deep-seated principle in British constitutional theory and practice: there is a preference for piecemeal attention to social and political issues and problems rather than the application of all-embracing principles, as reflected in the 1992 consultative document from the Northern Ireland Office, and the reluctance to adopt European law based on general principles.

There have been other criticisms of the RRA 1976 from both the extreme left and the extreme right of the political spectrum. What critics on the extreme right of politics have had to say about race relations law amounts to very little, and the little there is need not detain us. Suffice it to say that in general the extreme right in British public life see anti-racist initiatives as unnecessary, and for some, such as the Conservative Monday Club, black and brown Britons should be encouraged or forced to leave the country, presumably making it unnecessary for there to be laws guiding race relations (see, for example, The Conservative Party, 1984). A more sophisticated statement of much the same position was made by the economist E. J. Mishan in the conservative journal *The Salisbury Review* when he argued that

> the problems arising from race come to engage a quite disproportionate share of the nation's political energies – diverting its passions and its scarce resources from the main prevailing problems of the post-industrial era.   (Mishan, 1988, p. 26)

It is not that those on the far left of British politics do not recognise the need to fight against racism. Rather, it is a case of whether the law is sufficiently rigorous and can bring about change within the framework of what are regarded as irreconcilable class interests. The extreme left position was perhaps best stated by the American sociologist Ira Katznelson and variously re-stated by others such as Sivanandan and his associates at the Institute of Race Relations. The position is that race relations and the CRE are so many attempts to co-opt community radicals into the *status quo* in order to pre-empt radical solutions to a desperate situation (see, for example, Sivanandan, 1991).

Thus, although starting from opposite positions and with quite different concerns, both the left and the right would appear to converge at much the same point, namely, that race relations legislation and statutory bodies are not what are necessary to resolve problems of relations between different racial and ethnic groups. And, of course, the attraction of this position lies in the fact that it does point to the limitations of the law as an instrument of change or control. None the less, most commentators and observers of British race relations would agree that the truth of the matter lies somewhere between these extreme positions, and a few comments about this middle ground may be worthwhile here.

Among anti-racists of all political persuasions, it is not so much that there is any serious and widespread doubt about the necessity of law in this area of national life; rather, it is a case of whether the law is an entirely adequate instrument for necessary change. Criticism of the RRA 1976 tends, therefore, to be over the limitations of the law; but when push comes to shove, anti-discrimination lawyers, academics, activists and other progressive individuals will admit that anti-discrimination law has made a difference – however little – to the life chances of black and brown Britons and has, therefore, contributed to making the country a less unjust place for all members of society. None the less, the continued evidence of discrimination in employment, education, training, housing, and other areas of public life extensively documented by researchers, the courts, the CRE and others, suggests that too much confidence in the law would be unjustified. Hepple (1992) has correctly reminded us of the

> false assumption that law is simply an independent instrument of state power, a technical device that is capable of doing much for ethnic relations as the microchip has done for communications.
>
> (p. 19)

The law would appear to have 'driven underground' (ibid.) many of the overt acts of discrimination, but the law has not, and it would be naive to expect that it could or ever will, eliminate racial discrimination in society. This may be particularly so where competition is not only an economic necessity but is promoted as a social and moral public good, and in the spirit of competition legitimate differences may be mobilised in order to secure scarce resources. In his piece on twenty-five years of race relations legislation, Hepple persuasively argued that since law has to be located within the specific individual, and conflict – including racial conflict – has to be reduced in law to specific parties, the law has difficulty getting to grips with large claims of discrimination against whole groups of people. Thus, the failure of the police to do more against racial harassment, or the failure of employers to effect racial justice in the labour market, cannot be handled by the law unless and until this form of discrimination is individualised. The alternative approach which Hepple (1992) and Lacey (1992) have hinted at, is for the law to permit collective rights to be defended in the courts, but this is perhaps too radical a departure from well-established legal and constitutional norms, centred on the individual, to be seriously entertained. Arising from the individualising of acts of racial discrimination, Hepple goes on to argue that the law is directed at only one factor, namely, discrimination and the requirement of legal specificity, and this has led to a narrow understanding of racism, which in turn has proven to be illusory. In other words, as necessary as law against discrimination clearly is, there are definite limits to its effectiveness in bringing about substantial change in this area of social life. After all, the law cannot sensibly outlaw racism as such, only its manifestations as public action.

None the less, this recognition of the limitations of the law should not belittle its positive effects on social relations. Referring to a statement by the Race Relations Board which was set up under the 1965 Act, Hepple (1992) found a 'classic liberal definition of the aims of anti-discrimination legislation' stated as being that law is a clear statement of public policy; it supports those who do not want to discriminate but are pressured by social convention to do so; it provides redress and protection to minorities; it provides the procedures whereby peaceful solutions to grievances can be achieved and thereby releases social tensions; and the law limits the spread of prejudicial behaviour by discouraging the environment in which such behaviour thrives. Judged by these criteria, the law against racial discrimination has obviously been a success.

But this success has been limited. As the person who drafted the 1976 Act, Lester identified a number of drawbacks in the measure itself and its implementation. Following from what he saw as a failure to establish a coherent principle of anti-discrimination covering gender, religion and race, the beneficial effects of European law have not been felt in British race relations. In the area of equal opportunities, European Union laws have improved British practice, as Lester stressed, but this has not occurred in race relations law for two reasons. First, the British law has stood on its own, and as Bindman, (1996) the CRE and others have argued, it is in advance of European law; second, Parliament and government have not incorporated European law on equality in general into national law. The drawbacks of the Equal Opportunities law, in Lester's view, have been remedied by the application of European law to Britain, but this has not been the experience with respect to race relations law. If, however, there were appropriate challenges in the courts under the provisions of European law, such as the Convention of Human Rights, this could change.

The concerns involved here have been taken on board by the CRE themselves in their review of the law and their call for changes to take account of what they see as new developments. In a widely publicised and discussed document, the *Second Review of the Race Relations Act 1976: A Consultative Paper*, the Commission laid out in 1991 a comprehensive list about the working of the law, its drawbacks and the way forward. The intention was that the government of the day should seek all-party support as occurred in 1976 to address aspects of the Act which had, as noted earlier,

> become weakened or which have proved to be more complex and cumbersome in practice than was envisaged, or in extending the scope of the Act to cover those areas where there is shown to be no effective enforcement.   (CRE, 1991, p. 6)

The Commission had gone through the same process in 1985, and had submitted proposals for change to the government, but had not received a formal response from them. The 1991 consultation document pointed out, however, that race relations affairs had progressed in two ways, despite government inactivity. First, the CRE had taken steps to have specific provisions incorporated into broader legislation, including planning control, extension of the power to draw up codes of practice in the area of housing, and protection for work-experience trainees and training for non-employees without recourse to ministerial designation or training bodies. The second development between 1985 and 1991 was that a number of cases before the courts had brought about changes consistent with the Commission's recommendations. These included the Court of Appeal increasing the level of compensation for injury to feelings in *Alexander* v *Home Office* (1988 IRLR 190) and *Noone* v *North West Thames Regional Health Authority* (1988 IRLR 195); in *Hampson* v *Department of Education* (1990, 2 All ER 25) the Court reduced the circumstances when indirect discrimination may be justified, and the legal scope for immunity from racial discrimination law was also reduced; in *Aziz* v *Trinity Street Taxis* (1988, 2 All ER 860) the Court attempted to 'iron out' some of the difficulties in the law against victimisation. Even after these developments, many of the recommendations from 1985 remained problematic for the Commission. These covered such matters as the definition of indirect discrimination, the immunity of some government activities from action by the Commission or individuals under the RRA 1976, failure to extend legal aid to racial discrimination cases in tribunals, limitations on the Commission in instituting formal investigations, limited remedies in industrial tribunals, and so forth. The Commission summarised developments in these areas by stating that the

the overall conclusion is that although the review power concentrated minds inside the Commission, in particular in relation to ways
forward with a test-case strategy, and also was the inspiration for a
number of statutory changes, much more could have been achieved
had there been a positive, Governmental response in favour of wide
statutory change. The Commission renews the call for change in line
with the 1985 Review, as updated in this Review.    (CRE, 1991, p. 11)

Additionally, the 1991 review highlighted specific areas of national life in
which there was an abundance of evidence of discrimination on the
grounds of race. The Commission pointed to the labour market in
which researchers had provided clear evidence of discrimination at a
number of stages in recruitment, selection and promotion. Education,
one of the areas most focused upon in Britain, was no different, nor were
housing, health, the criminal justice system, and racial harassment of
individuals from minority ethnic groups. The 1991 review made a
particular point about religious discrimination. The context of this was,
as seen in an earlier chapter, the furore over Salman Rushdie's *Satanic
Verses* in Muslim communities throughout the country. The Commission
argued that religious discrimination was having a significant impact on
race relations in the country and, therefore, required consideration.
They argued that the Rushdie Affair brought out the tension between
freedom of speech and religious toleration; 'protection of religion was
seen to be in conflict with the notion of freedom of speech' (CRE,
1991, p. 17). There were other issues in the wider society which each
had significant impact on race relations, such as incitement to racial
hatred, the then impending transformation of the European Economic
Community (EEC) into the European Union and the absence of legislation in member states comparable to the RRA 1976 to ensure protection of British citizens and residents in the new Europe, and the more
general question of human rights provisions in the European Human
Rights Convention. With the Maastricht Treaty and the EEC becoming
the European Union in 1992, the CRE pointed out the drawbacks of
the Convention and the relevance of the Union adopting the criminal
sanctions under the RRA 1976, because, as they argued, Article 14 of
the Convention 'does not grant an independent right to freedom from
discrimination' (CRE, 1991, p. 69).

Overall, the recommendations for change from the 1985 and 1991 re-
views amounted to 204 clauses, covering such areas as discrimination
and the scope of the RRA 1976, exemption from the Act, proving discrimination and adjudication, formal investigations and law enforcement,

remedies, mechanisms for change, ethnic monitoring, employment, areas of non-employment, legal undertakings from specific bodies, local authorities, positive and affirmative action, criminal and civil law, economic incentives, barristers and solicitors, education, harassment on housing estates, criminal justice, religion and the law, Race Equality Council, and so forth. Over twenty specific recommendations were made covering these areas, under the rubric 'discrimination and the scope of the RRA 1976', including direct and indirect discrimination. There was the call for clarification, without recourse to case law, of what is meant by an absence of intention on the part of a person whose action constitutes discrimination under the Act. There was also a call for clearer provisions against indirect discrimination which has a 'significant adverse impact' on specific groups, and for this itself to be clearly stated. It was seen as desirable for the law to be amended to provide more adequate protection against victimisation. The Commission called for a debate over whether the law should be extended to provide against discrimination on grounds of religion, following the Rushdie Affair.

Altogether, the document detailed recommendations to cover the comprehensive range of issues that have long been the concerns of people working in communities, public bodies, and the Commission itself, in the field of race relations. One of the most interesting of these recommendations was for discussion to take place and for consideration to be given to whether there should not be a single human rights body dealing with all issues pertaining to equality – race, gender, and so forth. This would, of course, come close to Lester's views, mentioned above, for a coherent set of principles to underpin efforts to resolve problems of these kinds in the United Kingdom, and perhaps, ultimately, the European Union. As with the passing of the RRA 1976 and the EOA 1975, there would be strong and perhaps convincing political reasons for separately treating in legislation questions of inequality and discrimination on grounds of race, gender and disability.

## Conclusion

Whatever the outcome of this debate in the next few years, it is clear that the law is not likely to be the sole or perhaps even the single most relevant instrument in the fight for a fairer and more just society in Britain. But nor will promotional and educational work be able to bring about 'the good society', necessary as such efforts are. Therefore, whilst the law and the CRE have obvious limitations, for the moment and for the foreseeable future they remain important weapons in the fight against racial discrimination. It is therefore highly likely that efforts to combine or unify all forms of struggle against unjust discrimination and inequality will falter on the rock of difference around which many groups wish to organise their grievances. It may be useful at this point to consider whether the acquisition of verifiable knowledge is likely to erode racial discrimination and therefore make it uncesessary for us to speak about a set of social relations as race relations.

# 6 'Good Race Relations' and the Production of Knowledge

## Introduction

There is a strong view in Britain and elsewhere that the production of verifiable knowledge is in itself significant in the effort to reduce racial discrimination. In part, this came from the American experience of fighting Jim Crowism in the states south of the Mason–Dixon line in the state of Virginia and which formally sanctioned the universal incorporation of black Americans into the wider society. More generally, the belief appears to be rooted in an assumption that knowledge is likely to erase prejudicial values and therefore obnoxious and unacceptable social behaviour based on ignorance. It is worth remembering, however, that whilst this view has continued to be a fundamental assumption in British race relations theory and policy, some of the most knowledgeable sections of British and American societies – the academic and intellectual establishments – furthered racial theories and colluded with plans to discriminate against vulnerable groups. Fortunately, as we have seen, the view that knowledge is a corrective to the injustices of discrimination, has been balanced since 1965 by legislation against racial discrimination in British public life. None the less, the propositions that racial discrimination in Britain can and will be undermined by verifiable knowledge and that this knowledge is likely to inform policy, remain basic but partly erroneous principles. This is a disturbing hypothesis. It raises questions over the realisation of the multi-cultural society, because, as we noted earlier, education is at the centre of the effort to accomplish the ideals of multi-culturalism.

This chapter confines discussion to one aspect of the wider problem, that is, the relationship between academic research and policy in British race relations over the last three or more decades. It is, however, first necessary to situate the discussion within a more general concern over the relevance of research to policy in Britain. Finally, the perceptions of those who make links between research and policy, as well as researchers themselves, are brought into the discussion in order to convey the subjectivity of the relationship between the acquisition of varifiable knowledge and policy-making and implementation.

## Research Relevance in the Social Sciences

Perhaps no other country in the European Union has invested more in the rational inquiry of relations between groups of people who are distinguished by race or colour than the United Kingdom. This has been particularly so since 1970. In that year the Institute of Race Relations (IRR), which had started in 1957 to encourage the study of race relations within an international context, was taken over by radicals led by A. Sivanandan, the Institute's librarian (Mullard, 1985; Sivanandan, 1974). Earlier, in 1968, the Social Science Research Council (SSRC) had responded to a request from the IRR for funds to conduct research into British race relations specifically, but the SSRC had instead taken the initiative to establish its own Research Unit on Ethnic Relations (RUER) at the University of Bristol under Professor Michael Banton in 1970. Five years later, in 1975, a committee of prominent academics was asked by the then Home Secretary, Roy Jenkins, to give advice on 'a programme of research likely to be relevant to the formulation of policy' in race relations, and to advise him 'on the priorities for Government expenditure' on research (Home Office, 1975, p. 1).

The Home Office committee and Banton advanced three factors that were to continue to underpin research into British race relations into the 1990s. First, as Banton expressed the point in 1973, there was the need for intellectual clarity to be able to 'understand general processes and structures as they affect both the minorities and the majority society', because of the inadequacy of 'the conceptual apparatus available in this field' (Banton, 1973, p. 227). RUER was meant to provide this kind of intellectual clarity. The Home Office committee concurred, but stressed that research was necessary in race relations because government needed reliable and up-to-date statistical data to provide 'a necessary though of course not sufficient condition for rational discussion and understanding' (Home Office, 1975, p. 7). Second, reliable knowledge was necessary for the proper 'assessment and development of policy', as was 'good data', if arbitrary identification of needs and faulty implementation of policy were to be avoided (ibid.).

Race relations were soon to become what some on the left as well as the right of British politics in the 1970s daubed 'the race relations industry'. But, as Banton noted, already in the 1950s the work of those who were beginning the study of race relations in Britain – Kenneth Little, and his students Sydney Collins, Anthony Richmond, Sheila Patterson and others – were being 'unkindly called the "Negroes in Britain industry"' (Banton, 1973, p. 2). This expressed a distaste for the growth of employment of community radicals and others who were increasingly making a living from attempting to sort out the problems created by racial discrimination. Whilst this moral tone was perhaps understandable, it might have equally been borne in mind that society has overcome or chosen to ignore the distaste of there being several institutions such as banks, mortgage and insurance companies, established to manage uncertainties and misfortunes of individuals. Today, it is unlikely that most reasonable people would seriously doubt that laws against colour or racial discrimination and the desire to apply verifiable knowledge to this process constitute a progressive step in how a society manages and minimises the impact of exclusion and differential incorporation on some of its members. But inquiry into race relations must be located within the national framework of social and political research in order to determine whether there has been the wastage that individual commentators from both left and right of the 'chattering classes' of British society sometimes claim there is.

In Spring 1996, the Higher Education Funding Councils (HEFCs) for England, Scotland and Wales, and the Department of Education for Northern Ireland received submissions from all higher education institutions in the United Kingdom outlining their research activities for the years from 1992. Although the purpose of the exercise was to 'produce quality ratings of research which will be used ... in the determination of grants for research' (Higher Education Founding Council for England (HEFCE), 1994, p. 1), there was a widespread view that the rating gained by each institution would shape its profile within the academic community and the wider society. Research was understood to be 'original investigation undertaken in order to gain knowledge and understanding' (ibid.), and included a wide range of the activities universities have involved themselves in since the late 1980s, particularly since the abolition of the binary system involving universities and polytechnics in higher education at the beginning of the 1990s. Above all, however, emphasis was given to ' work of direct relevance to the needs of commerce and industry, as well as to the public and voluntary sectors' (ibid.).

This emphasis on relevance is no longer surprising nor seriously resisted in academic teaching and research. Students expect to be taught subjects which will help them to secure employment in a volatile and increasingly competitive labour market, and there is a more rigorous demand that all research should be relevant to at least one user group in society. Moreover, relevance is now a primary consideration in re-search financing and therefore the design of research projects. This is strongly emphasised by the Economic and Social Research Council (ESRC), the body that administers much of the state's funding of re-search in the social sciences in Britain.[1] Pressure from politicians and others has meant that from its inception the ESRC has had to justify its existence and work to others outside the academic community. Since the late 1980s, however, the ESRC went into over-drive to show aware-ness of their general public accountability. One way of demonstrating this awareness is to ask applicants for research funds to state what they see as the practical policy implications of their research projects. Ref-erees for each project are asked to comment on these features of applica-tions, as well as their timeliness. In the mid-1990s, academic referees were asked to comment on the theoretical, methodological and 'prac-tical significance' of projects, and to rate these as 'none', 'low', 'moder-ate' or 'high'. Where the ESRC advertise for tenders for contracts on their own programmes, applications were vetted in terms of whether they were 'wholly relevant', 'marginally/partially relevant', or 'irrel-evant' to the aims and objectives of the overall programme. It has also become the case that relevant non-academic bodies may be asked to comment on applications.

It therefore now seems like a lifetime ago when social science aca-demics could confidently speak of conducting research which would have no obvious relevance for policy and no relevant user group or com-munity. The distance between research and policy that obtained in the past has given way to what appears to be a convergence of interests between funders and researchers. This apparent convergence of inter-ests, however, is problematic. Some researchers still experience difficulty in reconciling their academic interests with the needs of policy-makers and implementers. Similarly, policy-makers and implementers some-times express frustrations over the seeming irrelevance, or inaccessibil-ity, of academic research.

In the main, however, there has been a change in perspective from what appeared to have been 'research for the sake of research' to 'the relevance of research' becoming an orthodoxy. The movement to-wards apparent convergence of academic and policy interests may be said to have started with Lord Rothschild's *A Framework for Government Research and Development* in 1971. This report suggested that the relation-ship between government funding and researchers should be that between customer and contractor: government sets out their research needs and the researcher contracts to conduct the research. Although this was to lead to much debate about who determined research priorities, it was not until the latter part of the 1980s that the customer/contractor relationship began to be an overriding factor in the funding of research. The environment within which this change of attitude was occurring was one established by Margaret Thatcher's concern about the relevance of the work universities were doing. Up to this point, the work of universities was assumed to be clear enough and, even if teaching and research were mysteries to the general public, it was taken for granted that their activities were legitimate and, in often undefined ways, useful to consuming individuals and a grateful country. The second Rothschild (1982) report, specifically on the social sciences, challenged these assumptions. The report, published in 1982, was commissioned by Sir Keith Joseph, then Secretary of State for Education and Science, and the person whom Thatcher herself credited with founding Thatcherism. But, on the whole and considering the general sceptical attitude towards the social sciences at that time, Rothschild was kind to these disciplines. None the less, he questioned whether social sciences, including the more well-known discipline of economics, were in fact sciences, and recommended that the Social Science Research Council, which had been established in 1965, should be renamed the Economic and Social Research Council[2] in order better to reflect the nature of the disciplines. Rothschild also called for research supported by the government to be relevant to the problems they and society faced.

Rothschild was followed by a number of statements from the ESRC, picking up the general theme of research relevance, and emphasising the dire need for the social sciences to be relevant to issues of the day. Relevance was rapidly being understood to mean relevance to policy, and the research assessment exercises of 1992 and 1996, perhaps unwittingly, emphasised this understanding within wider contexts. A major step in this direction was William Waldegrave's 1993 *White Paper on Science, Engineering and Technology* which wanted research in these areas to be more relevant to the needs of British industry and commerce. The ESRC under Howard Newby and his successors took up this understanding of relevance and made it part of Council's own brief, but in a manner that would not necessarily compromise academic rigour, wider concerns and independence. In January 1994, soon after the White Paper was published and was being widely discussed in educational and policy circles, the ESRC stated in its official publication that

While the shake-up of the natural science community is the more dramatic, it would be an unwise social scientist who dismissed the White Paper's implications as of no relevance to economic and social researchers.   (ESRC, 1994, p. 3)

Council saw their remit as including not only basic but also applied and strategic research, and declared that it was 'called on to engage more fully with the users of research in defining priorities, managing and conducting research and in applying its results' (ESRC, 1994, p. 1).

Earlier, in 1987, an ESRC Working Group of six British, one French and one Swedish academics drew up an influential document entitled *Horizons and Opportunities in the Social Sciences* (ESRC, 1987). The document set out some conditions for the development of a relevant and successful community of social scientists in Britain. These included, first, turning our backs on parochialism and embracing international collaboration in research. In a period when it appeared that British social science was in danger of neglecting broad international, comparative and theoretical issues, and the Council was the subject of Press and political lampooning (see Thomas, 1985, pp. 1–2), the report admitted that it is

> not wrong-headed to spend British money studying political institutions in developing African states, religious revivalism in Islam, the economic and social stability of oil-producing countries, the social and economic conditions which lead poor countries to be the big suppliers of illicit drugs to rich countries, the relationship between social and political conditions and economic success in the Pacific basin, and so on.   (ESRC, 1987, p. 4)

This recommendation has been actively taken up by the ESRC, as demonstrated in a number of their research programmes in the 1990s, such as their four-year population and household change and the Pacific Asia programmes from 1994. Moreover, the ESRC has supported a number of research centres over five-year periods which deal with British, wider European and international issues (see ESRC, 1995a). In the area of race relations research in Britain, the Centre for Research in Ethnic Relations at the University of Warwick was an example of research supported by the ESRC which was supposed to have an international programme of research around a common theme.

The second theme stressed by *Horizons and Opportunities* was that British social science should become more interdisciplinary. It was felt that some areas of British social science ran the risk of being left behind, because at the cutting edge of research in these fields researchers were making new discoveries from collaborative work with individuals in related fields, whilst in the UK social scientists were still stuck in their individual disciplines. The document stressed that

> Social science ... has to move forward from a period in which much was learnt about the disarticulated social parts, and address itself again to understanding the social whole. The splitting of the social sciences into tightly drawn specialities, each with its own professional organisation and flying its own flag over a proudly defended patch, is a comparatively recent happening. Perhaps such an organisation of the field was a necessary development to serve the needs of the time, but as a guild system it may not be apt to the needs of the future.
>
> (ESRC, 1987, p. 5)

This particular recommendation has been encouraged by the ESRC's promotion of multi-disciplinary research centres as a result of its annual centre competition exercises in the 1990s. One effect of the HEFCS' research assessment exercises, however, has been to encourage the older universities, and perhaps with time the new universities will also respond in a similar manner, to organise according to the arbitrary divisions of the social sciences the report spoke about.[3]

The third aspect of the Working Group's recommendation to which I want to refer was the emphasis it placed on the role between policy and theory. Research, they asserted, should be planned on a long-term basis to balance what many researchers saw as opportunistic, short-term, policy-oriented research. Many researchers saw policy research as intellectually impoverished and an imposition by funders; long-term basic research would, on the other hand, yield sound findings and provide a better basis for policy. For a decade or more, this was to be a debating point in the area of race relations research, and is discussed in that context below.

Taken together, these statements marked the increasing demand for social scientists from all disciplines to see their work to be relevant to the day-to-day activities of society. But given the contentious nature of the social sciences this call for relevance placed a burden on social scientists to demonstrate to people of practical affairs the utility of research. This has been particularly true for sociology, which, as Max Weber noted before World War One is 'a word which is used in many different senses' (Weber, 1995, p. 7). The observation could be applied equally to the utilitarian world of the late 1980s and the 1990s, and the uncertainty of what sociological investigation is about sometimes reinforces the inherently contentious nature of the discipline. But, of course, the choice and definition of current problems and issues are largely determined by politicians and other entrenched interests within a socio-political system. These choices and preferences are not necessarily those held by researchers. Moreover, the values or world views of researchers and those shared by actors in the policy world are not necessarily the same. What Weber (1995) and Myrdal (1944) respectively saw as the conflict of values or valuations have meant that many in the research community and the functionaries of the state have held varying views, which cannot always be reconciled. The uncertainty of the direction of the social sciences for much of the 1980s hinged on this inherent conflict of valuations of the aims and objectives of the social sciences or their role within a social order.

What administrators and politicians would see as relevant often conflict with a radical tradition in the social sciences. This is the view that social studies should seek to understand social patterns, problems and issues and offer a critical perspective on them. For example, Max Weber (1995), the single most influential sociologist of the twentieth century, argued that the purpose of sociology is 'to interpret the meaning of social action and thereby give a causal explanation of the way in which the action proceeds and the effects which it produces'. For some, it would appear that this meant maintaining a sense of neutrality, thereby isolating themselves from the subjectivity of sociological investigation that Weber stressed. It is difficult to determine the extent of this sense of neutrality in the British social science community, but undoubtedly in the 1970s there had been a concern on the part of some social scientists to be critical of all social processes, revealing the tension between the policy and academic communities that observers have commented on (Bulmer, 1987).

After all, the social sciences originated in a general context of social and political thinkers wanting to develop what they variously saw as a 'science' in order better to understand society and effect social change. Auguste Comte who, early in the nineteenth century, coined the telling phrase 'a science of society' (sociology) intended that this new science should mirror developments in the natural sciences which were adding considerably to human understanding of the environment. Karl Marx, one of the giant founding figures of political sociology, asserted that the main purpose or aim of social analysis was not so much to interpret or understand the world, but to change it. Marxist political sociology proclaimed this, particularly after the success of Leninism in Russia following the Revolution of 1918. Marxism in West Europe, however, not only lost sight of a radical relationship between the understanding of social processes and the will to change them; it also largely rejected the reformist perspective of change which informed much social reform in Western societies. Thus, the activist Marx and his followers came to have less impact on social policy than, as Myrdal suggested (1944, p. 1050, footnote b), the early socialist St Simon, and we might add Robert Owen, whose social prognoses Marx dismissed as Utopian. In Marxist social science, it might be expected that social researchers would want to support the class interests with which they have an affinity. The radical or revolutionary social researcher may therefore want to champion the cause of the class whose labour is exploited by the owners of capital. But in the Cold War period, most Marxists in the West were far more concerned with the totality of socio-economic and political systems than with the details of how these systems worked. There were, of course, exceptions. Those Marxists who were interested in development and change in the Third World often raised questions about the nuts and bolts of socio-economic and political systems with which policy is concerned (see, for example, Bettelheim, 1975; Thomas, 1974).

The tension between disinterested or impartial research and committed social research is perhaps nowhere more clearly dealt with than in the appendices to Gundar Myrdal's *An American Dilemma* (1944). In this seminal work on race relations in America, Myrdal argued that every work of science is imbued with the researcher's valuations, that is, what in moral philosophy is called 'ought' statements.[4] This is so because the social scientist

> is part of the culture in which he lives, and he never succeeds in freeing himself entirely from dependence on the dominant preconceptions and biases of his environment.   (Myrdal, 1944, p. 1035)

Moreover, the individual researcher is 'more or less entangled . . . in the web of conflicting valuations' (ibid.). From his study of race relations in the USA in the early 1940s Myrdal found that 'even the scientific biases will run against the Negroes most of the time' (ibid.), and in the 1960s, the influential Martiniquian/Algerian psychiatrist and politician Frantz Fanon argued that scientific objectivity is always used against the interests of the colonised person (see Fanon, 1968, 1970). From different intellectual perspectives, Fanon and Myrdal correctly related this situation of the bias in scientific inquiry to the distribution of power in society.

Weber described the relationship between the individual social scientist's value-judgements (whether based on ethical standards, cultural ideals, or some other kind of world view) as being 'irresolvable', because, he argued, the 'question cannot be discussed in scientific terms, since it is itself entirely dependent on practical value-judgements' (Weber, 1995, p. 69). Less pessimistic than Weber, and more experienced with policy research, Myrdal insisted that the duty of the social scientist is to strive to limit or control bias while recognising that the objectivity we seek to attain in our disciplines will never be fully achieved. Whether the social scientist is part of the group or culture they investigate or is outside of the group studied, bias cannot be erased by keeping to the so-called 'facts' which are themselves 'pervious'; whilst observation is necessary, it is insufficient. Like Weber, Myrdal insists that the social science researcher delimits the permeation of biases by first making explicit the researcher's own values, developing hypotheses, and drawing practical conclusions from findings. In a democratic society, where interest is recognised as being necessarily multiple or plural, it is important for the researcher to make clear what their values are so that readers can judge for themselves. Weber saw this as 'a straightforward requirement of intellectual integrity'; he also saw it as 'the absolute minimum that is required' (Weber, 1995, p. 70).

Like Marx and Weber, Myrdal had no doubt that social scientists should be conducting research that is relevant to contemporary problems. Relevance in social science research, for him was, therefore, the 'principle of selection' we apply in determining what are the 'practical aspects of social problems' as well as an alternative set of hypotheses (1944, p. 1060). Quite correctly, Myrdal was of what is ultimately an Aristotelean view that the social sciences are a political science, and therefore, practical. More confident than Weber, Myrdal emphasised, by using italic, that social research was relevant where it has the aim of showing

> *what should be the practical and political opinions and plans for ac-*
> *tion from the point of view of the various valuations if their holders*
> *also had the more correct and comprehensive factual knowledge*
> *which science provides.* (1944, pp. 1060–1)[5]

The necessity, therefore, for research to be relevant to felt needs in society is not new to social scientists. What is, however, new is the emphasis being given to relevance today, and a growing acceptance of relevance to be interpreted almost exclusively in terms of the relationship between research and policy. Social scientists can no longer refuse to say what they think the practical implications of their researches are, but as Myrdal correctly pointed out, the people most able to do so are social science researchers themselves. But, as noted, this was not new in

Myrdal's time and is even less so today in the social sciences. Weber's interpretive or subjective sociology in the early decades of the present century had taken great pains to make explicit what had been implicit in Marx, namely, the view that the social sciences are essentially subjective, because they are necessarily invested by or imbued with our values.

## Policy and Academic Research in Race Relations

This may be particularly so in the multi-disciplinary fields of race relations. There is a tendency for many well-informed people to assume that if an academic is conducting race relations research, that person's work is bound to have practical implications, and perhaps little theoretical relevance. Whilst, however, many researchers believe that their individual work has important policy implications, there is little evidence that there is a close and active relationship between academic research and policy at national level.

In order to have a closer understanding of this supposed close relationship between researchers and the policy process in race relations, a piece of research by Veena Vasista and myself was conducted in 1995 amongst relevant actors in this sector. Of the groups interviewed, academics and leaders of non-governmental organisations were by far the greater number of people who were willing to speak about their work. Indeed, the balance sought between the different groups was quickly overturned by academics, with many public figures being unable to spare the time for interviews, confirming Thomas's point that we are more likely to know what academics think about policy than what policy-makers think about research. The interviews centred around questions about the relevance of research to practical issues and problems of the day, knowledge and means of accessing data from researchers, the use made, and the funding, of research. Academics holding posts at universities accounted for sixteen of the thirty interviewees; the remainder were individuals from the CRE, the Home Office, and non-governmental organisations, but some of these individuals have straddled the academic and policy worlds at points in their careers. Others have been involved with research in institutions outside the universities, and sometimes there were overlaps with journalism. This overlapping of roles and the carrying out of multiple functions by individuals in the field of race relations would appear to resemble the relationship between academic and the world of policy in the USA. But, in comparison with the USA, the transparent relationship between the academic and the policy world in Britain is slight. This brushing relationship, however, may be enough to give British race relations studies in universities and policy in town halls, quangos and departments of state, that mien of instrumentalism or pragmatism associated with practice in the United States.

Our first hypothesis was that whilst much relevant research in race relations is being conducted in Britain, most of the findings do not have an influence on the decision-making process. One of the founding figures of contemporary race relations in Britain stressed that the field has tended to 'attract people with a reformist temperament (and often a leftist political commitment) rather than people who wish to pursue problems because of their intellectual interest'.[6] Whilst this does not reflect the variety of research interests that there are, none the less the statement does reflect the tendency on the part of many researchers in the field to claim that their research has relevance for policy, thereby contradicting a view attributed to Michael Posner, a senior ESRC officer in the 1980s, that 'if problems exist in the relationship between research and policy, it is because social scientists fail to address themselves to the right questions' (Thomas, 1985, p. 22). The interest in conducting policy-relevant research has been borne out by the testimony of all academics interviewed. In general, many researchers in this field have academic agendas drawn from questions and problems minority ethnic groups face within the wider British socio-economic and political context. Some, but by no means all, attempt to keep to one sociologist's stricture to see minority ethnic communities within the wider context of the society as a whole. Policy-makers and implementers also have their agendas, and the two sets do not necessarily correspond with each other. Perceptions of problems necessarily differ, and aims and objectives are not always the same. Differences between academic and policy research may not be as sharp as one well-known researcher with a policy background expressed the point, 'research and policy makers cross each other because they don't understand each other', but academic research agendas and those of policy-makers and implementers do not necessarily meet or inform each other. Nor, however, is the relationship between the research community and the policy process as divorced as has been suggested by the first respondent referred to above: this person argued that the 'one clear instance in which social research affected British policy in the field of race relations is that of the 1967 PEP report . . . [and that the] rest is more speculative'.

None the less, this statement reflects the impact of the American-like research organisations outside the universities which are now part of the research environment in Britain. On some topical questions of the day – such as some race relations issues – the largely quantitative outputs of the PEP, and, from the 1970s, the Policy Studies Institute (PSI) have been much more widely and rigorously disseminated and are therefore more likely to be influential than research in the universities. The PSI's work in the field of race relations is well known, and the PSI are credited with pioneering new ways of disseminating research so that policy-makers and implementers are easily exposed to findings. The PEP report of 1967 by W. Daniel and those by David Smith in the 1970s and Colin Brown in the 1980s were highly publicised, but as had been suggested, perhaps apart from Daniel's work, the policy impact of the others was largely speculative. In general, the picture that emerges of the relationship between policy and research in the area of race relations is a mixed one. It is worth illustrating this point from some of the responses researchers and individuals associated with the policy process gave to questions about the relevance of research for policy.

One prominent researcher with experience from the 1960s stated that whilst her research into youth, gender and work have included practical recommendations, 'they have made no difference' to policy-making. This respondent said that she often sent copies of her research findings to appropriate policy-makers, but she did not believe they bothered to read the material. She stressed, however, that she was aware that this is not how the policy process works; she pointed out that it is not simply a matter of information being made available to decision-makers 'and then change happens'. Another researcher, a senior educationalist, argued that from his experience 'research has no influence' on the policy process. He went on to stress that many community leaders and activists also believe that policy-makers take action on issues affecting new minority ethnic communities only after large-scale public disruptions such as the Brixton riots in 1981 and 1985. In this researcher's view, research findings will not shift policy: 'research serves as an afterward, it is not used in a proactive sense'.

Some researchers made the sensible distinction between the receptivity to research findings by civil servants and politicians. An experienced political science researcher who believes that his work on voting behaviour and the politics of immigration has been consulted by politicians and civil servants, stressed that 'politicians are less knowledgeable than civil servants and are less willing to be influenced'. Civil servants are relied upon for information and they are therefore more concerned to know what researchers are doing than are politicians.

Another researcher noted that politicians are more inclined to stay close to their agendas; he also stressed that 'politicians don't have time to read', and that they need 'authoritative, comprehensible and accessible reports'.

The varied experiences researchers have acquired in race relations studies cannot be easily categorised as simply successful or unsuccessful, or relevant or irrelevant, to the policy process. Distinguishing between policy and practice, the last researcher referred to above, who has worked mainly on health and minority ethnic groups, claimed that all the specific projects he has worked on for over a decade have been relevant to policy. But some of his findings have had more obvious policy implications than others, and he has taken the trouble actively to disseminate his findings through participation in community-based conferences, where he is also able to negotiate access to minority ethnic communities for his work. Indeed, some of his work has been done in collaboration with relevant community groups, and this mode is more accessible to policy-makers and implementers. However, this respondent, like a number of others, was of the view that whilst researchers are generally unaware of the needs of decision-makers, quite often the latter do not themselves have a clear view of what they want and will ask for guidance from researchers, as borne out by his own experience in the health field.

There is no clear and obvious relationship between the researcher and the policy-maker. For example, one researcher confessed that although he is frustrated by the high degree to which relevant research has been ignored in the policy process, including some of his own, he was of the view that academic 'researchers are not beholden' to groups and individuals outside the academy. This point was picked up by several senior figures in the field. None the less, another researcher who had also been a policy implementer, admitted that whilst academic researchers have no obligation to the policy process, they should 'bear in mind the user group and appropriately arrange a presentation of their material' so that policy-makers have the opportunity to know about researchers' findings. A researcher who has worked on the relationship between research and policy in the social sciences generally, argued that 'it is not the race relations academics' responsibility to be accessible' to the practitioners in race relations, such as local government workers. This respondent suggested that just as academics train social workers, but do not contribute directly to the social work process, so too academic researchers in the field of race relations should not be too directly involved in the process of race relations practice. He pointed out, however, that there is an indirect influence on the process through graduates who become practitioners. The role of the social scientist, this respondent argued, is to 'demonstrate the social and environmental factors which contribute to the placement of people in disadvantaged positions'.

Some respondents saw the dissemination of their work to be relevant to the influence that their work probably had on makers and implementers of policy. The last respondent referred to stressed that publicity in the media is essential if research findings were to be made known and be effective. In his view, non-academic work which purports to be research is likely to be more successfully disseminated by the media, presumably because such work is more easily accessible than research written for an academic constituency. He and other respondents also stressed that the academic publications which were likely to have some influence were those which enjoyed wide publicity in the media. Although not clearly expressed, there was something of a view that the most widely publicised research was not necessarily the best.

No respondent was able to measure with any degree of precision the impact of their work or the work of others on the policy process. Daniel's work, referred to earlier by one respondent, was the exception some pointed to as having had an influence on the policy-formulation of the 1968 Race Relations Act. One prominent sociologist who has done much to define the field of race relations in Britain, and whose work on housing influenced a generation of researchers, believed that his work on housing was at first ignored by the local authority in which research was conducted, but later his book became recommended reading for officers in the same local authority. In general, however, there is widespread agreement that it is hard to find evidence of research affecting policy at the national level. However, at the level of local government and in particular institutions, the situation is somewhat different, but it may be best to consider this within the broader context of our second hypothesis.

This hypothesis stated that whilst a great deal of research is being commissioned by public bodies, such research is often so specific and narrow in conception that it is of little value in generating theoretical or methodological discussions, and might be mainly serving to provide ideological justifications for preferred political and managerial options. This, however, must be set within the context of a long-running debate over the relationship or balance between policy-led or policy-relevant and fundamental or basic research, as noted earlier in this chapter. Similarly, the discussion over the relationship between policy-led research and basic or fundamental research just before and immediately after the 1992 Research Assessment Exercise, had earlier antecedents.

The Rothschild Report of 1982 sought to impress on social scientists that their work needs to be more closely related to finding answers to current and contemporary problems. In the area of race relations research, the balance between what the ESRC's *Horizons and Opportunities* called 'the play between policy and theory' became a contentious issue for much of the 1980s and into the 1990s. Speaking of the social science community as a whole, the panel found that researchers were wary of policy-oriented research, because such research 'becomes a series of *ad hoc* and opportunistic searchings after three-year grants' (ESRC, 1987, p. 6).[7] This kind of research was seen by the social science community to be 'the type of endeavour favoured by the dictates of funding agencies', whilst basic or fundamental research was seen to be 'what scientists themselves would like to pursue if direction could be got off their shoulders' (ibid.). This dichotomous approach to research, the panel felt, was too sharp and did not represent the process of actual research. None the less, it was noted that 'only if a discipline is able to develop sustained basic research is it possible for that subject to generate useful policy insights in the long term' (ibid.). In the late 1980s and the 1990s this debate became more urgent. However, this is no longer conducted in terms of whether there is a justifiable relationship between basic and policy research; it is no longer seriously questioned whether there is such a relationship, and that either should be seen as divorced from the other. What is now a problem is the practical question of how to organise and manage this relationship. In other words, as the research community grows and to a degree becomes divorced from teaching, is it possible for those involved in short-term policy research to be also trained and allocated time to relate such research to the broader questions faced by the social sciences in general.

The repercussion of this wider debate was keenly felt in the ESRC-funded Centre for Research in Ethnic Relations (CRER) at the University of Warwick, particularly between 1986 and 1992. This example is most relevant, because the Centre has enjoyed by far the greatest amount of public funds directed at research in this field over the past quarter-century. There were those who felt that a principal task of the Centre was to conduct contract-research, and thereby demonstrate the Centre's relevance to the policy process. On the other hand, there were those members who felt that research should be placed on a long-term basis, and that research should be basic or fundamental in nature, and thereby contribute to wider debates in the social sciences. Those who conformed to the first of these positions produced much specific research for a number of national and local government and other public bodies, as any list of the Centre's publications after 1984 will show (see, for example, CRER, 1997). Those who favoured the second approach produced work which the ESRC's independent evaluation panel in 1991 regarded as contributions to general debates in the social science community. In the main, however, CRER's theoretical work was divorced from its policy work, as the panel concluded. The relationship between policy and basic research appeared to be unresolved well into the 1990s. But the same concern between applied and theoretical considerations occupied the wider race relations research community in Britain during this period, as discussions with respondents revealed.

Research and policy do have a close link at the local and institutional level, but this is precisely because local authorities and statutory bodies commission specific pieces of research on issues relating to minority ethnic groups. The intent and scope of such research was usually determined by the institution commissioning the work and the terms and conditions became increasingly precise in the late 1980s and early 1990s in order to get value for money as well as persuade researchers to deliver on time. But, in the past, for the academic researcher the time-frame of research was not necessarily crucial in the design and delivery of a piece of work. For several reasons, the opposite is true for the policy-maker as politician, adviser or implementer. Thomas expresses the point well, when she states that

> the researcher's time-scale is long and the policy-maker's is short: civil servants cannot wait three years for the answer to a problem which is troubling them, or their political masters, today and which may be overtaken by a quite different set of problems next week.
>
> (Thomas, 1985, p. 4)

Additionally, the academic researcher must produce work to be favourably assessed by academic peers. This is, however, now changing. The report which follows much policy research will have definite target audiences and, if recommendation for action meets with official approval, there will be a clear relation between research and policy, as Martin Rein (1976, p. 11) correctly argued in what he called the optimistic view about the relationship between research and policy. This is what Rothschild described as the customer/contractor relationship in his 1971 report when he spoke about there being a relationship between researchers and sponsors (government). Without reference to Rothchild in the 1990s, this became the generalised form of relations between researchers and customers in all fields of academic enquiry. Of course, it is not always the case that the researcher submits what those who commissioned the research wish to hear. Sometimes this difference between policy-makers and researchers reflects the differences between policy-makers and community groups and the recommendations appear to support one side against the other. Where communities and organised community groups are involved, the researcher must of necessity also play the role of honest broker between the commissioning body and the community and their groups, and, as Weber and Myrdal noted, much depends here on how the individual researcher sets about explicating and controlling their own subjective views of the world and relations between different kinds of people. The satisfaction or frustration for the researcher which results from these exercises are part and parcel of the research–policy process, which some researchers, (mistakenly) concerned to contribute to our understanding of basic or fundamental research problems, sometimes find to be too costly a distraction.

## The Policy View

Our third hypothesis about the relationship between research and the policy process stated that whilst the academic and research community is in the main inspired by the Myrdalian desire to influence change, the overall political context, within which decision-making and implementation occur, may be hostile to the kind of intervention researchers might want to make. We have seen that researchers have a mixed view of the relationship between their research and the policy process. We have also seen that in the view of some researchers there is an important distinction between politicians and civil servants, as there is between central government and operators at local and institutional levels. There is, therefore, an apparent paradox here: whilst at national level the Conservative governments of Margaret Thatcher and John Major appeared to have consistently ignored the race relations research community, they appeared to have none the less been influenced by right-wing educationlists (see, for example, Honeyford, 1988) who appeared to oppose the ideals of a multi-cultural society which informed much research. In other words, shared ideological outlook and values, friendships, and other forms of discrete social network may have been more important in influencing the decision-making process than any particular aspect of the vast body of knowledge there is, however well disseminated and accessible. As Rein (1976), borrowing from the late Thomas Kuhn's notion of 'a scientific paradigm' argues, the relationship between research and policy is one of shared values, framework or policy paradigm. Research is not then 'generally designed to challenge the paradigm but to develop understanding within the framework of its assumptions' (p. 108). At national level there would appear to be a degree of suspicion and mistrust between the research and policy communities.

With respect to race relations research, whilst the former is imbued by the ideals of multi-culturalism, the latter appears to stand on an unstated assimilationist platform. Another way to look at the situation is that whilst the research community is concerned to see action being taken, policy-makers and implementers are not only passive but put their trust in the magic that can apparently be wrought by benign neglect of social problems arising from relations between racial and ethnic groups. In short, it is clear that researchers in race relations and Conservative governments from 1979 did not share what Rein called a common policy paradigm. Consequently, suspicion has been reflected in a number of ways. For example, the framers of the 1988 Education Reform Act appeared to have simply ignored the findings of many educationalists working in the field of race relations, as reflected in the Swann Report of 1985. Some of the main provisions – for example, the teaching of history in schools – entirely ignored the legitimate cultural and historic interests of new minority ethnic communities. In the first months of a new Labour Government, it remains an open question whether they will be in tune with the ideals of a multi-cultural society which pervades research in the field. If the response is a positive one, then it may be expected that the call for reform from the CRE and others may lead to a new act on the statute books.

If at national level there has been neglect of race relations matters, at the local and institutional levels there appears to have been commendable attention to problems. A multitude of research reports collect dust in town hall departments up and down the country (particularly in metropolitan but also in provincial cities and towns) and statutory bodies commission an impressive body of research to help them justify, explain and clarify preferred policy initiatives. But as political analysts of decision-making and implementation know well, there are, as Rein (1976, p. 97) reminds us, several 'paths between research and policy' in which research serves different purposes, including 'research as containment, research as power, research as legitimation, research as policing and research as social reform'

But, in addition, an important aspect of the policy process is the impact or influence of non-governmental organisations concerned with race relations affairs in multi-cultural Britain. These include the Runnymede Trust, the Joint Council for the Welfare of Immigrants, the Institute of Race Relations, and several less-well-known bodies at national and local levels throughout Britain. A number of officers in some of these organisations were also interviewed. Unlike in the American political system, in Britain functionaries in non-governmental organisations tend not to overlap with government, but they sometimes do overlap with the academic world. Many officers from non-governmental organisations produce important academic books which are regularly used in university courses. Some of these organisations make use of academic research, often making research more easily accessible to non-academic audiences. Nor is it unusual for these non-governmental organisations to collaborate with academic researchers on research that is of mutual benefit. These non-governmental organisations may be said to form a fourth member in what Patricia Thomas saw as a tripartite relationship between researchers, funders and policy-makers. The present emphasis on research-relevance and the need for academic researchers to have user communities and collaborators mean that members from this fourth group or constituency have the potential to play the game in all directions.

In general, however, both government and non-governmental organisations as consumers of academic race relations research stress much the same points: they wish to have what they nearly all describe as 'information', preferably in a statistical form. A key user of research who serviced the All-Party Parliamentary Group on Race and Community (APPGRC) in 1994, stressed that he looked to researchers for 'salient points to inform arguments, including empirical information', but also for 'statistics and interpretation'. Although he found some research to be inaccessible, he thought that APPGRC could 'act as a conduit to distil the essence from research', and referred to several pieces of research which the group had used in its attempt to influence legislation in Parliament, such as those affecting education, immigration and housing. One prominent Home Office adviser on race relations issues said that the research he relies upon is primarily statistical and he is alerted to such research by reports in the Press, work at the Universities of Warwick, Liverpool and Aston, and from senior community officers around the country. The officer is, however, aware that minority ethnic communities 'see that there is too much research and too little effect'. Community spokespersons often express this view to researchers, particularly at the local level (see Goulbourne et al., 1995).

A central government officer, who operated between the research and policy communities, stressed the importance of the overall attitude to research on the part of the government of the day. She believes that her own research has been influential in both the academic and policy communities. This officer stressed that for a piece of academic research to attract attention it must have 'a selling angle', such as providing a group of administrators or politicians with an advantage which can cause embarrassment to opponents. She also pointed out that from her experience research can be used to persuade politicians to take a course of action other than that determined by lack of knowledge or even ideology.

One long-serving researcher in a central government department drew upon his extensive experience to make a number of incisive points about the relationship between research and policy. Like academic researchers, this officer felt that it is difficult to say what has been the direct effect of research on policy, but noted that in his department research was not intended to change policy but rather to help with clarification, understanding and improvement within the context of policy already determined. In other words, there was already in place what Rein calls the policy paradigm. The officer gave the example of a long-standing policy against harassment, and the departmental researcher's task was therefore to show how best to implement this policy. More tellingly, this officer pointed out that in his experience of over twenty years, some of the people responsible for policy often feel that they do not have sufficient ownership of research. Moreover, policy people rapidly move from one issue to another, and they tend to feel that researchers do not keep pace with shifting events. When the policy person has moved onto another problem, they sometimes forget the relevance of what the researcher is doing researching past issues. In the end, as Thomas noted and this officer's testimony validated, policy folks need quick answers, whilst researchers are necessarily slow. But at the annual meeting between policy and research people in his department, the one is able to inform the other about their preferences. Like academic researchers, this officer stressed that research findings 'must be presented clearly and simply because ministers come in and out and usually come to an issue without background'. He went on to stress that policy research is an activity which takes place within the 'backdrop' of established policy; research, therefore, is not 'pro-active', but re-active. As noted earlier, this view is not entirely unknown in academic circles.

This point was most clearly expressed in the report to Roy Jenkins on race relations research in 1975, when it stated that

In general the role of research is clear cut and straightforward when policy makers come forward with explicit aims and ask researchers either to establish more precisely the nature of the present situation or to identify the steps by which a desired situation may be brought into being. (Home Office, 1975, p. 2)

The committee identified equality and social harmony as the cornerstones of race relations policy in Britain. They suggested that some areas which could have relevance to policy were not at that time high priorities. These non-priority areas included specific minority ethnic groups, family life, problems of adjustment to a new society, and evaluations of the 'agencies established as instruments of race relations policy' (ibid., p. 7). These, of course, have now become familiar terrain for researchers, alongside the committee's key recommendation that government needed reliable statistics about the structural position of minority ethnic groups in Britain. The specific areas in which statistical data were needed included education, employment, the Home Office, and health and social security, through the General Household Survey, the national census and other large data sets. They also saw the need for these data sets to differentiate between people who were generally entered as 'coloured'; and, in perhaps the only place in British race relations literature, they pointed out the obvious, which is too often ignored, that the word coloured 'is of doubtful acceptability since, in the sense that white is also as much a colour as black, everyone is coloured' (ibid., p. 12).[8] It was not, however, until the 1991 national census that the committee's recommendation to identify different groups in more acceptable terms was implemented by the Office of Population and Census Surveys (now National Statistics).

## Conclusion

Research into the state of contemporary race relations issues in Britain is being complemented by much valuable research in historical studies, and research over the last fifteen years or so has gone beyond the priorities set by the Home Office committee in 1975. The field is multi-disciplinary in nature, and some disciplines – in particular, sociology, social geography, education and politics – have made considerable contributions to our understanding of these relations. But the relationship between the research and policy communities is complex. A good deal of research findings have no obvious or tangible effect on the policy process, and this is partly due to the different paradigms in which policy-makers and implementers and researchers operate, particularly during the Conservatives' long tenure in office (from 1979 to 1997). Clearly, research is not the only or even the most powerful influence bearing on the decision-making process in any field of public and social policy. Nor is policy the only objective of sound research.

But the race relations community has taken seriously the challenge to create a more just and equal society in Britain and has performed a remarkable task of – in Weber's sense – explaining social and political phenomena in a manner that questions what many people take for granted. What, however, policy-makers and implementers may be looking for from research are acceptable or implementable recommendations which meet the conditions determined by pressing political exigencies. The questioning of myths, prejudices and what passes for common-sense or certain knowledge remains a valid objective of social research. Whilst it is of primary importance to recognise the different purposes of social research and policy-making, there can be little doubt that in the field of race relations there is a need for greater correspondence between the world of research and the world of policy.

# 7 British Race Relations in Perspective

This essay started with a discussion of whether it is possible to demarcate an area, or identify some patterns of social and political life that may be properly, or at least acceptably, described as a field of race relations. In Chapter 1 we saw that the term itself is unacceptable to some writers who prefer to speak about racism and racialisation, and there are any number of books with titles to suggest that these concepts are becoming more widely preferred to the notion of race relations. When, however, we looked into the matter more closely it became difficult to avoid the concept where relations between groups of human beings who believe themselves or are believed by others to be different from other groups of human beings are concerned.

The discussion then moved on to suggest that it was not so much a question of there being races, but that there are social relations premised on perceived or actual differences between groups of people. It follows, then, that since social action arises from these actual or perceived differences, it is possible sensibly to speak about a sub-field of race and ethnic relations. These relations intertwine with, but are not reducible to, class relations, and are of historical and contemporary sociological significance. Additionally, these relations are often compressed together despite careful distinctions, such as that made by M. G. Smith and discussed in the first chapter of this book. With their concern in and enthusiasm to oppose racialism and racism, some social scientists too easily forget that whether race is natural or not, people who have suffered from racism have to fight largely on the terrain established by those who control and exercise the power to exclude. Moreover, as Smith argued, it will not do simply to dismiss the fact that there are some physical differences between groups of people. The mistake is to make such physical differences the basis for differential treatment in society.

Crick and others who advocate that we should avoid using the word and concept of 'race' are therefore denying the unpleasant history of race and racism; they are also missing a sociological point, through a confusion of sociological fact and moral proclivity. It is a sociological

146

fact that very many people associate social behaviour, and individual and collective worth with skin colour and other phenotypic similarities and differences. Status and class positions, rights and the allocation of property and other goods within a social order are too often differentially conferred in accordance with perceived or actual racial characteristics to be ignored by those who wish to maintain the *status quo* as well as by those who are benignly, but also blithely, inclined to put an end to racism. The beliefs, attitudes and subjective perceptions of individuals and collectivities are more important than large, impersonal and abstract forces in determining social norms, and, as Weber stressed, these constitute the proper province for sociological inquiry.

In discussing aspects of race relations in Britain I have drawn on a number of concepts from the work of social anthropologists and political analysts to suggest that the mobilisation of racial and ethnic affinities for preferred ends has become the most pronounced aspect of race and ethnic relations. I have suggested that in the present British situation such mobilisation is not checked but is perhaps encouraged by the ideology of multi-culturalism. At the same time the virtues of multi-culturalism – recognition and toleration of difference and rejection of what Jenkins called a flattening assimilation – are to be welcomed in a post-imperial society trying to reconstruct the present for a fairer and more equal society. At the political level there is no general official sanction of structural differential incorporation of black and brown citizens and residents. But whilst they were members of the franchise, aspirant politicians from African-Caribbean and Asian communities had to struggle to find places in local government and in Parliament. There is still a considerable way to go, however, before it becomes commonplace for Britain to be represented abroad in political circles (as ambassadors, ministers, and so forth) in the same way as the country is represented by black sportsmen and women, journalists and others. Differential treatment of black and brown citizens is to be found in the criminal justice system, the labour market, housing and so forth where behaviour defies stated intentions to build a fairer and a more just society. Problems over the provision of services and health care demonstrate the distance between the vision and the reality of the multi-cultural society. There are, however, enough non-governmental organisations and concerned individuals actively engaged in relevant activities to give hope that some of the ideals of the multi-cultural society will be realised.

In describing aspects of these questions, I did not seek to offer a comprehensive coverage of the problems, because there is already an abundance of data and analyses or commentary available on them. For example, the various PEP and PSI reports from 1968, reports by the CRE, the Runnymede Trust, the Joint Council for the Welfare of Immigrants, research institutions such as CRER at the University of Warwick have produced an impressive body of accessible literature. The multi-disciplinary nature of the sub-field made it necessary to discuss the issues in a general way that may be useful to a non-specialist readership. It was also necessary, however, to point to certain factors about the imperial past which form a background to contemporary race relations in Britain. This was not to suggest that race relations everywhere have common historical origins in the trans Atlantic slavery of early capitalism, but simply to reassert the link that has long been recognised between that historical experience, later colonialism and contemporary race relations within the English-speaking, particularly the British, world.

I have no doubt that some commentators will suggest that insufficient attention has been paid here to the experiences of groups who did not share the British colonial experience. Similarly, it may be pointed out that the experiences of Southern Europeans who came under British rule have been set aside in this account of British race relations. Early in the discussion I suggested that the central aspects of British race relations have to do with the presence and assertion of African-Caribbean and South Asian communities over the past half a century or so. There have long been black and brown people in Britain and this is now being recognised and celebrated by some (CRE, 1996b). Britain has long been the destination for refugees from Europe and immigrants from Ireland and elsewhere, and these groups have all experienced discrimination. There can be no serious contention about these facts, and the experiences of these groups are being drawn upon to reconstruct a more diverse history of the British people, a history that goes beyond the core of England and Englishness as well as beyond the other major national communities of Scotland, Wales and Northern Ireland. My suggestion, however, was that whilst these developments provided a broad background for the multi-cultural society, it was the arrival in significant numbers of African-Caribbeans and South Asians that have led to the making of a multi-cultural Britain. Their very presence and the issues raised by this were utilised by those in the indigenous population seeking to mobilise and redefine British identity in a post-imperial age, as we noted. The new minorities themselves both responded to this and independently created their own separate identities within the context of the ideology of multi-culturalism. The future presence of South Asians and Chinese British citizens from Hong Kong which reverted to

China in July 1997 is more then likely to contribute to the changing British character or identity, however this is understood, by making it more diverse and cosmopolitan.

In an age of globalisation, the world's population at the nodal points of great social, economic and political activities increasingly involves mixing. But to use Furnivall and M. G. Smith's notion of social and cultural pluralism, the increase in diasporic communities (see Cohen, 1997) may enable groups to continue to mix in the market-place but resist combining or integrating with each other. None the less, new groups and cultures have enriched British society in ways unforeseen in the imperial age. The regeneration of the inner cores of Britain's great cities such as London, Manchester, Birmingham, Bradford, Leicester and Coventry is largely attributable to South Asians and African-Caribbeans. On the other hand, many in the indigenous population who could have participated in this regeneration contributed instead to the suburban sprawl taking place throughout the country. New communities have sprung up in the inner cities, rejuvenating and transforming the traditional family corner-shop, introducing what was once novel cuisine and new restaurants and social clubs. Muslim mosques, Sikh gurdwaras, Hindu temples and African-Caribbean-led churches have revived and enriched important areas of British life. This renewal contributes to the nation's traditional passion for sports, communal recreational areas and market-places where the mixing of different groups occurs despite difficulties. In these areas, cars blasting reggae or bhangra music, individuals displaying syncretised personal styles of adornment, talk and walk, appear to suggest the shifting boundaries of identities that some cultural theorists speak about (see, for example, Hall, 1988). This gives an impression that whilst different ethnic groups may sometimes be involved in maintaining what Barth described as 'boundary maintenance', others are also engaged in storming and breaking down, however tentative this may be, the boundaries separating communities which share common territory, some political allegiances, some social and moral values, and a degree of mutual respect.

But if multi-ethnic, multi-cultural, post-imperial Britain sometimes appears to be making progress in these and other terms, it is always sobering to bear in mind that it is the same society in which legal justice still appears to be differentially administered, as the case of Stephen Lawrence highlighted. Like the criminal and civil trials in the US of the African-American former football star O. J. Simpson, in 1996 and early 1997, for the murder of his wife Nicole and her friend in 1994, the murder of Stephen Lawrence in April in 1993 in Eltham, South London, triggered a nationwide debate over race relations in the Atlantic/Caribbean African diaspora. In America the criminal trial of Simpson turned, not so much on whether he was guilty, as on whether, as a black man of some prominence, he was receiving the same consideration as a white male would, and the case became one about the state of relations between black and white America. In Britain, Stephen the black teenager was set upon unprovoked and stabbed to death at a bus stop, but the police apparently failed to take appropriate action in time, and the five young white men accused of the murder escaped through the plea of silence, because, they held, to speak would be to incriminate themselves. For a criminal case to have a chance of success the jury has to be certain beyond a doubt about the guilt of the accused, and in this situation the Crown Prosecution Service decided that there was insufficient evidence to go to the trial of the young white men. The finding, however, of the inquest on 13 February 1997 amounted to a stunning indictment of the police; the Coroner, Sir Montague Levine, made the statement that

> This was a horrific crime, totally unprovoked. A group of white youths killed a young man in cold blood and for no other reason, it would appear, than that the colour of his skin was black. (*Daily Mail*, 14 February 1997, p. 6)

On St Valentine's day, the morning after the inquest, the newspapers and news reports on television and radio all covered the story, pointing to the injustice to the young man, his family and good race relations in the country. The front page of the *Guardian* newspaper carried a full picture of Stephen and detailed the events leading to his death and the lack of effort to find the murderers. The BBC Radio 4 morning news was dominated by the extraordinary story, thereby over-shadowing the phoney war between the Conservatives and Labour in the campaign for the general election which had not been formally announced by the Prime Minister, John Major. The media reported a 'wall of silence' in the community about speaking against the white gang which terrorised the neighbourhood and was widely known for their racist activities. Some commentators made mention of the fact that when a white person had been killed by two Asians they were quickly apprehended and were serving time in prison. Another comparison made with Stephen Lawrence's death was the outrageous murder of the headmaster Philip Lawrence in North London. The case was highlighted across the nation, and again the police quickly and successfully apprehended and secured conviction of Mr Lawrence's murderer. The other Lawrence had no such luck because, as his mother repeatedly pointed out, Stephen was another 'black boy' and the police could not be bothered to take action at the appropriate time. This prompted Sir Herman Ousley, Chairman of the Commission for Racial Equality, to call for an independent inquiry into the police's handling of the case (*Guardian*, 14 February 1997). The *Daily Mail* newspaper took the unprecedented step of accusing the five young white men of the murder and invited them to sue the newspaper so that the full facts could be brought into the open (*Daily Mail*, 14 February 1997).

The tragic case of Stephen Lawrence and his family led many commentators to speak in terms of the undermining of 'good race relations' in the country, just as observers in America were aware that Simpson's case was, in effect, American racial justice – which goes beyond the criminal justice system – on the stand. The fact that this question can be so dramatically brought into the public arena in Britain and the USA suggests that race relations are not at a point of equilibrium, to use a phrase from Park. These relations cannot be wished away, as some commentators would appear to suggest. On the contrary, problems of race relations are uncomfortably and disturbingly too close to the surface of everyday life in these societies.

The connections between the USA, the Caribbean, Africa and South Asia have featured in this discussion, but from a British perspective. I have stayed clear of the new and dynamic dimension that has arisen in continental Europe, partly as a result of the fall of the Iron Curtain and the demise of state socialism in East and Central Europe, and partly as a result of migration from Southern Europe to more prosperous North European destinations during the period Caribbeans and South Asians were migrating to Britain after World War Two. In particular, attention is being turned to the situation in Germany where over two million Muslims, with backgrounds in Turkey but many born in Germany, are excluded from the mainstream of society (see, for example, Brandt, 1996; Dummett, 1994; Kepel, 1994). Clearly, there is a case here of differential incorporation. In other West European states, from Sweden (see, for example, Alund and Schierup, 1991) in the north to Italy in the south and from France (see, for example, Grillo, 1985; Martin, 1994) in the west to the states bordering East Europe, there have been significant levels of migration from within other European states and from without, and these developments have posed new challenges and problems (see, for example, Layton-Henry, 1990; Wrench, 1996). The question of their incorporation into society is approached in different ways from in the UK, but also presents problems of identity (see, for example, Kastoryano, 1994), integration or exclusion.

The British experience has drawn significantly on the American experience both in terms of theory and practice, and this will continue, given the range of common features shared across the Atlantic. However, a new dialogue is emerging between the British experience and member states within the European Union. It will, however, take time and effort to arrive at a degree of understanding between the different traditions of member states. For example, the Franch state's adherence to the principle of universalism (a convenient way of hiding flattening assimilationism) has been strong since the Revolution of 1789, and stands in sharp contrast to the British inclination to treat issues in a piecemeal manner. There are issues here requiring detailed analysis which is beyond the scope of this discussion.

Finally, the impression is sometimes given in the emerging literature and popular discourses that what we have understood as the substance of race relations in Britain is giving way to new patterns of ethnic conflict including traditional European minorities. The post-Cold-War situation in which Europe once again faces the mass movement of people within her borders should not, however, be confused with the situation of black and brown people with historic backgrounds outside Europe. Whilst East and Central European groups will, like others before them, face great difficulties of entry and settlement in the more prosperous countries of the European Union, as in the USA, after a generation these groups are likely to be integrated into the class and status structures. African-Caribbeans and perhaps some South Asian groups are likely to remain almost as pariah groups in the social order. Their differential incorporation is likely to continue to generate problems, questions and issues from which new European groups are likely to be shielded; it will be enough for the new groups to perform competitively in the market to be universally incorporated into the overall social structure. After all, the history of mass migration of Europeans to the USA, particularly from the nineteenth century, and migration within Europe are clear examples of how Anglo-American societies can and do universally incorporate groups that are, as M. G. Smith argued, racially much the same even though they may be ethnically different. Much the same may be said about the experiences of Irish, Jewish and other European groups who have migrated to Britain. The paradox is that black and brown people often share the same culture with whites who determine the nature of incorporation, but the racial affinity is nearly always stronger than the cultural ties. Indeed, the fact of proximity of Caribbean culture to the culture of the dominant group may be said to place Caribbean groups at a greater disadvantage than groups whose cultures are relatively distinctive. It may be suggested, therefore, that whilst the general framework of race relations in Britain is changing, like much of the modern world, to include a wider spectrum of excluded peoples and communities, race relations pivoted upon the divide of the colour-line remains relevant in Britain.

It is important to stress, however, that differences in the forms of incorporation into British society do not exclude the possibility of a common fight against exclusion. It is too often the case that when the differential forms of incorporation between white and black groups are discussed the conclusion is drawn that the pain and sufferings of oppressed white groups are not being recognised and that there is an attempt to belittle these groups' struggles for equality. This is a mistake. The analysis of differential experiences of exclusion does not foreclose possibilities for unity of purpose and common endeavour against injustice. Indeed, the history of the struggle against racism in British life, particularly in the law, is incomplete without the clear recognition of the paramount role played by individuals from the Jewish, Irish and other communities, including individuals from the majority indigenous society. The discussion here has not focused on this dimension of British race relations, but at several points in the account there is clear recognition of the fact that the changes that have occurred over the past two or three decades have been brought about through combined, not isolated, social action.

A central theme of the discussion has been that differential incorporation (on the basis of race) is very much alive in British society. And to conclude the discussion another reference to DuBois is highly relevant. Speaking of the decline of nineteenth-century racist theories, already in 1946 he stressed that there was none the less a 'persistent exception' (DuBois, 1969, p. 116) to this general development. He pointed out that whilst the term 'Caucasoid race' came to include people of 'widely different physique inhabiting Europe', and the term 'Mongoloid race' which 'was even more vague and indefinite nearly fell into disuse', the concept of 'the negro'

> as a definite and scientific race designation, persisted, and its use was defended with bitter determination by men who otherwise ranked as leading scientists. Despite the fact that the number of human beings corresponding to the current definition of the word 'Negro' was narrowed again and again in space and number to a small remnant even in Africa, nevertheless in the usage of many distinguished writers there really emerged from their thinking two groups of men: Human Beings and Negroes.    (ibid.)

More than half a century after DuBois wrote these words, there is still sufficient exclusion of black and brown people in Britain to suggest that, public declarations to the contrary notwithstanding, there is a distinction between 'Human Beings and Negroes' for many of the people who control the resources of society. Clearly, DuBois had the Anglo-American and African world in view when he wrote these particular words. But we must not forget that his was a universal vision bred of the sufferings of exclusion despite immense personal academic, moral and ethical achievements. As we approach a new century and a new millennium within the context of a significantly globalised and post-imperial world we cannot assume that 'the colour-line' is about to disappear.

Even at century's end the colour-line holds against the development of the humanity that many in both minority and majority communities have long striven to attain.

# Notes

## Chapter 1. The Question of a Field of Race Relations

1. The book was first published in 1776, the year of the Declaration of Independence by the Thirteen Colonies in North America against England.
2. Several of Marx's works are drawn upon in this section of the discussion, but the most relevant for the point being made is his *Capital* (1867), vol. 1; other texts by and about Marx are also to be found in the bibliography at the end of this book.
3. It is not surprising, therefore, that in recent years in Africa and the African diaspora groups demands are being made for reparations to be paid to the African people for the damage caused by European slavery. In Britain this call is being led by Bernie Grant, Labour MP for Tottenham.
4. In the US debates over slavery from the 1830s to Emancipation in 1863, the point was frequently made by slave owners that slaves were well looked after by their masters, whereas freedom would place the responsibility of care on freed persons themselves, and this was nothing more or less than a new form of slavery.
5. Lord Scarman in his influential report on the Brixton disturbances stated that:

   > It was alleged by some of those who made representations to me that Britain is an institutionally racist society. If by that is meant that it is a society which knowingly, as a matter of policy, discriminates against black people, I reject the allegation. If, however, the suggestion being made is that practices may be adopted by public bodies as well as by private individuals which are unwittingly discriminatory against black people, then this is an allegation which deserves serious consideration, and, where proved, swift remedy.
   > (Scarman, 1982, p. 11)

6. Barbara Ballis Lal (1988, p. 283) has suggested that Park's 'race relations cycle' is of minor value when compared with his contributions to

the understanding of the socio-psychological, ecological and other aspects of race relations.

7. The works of Best (1968), Beckford (1972), Girvan (1971), Jefferson (1972), and Lewis (1950) are some of the relevant literature that are surprisingly absent from analyses that purport to be informed.

## Chapter 2. Imperial and Post-imperial Backgrounds

1. Scottish devolution was a key issue in the May 1997 general elections campaign, and featured in the manifestos of the relevant political parties. Within weeks of assuming office, Tony Blair's New Labour government informed Parliament of its intention to publish a White Paper on the question. This was done in the summer of 1977, and in September voters in Scotland cast a decisive 'yes' vote in favour of both a Parliament in Edinburgh and the power to vary national taxation within a narrow margin set by Westminster.

2. Proponents of multi-culturalism have not been forthcoming in making links of this kind with the British past, even although the effort might strengthen their case.

3. Early Pan-Africanists such as Alexander Crummell and Edward Blyden, who saw European colonialism as unavoidable in their time, would have been happy to see Britain undertaking in Africa the massive feats of engineering undertaken in India (see, for example, Lewis, 1993, Chapter 7; Lynch, 1970).

4. In the Caribbean, the word 'brown' refers to people of mixed black and white parentage, not people of South Asian backgrounds, as is the case in East Africa and Britain. Caribbean people of South Asian backgrounds are generally referred to as East Indians, but this may be changing as they became politically more assertive.

5. Independence could have been achieved in Jamaica much earlier, but for the class and colour interests articulated in the politics of the decades of the 1940s and 1950s (for a thorough discussion, see Munroe, 1971).

6. Williams' notion of 'froudacity' is a play on the name of Anthony Froude and was a deliberate attempt to show disapproval of his book which portrayed the West Indies in the most negative terms possible.

7. For cultural reasons, Guyana is generally counted as part of the Commonwealth Caribbean, although it is physically on the north-eastern tip of the South American continent.

8. President Woweri Musoveni, who established a stable government in hitherto war-torn Uganda during the decade from the late

1980s, has asked Asian families to return to Uganda and take charge of the properties taken from them by Idi Amin. In general, the relative stability of the country appears to be encouraging many people who fled to return or at least visit.

9. *Keshadhari* Sikhs adhere to the 'Five Ks' of Sikhism; *sahajdhari* Sikhs do not adhere to the Five Ks and refer to themselves as 'slow adopters'.

10. In independent India these same skills were later to be used to good effect. The agricultural skills of the Sikhs brought about the Green Revolution and enabled India to feed and free herself from the centuries-old periodic scourge of famine. Second, Sikhs have been proud of the fact that they formed a disproportionately high percentage of the Indian army. Both factors were later to feature in the rise of militant and violent Sikh ethnic nationalism, which brought about the death of Indira Ghandi in the 1980s (see, Rai, 1986; Sidhu, 1977; Singh and Kuar, 1986)

## Chapter 3. The Political Context

1. During the election campaign in 1997, the most likely candidates for office appeared to be Paul Boateng, a Brent MP of Ghanaian and English backgrounds who had been a member of Labour's treasury team and spokesman on legal affairs, and Keith Vaz, a Leicester MP of Goan background and also a shadow spokesman. Boateng was made a junior minister in the Blair government, but overall it was surprising that neither of these men were offered visible places in the government. Given how the UK mimics developments in the USA, until there is a black president of the USA (probably General Colin Powell) it is unlikely that there will be a British prime minister from either the African-Caribbean or Asian communities, irrespective of the talents individuals may possess.

2. At the time of writing, the assessments of the performances of the parties' candidates from the minority ethnic communities had not been completed by observers. These will become available soon, and I am aware that Muhammad Anwar is conducting research into these matters for the BBC.

3. I am grateful to Muhammad Anwar for discussing his work on these matters with me.

4. For a detailed discussion of the participation of new minority ethnic groups in the political parties and the broader implications of

such participation for these organisations, see H. Goulbourne (1998)
5. Margaret Wright's forthcoming doctoral thesis for the University of London on the West Indian Standing Conference and other Caribbean associations should therefore fill a gap.

## Chapter 4. Practical Problems of the Multi-cultural Society

1. Of course, the situation varied enormously from colony to colony. For example, from the 1880s there were discussions in the Caribbean colonies about providing universal free primary education. In Jamaica, this was initiated in 1892 but economic decline brought such considerations to an end before World War One, and it was not made compulsory, as reformers in the 1890s intended. Barbados was able to maintain high educational standards. Although discussed from the 1890s, university education was provided in the region only from as recently as 1948 with the founding of the University of the West Indies. These developments were in something of reverse order in India, where universities were established from the nineteenth century but primary education not provided for all.
2. These reports were *Racial Disadvantage in Employment*, PEP Report No. 544 (June 1974) and *Racial Minorities and Public Housing*, PEP Report No. 560 (February 1976).
3. The latest PSI report was published in 1997, but came too late to be incorporated into the analysis outlined here. However, in general, the report underscored the main trends of earlier reports. The new report draws on the 1991 census data as well as new data collected by the authors of the report (for further details see Modood and Berthoud, 1997).
4. 'Partnerships' were where individuals pooled their savings on a weekly basis and each week one member of the group would take the 'hand', that is, the money contributed by all members. The system was based on trust, and was usually headed by a person of considerable stature in the community.
5. But the 1991 census also provided data on other aspects of the quality of life such as car and television ownership per household (Owen, 1994).
6. At this time the figures would have included white Indians because place of birth, not ethnicity, was used to determine the size and so forth of the black and brown communities.

7. Ray Honeyford (1996), the controversial Bradford headteacher in the 1980s, has suggested that the changes show that this one group is more successful in the competition for public housing than other groups.

8. This reflected the mass expulsion of Asians from Uganda; the country lost many of her skilled and professional citizens and residents through the actions of Idi Amin in the early 1970s.

9. The now defunct CRE journal, *New Community*, was an invaluable forum for debates on these issues, particularly during the period under the editorship of Malcolm Cross from the late 1980s to the mid-1990s

10. Bill Morris is still the only person from either minority ethnic communities who heads a union.

11. Self-employment among Asians increased from 8 per cent in 1974 to 14 per cent in 1982, and from 7 per cent to 12 per cent among Asian women during the same period. This trend continued into the 1990s (Owen, 1994). Caribbean people are the least likely to be self-employed, and this pattern has been reported for the whole post-war period.

12. The general link between education and employment was recognised by the government in 1995, when they combined the Departments of Education and Employment under the same minister, Gillian Sheppard, but this does not change the fact that education and employment are still relatively divorced from each other where discussions over multi-culturalism are concerned.

13. Bernard Coard was later to return to the Caribbean and played a prominent part in the New Jewel Movement's revolution in Granada in the 1980s. He has been in detention since the brutal murder of Prime Minister Maurice Bishop in 1983. The murder provided the US with a reason for invading a Commonwealth country that the then US Secretary of State, George Shultz, would describe as a 'very nice piece of real estate'.

14. And presumably this would have been true too for some children from white working-class families

15. These patterns of educational success by children of Asian backgrounds and under-achievement by children of Caribbean backgrounds have continued into the 1990s.

16. It is also invaluable to see Tomlinson's coverage of developments in British schools in the CRE's journal *New Community* in the late 1980s and into the 1990s

17. There are, of course, other vitally important areas of concern, such as provision for the disabled (see Stuart, 1996).
18. For discussions of these and related issues, see *New Community*, vol. 15, no. 3 (1989); this is a special issue of the journal focusing on race and the health and social services, and contains some excellent articles.

## Chapter 5. Outlawing Racial Discrimination

1. Provisions were made for allegations of acts of indirect discrimination to come into effect in September 1977.
2. The media frequently report instances of gross discrimination based on convention but which are not always visible to the public nor to the victims of discrimination. A case in point is that of the Ford Motor Company at Dagenham which was long hidden from view and under the cloak of convention. It appears that the job of truck driving is much coveted, but has been passed down from fathers to sons to the effective exclusion of African-Caribbean and Asian workers who made up in 1996 about 45 per cent of the work force but only 1.8 per cent of drivers. Bob Purkiss, national equality officer of the Transport and General Workers' Union, chairman of the TUC's Race Committee and a CRE commissioner had a tough fight with the employers and the 300-strong white workers for whom the fleet was a preserve before the company agreed a fair procedure of recruitment (see, for example, the *Guardian*, 28 January 1997, p. 6).
3. This last aspect of the exemption has more than a vague echo of the Somerset case about slavery in eighteenth-century England, where freedom was not automatically conferred on all individuals on British soil, but was determined by the individual's status prior to entry (for a contextual discussion see Fryer, 1984, Chapter 6).
4. So far, Chairs have been men, perhaps balancing the preponderance of women in similar positions at the Equal Opportunities Commission, but there is no good reason why this should be so. Chairs have also been of different political persuasions, perhaps reflecting a general desire to make the Commission a cross-political body.
5. This ceasefire, on which much hope rested, was to be dramatically shattered by IRA bombs in London in February 1996.

## Chapter 6. 'Good Race Relations' and the Production of Knowledge

1. Although the ESRC's expenditure on research has grown over the years to over £60m by the mid-1990s (ESRC, 1995a), in the 1980s Thomas noted that central government remained the major spender on social studies research (Thomas, 1985, p. 3).
2. The SSRC was renamed the ESRC in 1984.
3. For example, between the 1992 and the 1996 research assessments, several universities brought departments of politics and international relations together in order to create a single unit of assessment, as the HEFCs had done.
4. Myrdal's discussion of this and related points may be more accessible in his later work, *Objectivity in Social Research* (1969).
5. By using the italic as emphasis Myrdal obviously intended to stress the importance of this point of view in the understanding social structure and social action.
6. For purposes of confidentiality the names of respondents are not reported here.
7. The notion that three-year research grants are short-term, *ad hoc* money shows how rapidly the research community has changed during the late 1980s and the 1990s. In the 1990s three-year social science research projects funded from the public purse are regarded as substantial awards, which should yield new theoretical insights into complex social issues and should also introduce novel research methods and techniques. Not so many years ago the absurdity of this view would have been readily grasped by experienced academics and researchers.
8. It remains the case that very many people continue to speak about 'coloureds' when they mean people who regard themselves as black, brown and so forth, but not white people. White is still regarded as a non-colour. This is paradoxical. After all, the designation of colours to groups of humanity was an important European enterprise.

# Bibliography

Ahmad, W. I. U. (ed.) (1993), *'Race' and Health in Contemporary Britain* (Buckingham: Open University Press).

Ahmad, W. I. U. and Atkin, K. (eds) (1996), *'Race' and Community Care* (Buckingham: Open University Press).

Allen, D. E. (1971), 'Introduction' to reprint of John Beddoe (1885), *The Races of Britain: A Contribution to the Anthropology of Western Europe* (London: Hutchinson).

Allport, G. W. (1958), *The Nature of Prejudice* (New York: Doubleday).

Alund, A. and Schierup, C. U. (1991), *Paradoxes of Multi-Culturalism: Essays on Swedish Society* (Aldershot: Avebury).

Anionwu, E. N. (1993), 'Sickle Cell and Thalassaemia: Community Experiences and Official Response', in Ahmad (ed.) (1993).

Anwar, M. (1979), *The Myth of Return* (London: Heinemann).

— (1994), *Race and Elections: The Participation of Ethnic Minorities in Politics* (Coventry: Centre for Research in Ethnic Relations, University of Warwick).

— (1996), *British Pakistanis: Demographic, Social and Economic Position* (Coventry: Centre for Research in Ethnic Relations, University of Warwick).

Ashley, M. (1972), *Statement on Race* (London: Oxford University Press).

Atkin, K. and Rollings, J. (1996), 'Looking after their Own? Family Care-giving among Asian and Afro-caribbean Communities', in Ahmad and Atkin (eds) (1996).

Augier, R. (1966), 'The Consequences of Morant Bay: Before and After 1865', *New World Quarterly*, vol. ii, no. ii.

Azim, W. (1996), *Ethnic Socialisation and Political Behaviour: The Case of South Asians in Britain*, Social Science Occasional Papers 7 (Southampton: Southampton Institute).

Ballard, R. (1994), 'Differentiation and Disjunction among the Sikhs', in Ballard (ed.), *Desh Pardesh: The South Asian Presence in Britain* (London: Hurst).

Ballis Lal, B. (1988), 'The "Chicago School" of American Sociology, Symbolic Interactionism, and Race Relations Theory', in Rex and Mason (eds) (1988), *Theories of Race and Ethnic Relations*.

Banks, M. (1994), 'Why Move? Regional and Long Distance Migrations of Gujarati Jains', in J. M. Brown and R. Foot (eds) (1994), *Migration: The Asian Experience* (London: Macmillan).

Banton, M. (1967), *Race Relations* (London: Tavistock).

— (1968), 'The Use of the Useful', *SSRC Newsletter*, no. 3, May, pp. 24–30.

— (1973), 'The Future of Race Relations Research in Britain: The Establishment of a Multi-Disciplinary Research Unit', *Race*, vol. xv, no. 2, pp. 222ff.

— (1983), 'Race, Prejudice and Education: Changing Approaches', *New Community*, vol. 10, pp. 373 ff.

— (1984), 'Transatlantic Perspectives on Public Policy Concerning Racial Disadvantage', *New Community*, vol. 11, pp. 28–35.

Barth, F. (ed.) (1969), *Ethnic Groups and Boundaries* (London: George Allen and Unwin).

Beckford, G. (1972), *Persistent Poverty: Underdevelopment in Plantation Economies of the Third World* (New York: Oxford University Press).

Berrington, A. (1996), 'Marriage Patterns and Inter-ethnic Unions', in Coleman and Salt (eds).

Best, L. (1968), 'A Model of Pure Plantation Economy', *Social and Economic Studies*, vol. 17, no. 3.

Bettelheim, C. (1975), *The Transition to Socialist Economy* (Hassocks: The Harvester Press).

Bhachu, P. (1986), *Twice Migrants* (London: Tavistock).

Bindman, G. (1996), 'When Will Europe Act Against Racism?', *New Law Journal*, February, pp. 170–1.

Blakemore, K. and Boneham, M. (1994), *Age, Race and Ethnicity: A Comparative Approach* (Buckingham: Open University Press).

Bourne, J. (1980), 'Cheerleaders and Ombudsmen: The Sociology of Race Relations in Britain', *Race and Class*, vol. 21, no. 4.

Boyce, D. G. (1993), *The Irish Question, 1868–1986* (London: Macmillan).

Braithwaite, L. (1953), 'Social Stratification in Trinidad: A Preliminary Analysis', *Social and Economic Studies*, vol. ii, no. ii, pp. 5–175.

Brandt, B. (1996), 'The Policy of Exclusion: The German Concept of Citizenship', *Migration*, Sondernummer.

Brathwaite, E. (1978), *The Development of Creole Society in Jamaica, 1770–1820* (Oxford: Clarendon Press).

Brown, C. (1984), *Black and White Britain* (London: Policy Studies Institute).

Brown, J. M. and Foot, R. (eds) (1994), *Migration: The Asian Experience* (London: St Martin's Press).

Bulmer, M. (ed.) (1987), *Social Science Research and Government: Compara-tive Essays on Britain and the United States* (Cambridge: Cambridge University Press).

Cabinet Papers (CP) (1946–1952) *passim* (Public Records Office, Kew Gardens, London).

Carter, R., Harris, C. and Joshi, S. (1987), 'The 1951–55 Conservative Government and the Racialisation of Black Immigration', *Immigrants and Minorities*, vol. 6, no. 3, November.

Central Community Relations Unit (1992), *Race Relations in Northern Ireland* (Belfast: Central Community Relations Unit).

Centre for Research in Ethnic Relations (nd, but presumably 1997), *Annual Report 1995–1996* (Coventry: CRER, University of Warwick).

Chamberlain, M. (1997), *Narratives of Exile and Return* (London: Macmillan).

Charman, P. (1979), *Reflections: Black and White Christians in the City* (London: Zebra Project).

Cherns, A. (1967), 'The Use of the Useful', *SSRC Newsletter*, no. 1, November, pp. 12–17.

Clarke, C., Peach, C. and Vertovec, S. (eds) (1990), *South Asians Overseas: Migration and Ethnicity* (Cambridge: Cambridge University Press).

Cleaver, E. (1968), *Soul on Ice* (New York: McGraw-Hill).

Coard, B. (1971), *How the West Indian Child is Made Educationally Sub-normal in the British School System* (London: New Beacon Books).

Cohen, N. (1997), 'The Sin of Whose Father?', *The Observer*, 26 January, p. 30.

Cohen, R. (1987), *The New Helots: Migrants in the International Division of Labour* (Aldershot: Gower).

— (1994), *Frontiers of Identity: The British and Others* (London: Longman).

— (1997), *Global Diasporas: Introduction* (London: UCL Press).

Cohen, R. and May, R. (1975), 'The Interaction between Race and Colonialism: A Case Study of the Liverpool Race Riots of 1919', *Race and Class*, vol. 16, no. 2.

Coleman, D. and Salt, J. (eds) (1996), *Ethnicity in the (1991) Census: Demo-graphic Characteristics of the Ethnic Minority Populations* (London: Office of Population, Censuses and Surveys (OPCS)), vol. 1.

Community for Racial Equality (1983–1993), *New Community: A Journal of Research and Policy on Ethnic Relations*, Commission for Racial Equality, *passim*).

— (1990a), *Britain: A Plural Society, Report of a Seminar*, Discussion Papers, No. 3 (London: Commission for Racial Equality).

Community for Racial Equality (1990b), *Law, Blasphemy and the Multi-faith Society, Report of a Seminar*, Discussion Papers, No. 1 (London: Commission for Racial Equality).

— (1991), *Second Review of the Race Relations Act 1976: A Consultative Paper* (London: CRE).

— (1992), *Annual Report (1991)* (London: CRE).

— (1995), *Annual Report (1994)* (London: CRE).

— (1996a), *Annual Report (1995)* (London: CRE).

— (1996b), *Roots of the Future: Ethnic Diversity in the Making of Britain* (London: CRE).

Conservative Party (1960–72), *Annual Conference* (London: Conservative Party).

Conservative Party (1984), *The Monday Club, The Law, Order and Race Relations*, Policy Paper IR3 (London: Conservative Party).

Constantine, S. (ed.) (1990), *Emigrants and Empire: British Settlement in the Dominions between the Wars* (Manchester: Manchester University Press).

Cox, O. C. (1959), *Caste, Class and Race* (New York: Monthly Review Press).

Crick, B. (1996), 'Throw the R-word Away: We Should Attack Racism by Ceasing to use the Word "Race"', *New Statesman*, 18 October.

Cumper, G. E. (1956), 'Population Movements in Jamaica 1830–1950', *Social and Economic Studies*, vol. v, no. iii.

Dahrendorf, R. (1959), *Class and Class Conflict in Industrial Society* (London: Routledge and Kegan Paul ).

Daniel, W. (1968), *Racial Discrimination in Britain* (Harmondsworth: Penguin).

Deakin, N. (1970), *Colour, Citizenship and British Society* (London: Panther Modern Society).

Dean, D. W. (1987), 'Coping with Colonial Immigration, the Cold War and Colonial Policy: The Labour Government and Black Communities in Great Britain, 1945–51', *Immigrants and Minorities*, vol. 6, no. 3, November.

Dench, G. (1986), *Minorities in the Open Society: Prisoners of Ambivalence* (London: Routledge and Kegan Paul).

Deutsch, K. (1968), *The Nerves of Government* (New York: The Free Press).

DuBois, W. E. B (1903), *The Souls of Black Folk: Essays and Sketches* (London: Longmans, Green).

— (1946), *The World and Africa: An Inquiry into the Part which Africa has Played in World History* (New York: International Publishers).

Dummett, A. (1994), *Citizens, Minorities and Foreigners: A Guide to the EU* (London: CRE).

Dummett, A. and Nicol, A. (1990), *Subjects, Citizens, Aliens and Others: Nationality and Immigration Law* (London: Weidenfeld and Nicolson).

Durkheim, E. (1993) [1893], *The Divisions of Labour in Society* (New York: The Free Press).

Dutton, G. (1967), *The Hero as Murderer* (London: Collins and Cheshire).

Economic and Social Research Council (1987), *Horizons and Opportunities in the Social Sciences* (London: ESRC).

— (1991), *1991–1996 Corporate Plan* (London: ESRC).

— (1994), 'White Paper Prompts Wide-Ranging Review', *Social Sciences*, no. 22, January, p.1.

— (1995a), *Facts and Figures 1994–1995* (Swindon: ESRC).

— (1995b), *Thematic Priorities* (Swindon: ESRC).

Edwards, J. (1987), *Positive Discrimination, Social Justice, and Social Policy: Moral Scrutiny of a Policy Practice* (London: Tavistock).

Egbuna, O. (1971), *Destroy this Temple: The Voice of Black Power in Britain* (London: Macgibbon and Kee).

Eisner, G. (1961), *Jamaica 1830–1930: A Study in Economic Growth* (Manchester: Manchester University Press).

Elkins, S. M. (1963), *Slavery* (New York: The Universal Library, Grosset and Dunlap).

Evans, J. M. (1983), *Immigration Law* (London: Sweet and Maxwell).

Emmanuel, P. (1993), *Governance and Democracy in the Commonwealth Caribbean: An Introduction* (Cave Hill: Institute of Social and Economic Research).

Fage, J. D. and Oliver, R. A. (eds) (1970), *Papers in African Prehistory* (Cambridge: Cambridge University Press).

Fanon, F. (1968), *Black Skin, White Masks* (London: Macgibbon and Kee).

— (1970), *A Dying Colonialism* (London: Penguin).

Foot, P. (1969), *The Rise of Enoch Powell* (Harmondsworth: Penguin).

Froude, J. A. (1888), *The English in the West Indies, or, The Bow of Ulysses* (London: Longmans, Green).

Frucht, R. (1967), 'Caribbean Social Type: Neither Peasant nor Proletarian', *Social and Economic Studies*, vol. xvi, no. iii.

Fryer, P. (1984), *Staying Power: The History of Black People in Britain* (London: Pluto Press).

Furnivall, J. S. (1948), *Colonial Policy and Practice* (Cambridge: Cambridge University Press).

Fusaro, A. (1979), 'Two Faces of British Nationalism: The Scottish Nationalist Party and Plaid Cymru Compared', *Polity*, vol. xi, no. 3.

Gay, P. and Young, K. (1988), *Community Relations Councils: Roles and Objectives* (London: Commission for Racial Equality).

Geertz, C. (1963), *Old Societies and New States* (Glencoe: The Free Press).

George, M. D. (1965), *London Life in the Eighteenth Century* (London: Penguin).

Gerloff, R. (1992), *A Plea for British Black Theologies*, 2 vols (London: Peter Lang).

Ghai, Y. P. and McAuslan, J. P. B. (1970), *Public Law and Political Change in Kenya: A Study of the Legal Framework of Government from Colonial Times to the Present* (Nairobi: Oxford University Press).

Girvan, N. (1971), *Foreign Capital and Economic Underdevelopment in Jamaica* (Kingston: Institute of Social and Economic Research, University of the West Indies).

Gordon, S. (1963), *A Century of West Indian Education: A Source Book* (London: Longmans, Green).

Goulbourne, H. (1980), 'Oral History and Black Labour in Britain: An Overview', *Oral History Journal*, vol. 8, no. 1.

— (1988), *Teachers, Education and Politics in Jamaica, 1882–1972* (London: Macmillan).

— (1991a), *Ethnicity and Nationalism in Post-imperial Britain* (Cambridge: Cambridge University Press).

— (1991b), 'Varities of Pluralism: The Notion of a Pluralist Post-imperial Britain', *New Community*, vol. 17, no. 2.

— (1997), 'Ethnic Mobilisation, Multi-culturalism and War', in D. Turton and G. Ausenda (eds), *Ethnicity and War* (Woodbridge: Bodell Press/CIRSS).

— (1998), 'The Participation of New Minority Ethnic Groups in British Politics', in Bhikhu Parekh, Tessa Blackstone and Peter Sanders (eds), *The Politics of Race Relations* (London: Routledge).

— Cowen, H. and Owen, D. (with assistance from J. Blake) (1995), *The Needs of the African Caribbean Community in Coventry: A Report* (Centre for Policy and Health Research, Cheltenham and Gloucester College of Higher Education).

Goulbourne, S. (1990), 'The Recent History of Black Ethnic Minorities in the Solicitors' Profession', in M. King, S. Goulbourne and M. Israel (eds), *Ethnic Minorities and Recruitment to the Solicitor's Profession: A Report* (London: The Law Society / CRE).

— (ed.) (1997), *Law and Migration* (Cheltenham: Edward Elgar).

Greene, J. E. (1974), *Race vs Politics in Guyana: Political Cleavages and Political Mobilisation in the 1968 General Election* (Mona: Institute of Social and Economic Research).

Grillo, R. (1985), *Ideologies and Institutions in Urban France: The Representation of Immigrants* (Cambridge: Cambridge University Press).

Hall, S. (1988), 'New Ethnicities', in K. Mercer (ed.), *Black Films and British Cinema: ICA Documents* (London: British Film Institute).

Hall, S., Critcher, C., Jefferson, T., Clarke, J. and Roberts, B. (1978), *Policing the Crisis: Mugging, the State, and Law and Order* (London and Basingstoke: Macmillan).

Hamilton, C. V. and Carmichael, S. (1967), *Black Power: The Politics of Black Liberation in America* (New York: Random House).

Hanham, H. J. (1969a), *Scottish Nationalism* (London: Faber and Faber).

— (1969b), 'The Development of the Scottish Office', in N. J. Wolfe (ed.), *Government and Nationalism in Scotland* (Edinburgh: Edinburgh University Press).

Heath, A. and McMahon, D. (1996), 'Education and Occupational Attainments: The Impact of Ethnic Origins', in V. Karn (ed.), *Education, Employment and Housing among Ethnic Minorities in Britain* (London: HMSO).

Hepple, B. (1992), 'Have Twenty-five Years of the Race Relations Acts in Britain been a Failure?', in Hepple and Szyszczak (eds), *Discrimination: The Limits of the Law* (London: Mansell).

Herskovits, M. (1970), *The Myth of the Negro Past* (Gloucester, MA: Peter Smith).

Heuman, G. (1994), *'The Killing Time': The Morant Bay Rebellion in Jamaica* (London: Macmillan).

Higher Education Council for England (1994), *1996 Research Assessment Exercise, RAE96/194* (London: HEFCE).

— (1995), *Generic Research: Method and Data Collection, Circular 10/95* (London: HEFCE.).

Hindess, B. and Hirst, P. (1975), *Pre-capitalist Modes of Production* (London: Routledge and Kegan Paul).

Hintjens, H. M. (1995), *Alternatives to Independence: Explorations in Post-colonial Relations* (Aldershot: Dartmouth).

Hobsbawn, E. (1973), *Industry and Empire: An Economic History of Britain since 1750* (London: Weidenfeld and Nicolson).

Holmes, C. (ed.) (1978), *Immigrants and Minorities in British Society* (London: George Allen and Unwin).

— (1988), *John Bull's Island: Immigration and British Society, 1871–1971* (London: Macmillan Education).

Home Office (1975), *Race Relations Research: A Report to the Home Secretary by the Advisory Committee on Race Relations Research* (London: HMSO).

— (1977), *Racial Discrimination: A Guide to the Race Relations Act 1976* (London: Home Office/HMSO).

— (1992), *British Crime Survey* (London: HMSO).

Honey, M. (1982), 'The History of Indian Merchant Capital and Class Formation in Tanganyika, *c.* 1840–1940', unpublished PhD thesis, University of Dar es Salaam.

Honeyford, R. (1996), 'Housing and Race Relations', *The Salisbury Review*, vol. 15, no. 1

—— (1988) *Integration or Disintegration? Towards a Non-Racist Society* (London: The Claridge Press).

House of Commons (1978), *First Report from the Select Committee on Race Relations and Immigration, Session 1977–78: Immigration,* vol. 1 (London: HMSO).

—— (1993), *Realising our Potential: A Strategy for Science, Engineering and Technology*, Cm 2250 (London: HMSO).

Humphry, D. (1972), *Police Power and Black People* (London: Panther).

Humphry, D. and John, G. (1971), *Because they're Black* (Harmondsworth: Penguin).

Huntington, S. P. (1968), *Political Order in Changing Societies* (New Haven: Yale University Press).

Jackson, G. (1970), *Soledad Brother: The Prison Letters of George Jackson* (London: Jonathan Cape).

—— (1972), *Blood in my Eye* (London: Jonathan Cape).

James, C. L. R. (1938), *The Black Jacobins: Toussaint L'Ouverture and the San Domingo Revolution* (New York: Vintage Books).

Jefferson, O. (1972), *The Post-War Economic Development of Jamaica* (Kingston: Institute of Social and Economic Research, University of the West Indies).

Jenkins, R. (1967), 'Racial Equality in Britain', in Anthony Lester (ed.), *Essays and Speeches by Roy Jenkins* (London: Collins ).

John, DeWitt (1969), *Indian Workers Associations in Britain* (London: Oxford University Press).

Johnson, M. and Songster, D. (1995), *A Measure of Equity: The Health Needs of African Caribbean People in the City of Peterborough* (Coventry: Centre for Research in Ethnic Relations, University of Warwick).

Jones, E. (1965), *Othello's Countrymen: The African in English Renaissance Drama* (Oxford: Oxford University Press).

—— (1971), *The Elizabethan Image of Africa* (Charlottesville: University of Virginia).

Josephedes, S. (1990), 'Principles, Strategies and Anti-racist Campaigns: The Case of the Indian Workers Associations', in Goulbourne (ed.), *Black Politics in Britain* (Aldershot: Avebury).

Kapur, R. A. (1986), *Sikh Separatism: The Politics of Faith* (London: Allen and Unwin).

Kastoryano, R. (1994), 'Construction de Communautes et Negociation des Identites: les Migrants Musulmans en France et en Allemangne', in D.-C. Martin (ed.), *Cartes d'identite: comment dit-on 'nous' en politique?* (Paris: Presses de la Fondation nationale des sciences politiques).

— (1997), *La France, L'Allemangne et Leuers Emmigres: Negocier L'identite* (Paris: Armand Colin).

Katznelson, I. (1973), *Black Men, White Cities: Race, Politics and Migration in the United States, 1900–30, and Britain, 1948–68* (London: Oxford University Press).

Kepel, G. (1994), *The Revenge of God: The Resurgence of Islam, Christianity and Judaism in the Modern World* (Cambridge: Polity Press).

Keith, M. (1990), 'Misunderstandings? Policing, Reform and Control, Co-optation and Consultation', in H. Goulbourne (ed.), *Black Politics in Britain*.

— (1993), *Race, Riots and Policing: Lore and Disorder in a Multi-racist Society* (London: UCL Press).

Kiernan, V. G. (1969), *The Lords of Human Kind: European Attitudes Towards the Outside world in the Imperial Age* (London: Weidenfeld and Nicolson).

Kuhn, T. (1970), *The Spreading of Scientific Revolutions* (Chicago, IL: University of Chicago Press).

Labour Party (1962), *The Integration of Immigrants: A Guide* (London: Labour Party).

— (1965), *National Executive Committee Report* (London: Labour Party).

— (1972), *Citizenship, Immigration and Integration: A Policy for the 1970s* (London: Labour Party).

Lacey, N. (1992), 'From Individual to Group', in Hepple and Szyszczak (eds).

Laski, H. (1921), *The Foundations of Sovereignty and Other Essays* (London: George Allen and Unwin).

Layton-Henry, Z. (1987), 'The State and New Commonwealth Immigrants: 1951–56', *New Community*, vol. VIV, nos 1/2.

— (ed.) (1990), *The Political Rights of Migrant Workers in Western Europe* (London: Sage).

— (1992), *The Politics of Immigration* (Oxford: Blackwell).

Leech, K. (1988), *The Birth of a Monster: The Growth of Racist Legislation since the 1950s* (London: The Runnymede Trust).

LeFranc, E. (1997), 'Family Structures, Health Status and Health Behaviour', mimeo (Oxford Brookes University and CEPHAR, Cheltenham and Gloucester CHE).

Lester, Lord Anthony (1994), 'Discrimination: What can Lawyers Learn from History?', *Public Law* (Summer) pp. 224–37.

Lewis, D. L. (1993), *W. E. B. DuBois: Biography of a Race, 1868–1919* (New York: Henry Holt).

Lewis, W. A. (1950), 'The Industrialisation of the British West Indies', *Caribbean Economic Review*, vol. 2.

Little, K. (1947), *Negroes in Britain* (London: Kegan Paul).

Lugard, Sir F. D. (1922), *The Dual Mandate in British Tropical Africa* (Edinburgh and London: William Blackwood).

Lynch, H. R. (1970), *Edward Wilmot Blyden: Pan-Negro Patriot* (London: Oxford University Press).

Macdonald, I. (1977), *Race Relations: The New Law* (London: Butterworths).

Machiavelli, N. (1970), *The Discourses*, introduction by Bernard Crick (London: Penguin Classics).

— (1981), *The Prince*, trans. with an introduction by George Bull (London: Penguin Books). [First translated into English 1640.]

Mackenzie, J. (1984), *Propaganda and Empire* (Manchester: Manchester University Press).

Mair, L. (1965), 'African Chiefs Today', in P. J. M. McEwan and R. B. Sutcliffe (eds), *The Study of Africa* (London: Methuen).

Major, J. (1997), 'Britain: The Best Place in the World', speech by the Prime Minister, the Rt Hon John Major, MP, *Conservative Party News*, 54/97, 18 January.

Malinowski, B. (1961), *The Dynamics of Culture Change* (Westport, CT: Greenwood Press).

Mamdani, M. (1973), *From Citizen to Refugee: Uganda Asians come to Britain* (London: Frances Pinter).

Marshall, P. J. (1985), 'The Moral Swing to the East: British Humanitarianism, India and the West Indies', in C. Abel and M. Twaddle (eds), *Collected Papers on Caribbean Societies*, mimeo, Institute of Commonwealth Studies, University of London.

Martin, D.-C. (ed.), (1994), *Cartes d'identite: Comment dit-on 'Nous' en Politique?* (Paris: Presses de la Fondation nationale des sciences politiques).

Marx, K. (1974), *Capital: A Critique of Capitalist Production*, vol. 1 (Moscow: Progress Publishers; originally published in 1867).

Marx, K. and Engels, F. (1969), *Selected Works* (Moscow: Progress Publishers).

Mason, D. (1995), *Race and Ethnicity in Modern Britain* (Oxford: Oxford University Press).

Messina, A. M. (1989), *Race and Party Competition in Britain* (Oxford: Clarendon Press).

Miles, R. (1989) *Racism* (London: Routledge).

— (1993), *Racism after 'Race Relations'* (London: Routledge).

Mintz, S. (1993), 'Goodbye, Columbus: Second Thoughts on the Caribbean Region at Mid-millennium', *Walter Rodney Memorial Lecture* (Coventry: University of Warwick).

Mintz, S. and Price, R. (1992), *The Birth of African-American Culture: An Anthropological Perspective* (Boston, MA: Beacon Press).

Mishan, E. J. (1988), 'What Future for a Multi-racial Britain? Part I and Part II', *The Salisbury Review*, June, pp. 18 ff., and September, pp. 4 ff., respectively.

Monroe, T. (1971), *The Politics of Constitutional Decolonisation* (Mona: Institute of Social and Economic Research).

Modood, T., and Berthoud, R. (1997), *Ethnic Minorities in Britain: Diversity and Disadvantage* (London: Policy Studies Institute)

Mullard, C. (1985), *Race, Power and Resistance* (London: Routledge and Kegan Paul).

Myrdal, G. (1944), *An American Dilemma: The Negro Problem and Modern Democracy* (London and New York: Harper and Brothers).

— (1969), *Objectivity in Social Research* (London: Gerald Duckworth).

Nairn, T. (1981), *The Break-up of Britain* (London: Verso).

National Association for the Care and Resettlement of Offenders (NACRO) (1989), *Replacing Custody* (London: NACRO).

Nayar, B. R. (1966), *Minority Politics in the Punjab* (New Jersey: Princeton University Press).

Nayar, K. and Singh, K. (1984), *Tragedy of Punjab: Operation Bluestar and After* (New Delhi: Vision Books).

Newton, H. P. (1974), *Revolutionary Suicide* (London: Wildwood House).

National Health Service (1996), *Good Practice and Quality Indicators in Primary Health Care: Health Care for Black and Minority Ethnic People* (London: NHS Ethnic Health Unit).

Owen, D. (1993), *Ethnic Minorities in Great Britain: Housing and Family Characteristics* (Coventry: National Ethnic Minority Data Archive, Centre for Research in Ethnic Relations, University of Warwick).

— (1994), *Black People in Great Britain: Social and Economic Circumstances* (Coventry: National Ethnic Minority Data Archive, Centre for Research in Ethnic Relations, University of Warwick).

— (1996), 'Size, Structure and Growth of the Ethnic Minority Populations', in Coleman and Salt (eds), *Ethnicity in the 1991, Census: Demographic Characteristics of the Ethnic Minority Populations.*

174 BIBLIOGRAPHY

Patterson, H. O. (1967), *The Sociology of Slavery* (London: Macgibbon and Kee).

Park, R. E. (1950), *Race and Culture* (New York: The Free Press).

Peach, C. (1968), *West Indian Migration to Britain: A Social Geography* (London: Oxford University Press/Institute of Race Relations).

— (1991), *The Caribbean in Europe: Contrasting Patterns of Migration and Settlement in Britain, France and the Netherlands*, Research Papers in Ethnic Relations no. 15 (Coventry: Centre for Research in Ethnic Relations).

Phillips, M. (1974), 'Landfall', *The Listener*, 21 November.

Phizacklea, A. and Miles, R. (1980), *Labour and Racism* (London: Routledge and Kegan Paul).

Pilkington, E. (1988), *Beyond the Mother Country: West Indians and the Notting Hill White Riots* (London: I. B. Tauris).

Political and Economic Planning (1974), *Racial Minorities and Public Housing* (London: PEP).

— (1976), *Racial Disadvantage in Employment* (London: PEP).

Premdas, R. (1995), *Ethnic Conflict and Development: The Case of Guyana* (Aldershot: Avebury).

Rai, S. (1986), *Punjab since Partition* (Delhi: Durga Publications).

Rampton, A. (1981), *West Indian Children in our Schools: Interim Report of the Committee of Inquiry into the Education of Children from Ethnic Groups*, Cmnd 8273 (London: HMSO).

Rein, M. (1976), *Social Science and Public Policy* (Harmondsworth: Penguin).

Rex, J. (1983), *Race Relations in Sociological Theory* (London: Routledge and Kegan Paul).

Rex, J. (1987), 'The Concept of a Multi-cultural Society', *New Community*, vol. XXIV, nos 1/2, pp. 218 ff.

Rex, J. and Mason, D. (eds) (1988), *Theories of Race and Ethnic Relations* (Cambridge: Cambridge University Press).

Rex, J. and Moore, R. (1967), *Race, Community and Conflict* (London: Oxford University Press).

Rex, J. and Tomlinson, S. (1979), *Colonial Immigrants in British City: A Class Analysis* (London: Routledge and Kegan Paul).

Rich, P. (1986), *Race and Empire in British Politics* (Cambridge: Cambridge University Press).

Richmond, A. H. (1955), *The Colour Problem: A Study of Racial Relations* (Harmondsworth: Penguin Books).

Ringer, B. (1983), *We the people . . . and Others: Duality and America's Treatment of its Racial Minorities* (New York and London: Tavistock).

Roberts, G. W. and Mills, D. O. (1958), *Study of External Migration Affecting Jamaica: 1953–55* (Mona: Institute of Social and Economic Research).

Robinson, R. and Gallagher, J. with Denny, A. (1965), *Africa and the Victorians: The Official Mind of Imperialism* (London: Macmillan).

Rodney, W. (1981), *A History of the Guyanese Working People, 1881–1905* (London: Heinemann Educational Books).

Rothchild, D. (1973), *Racial Bargaining in Independent Kenya* (New York: Oxford University Press).

Rothschild, Lord (1971), *A Framework for Government Research and Development*, Cmnd 4824 (London: HMSO).

Ryan, S. D. (1972), *Race and Nationalism in Trinidad and Tobago: A Study of Decolonisation in a Multi-racial Society* (University of Toronto Press).

Saha, P. (1970), *Immigration of Indian Labour, 1834–1900* (Delhi: People's Publishing House).

Sashidharan, S. P. and Francis, E. (1993), 'Epidemiology, Ethnicity and Schizophrenia', in Ahmad (ed.) (1993).

Scarman, Rt Hon The Lord (1982), *The Brixton Disorders, 10–12 April 1981,* Cmnd 8427 (London: HMSO).

Schattschnieder, E. (1967), *The Semi-sovereign People* (Hinsdale: The Dryden Press).

Schermerhorn, R. A. (1970), *Comparative Ethnic Relations: A Framework for Theory and Research* (New York: Random House).

Semmel, B. (1962), *The Governor Eyre Controversy* (London: Macgibbon and Kee).

Sewell, G. W. (1861), *The Ordeal of Free Labour in the West Indies* (New York: Harper Bros).

Sewell, T. (1993), *Black Tribunes: Black Political Participation in Britain* (London: Lawrence and Wishart).

Shaw, A. (1994), 'The Pakistani Community in Oxford', in Ballard (ed.).

Sheridan, R. B. (1974), *Sugar and Slavery: An Economic History of the British West Indies, 1623–1775* (Barbados: Caribbean Universities Press).

Sherwood, M. (1991), 'Race, Nationality and Employment among Lascar Seamen, 1660 to 1945', *New Community*, vol. 17, no. 2.

Shukra, K. (1990), 'Black Sections in the Labour Party', in H. Goulbourne (ed.), *Black Politics in Britain*.

Shyllon, F. O. (1974), *Black Slaves in Britain* (London: Oxford University Press).

Sidhu, G. S. *et al.* (1974), *The Soldier-Saint: Guru Gorbind Singh* (Gravesend: The Sikh Missionary Society).

Singh, K. (1966), *A History of the Sikhs* (Oxford: Oxford University Press).

Singh, D. and Kaur, A. (1986), *Rehat Maryada: The Sikh Code of Discipline*, no publisher, but printed in the United Kingdom.

Sires, R. V. (1955), 'The Experience of Jamaica with Modified Crown Colony Government', *Social and Economic Studies*, vol. iv, no. ii.

Sivanandan, A. (1974), *Race and Resistance: The IRR story* (London: Race Today Publications).

— (1991), *A Different Hunger: Writings on Black Resistance* (London: Pluto Press).

Smith, A. (1973), *The Wealth of Nations* (Harmondsworth: Penguin Books).

Smith, D. (1977), *Racial Disadvantage in Britain* (Harmondsworth: Penguin).

Smith, M. G. (1965), *The Plural Society in the British West Indies* (Berkeley, CA: University of California Press).

— (1974), *Corporations and Society* (London: Duckworth).

— (1988), 'Pluralism, Race and Ethnicity in Selected African Countries', in Rex and Mason (eds).

Smith, R. T. (1962), *British Guiana* (London: Oxford University Press).

Smith, S. (1989), *The Politics of Race and Residence: Citizenship, Segregation and White Supremacy in Britain* (Cambridge: Polity).

Solomos, J. (1988), *Black Youth, Racism and the State: The Politics of Ideology and Policy* (Cambridge: Cambridge University Press).

— (1993), *Race and Racism in Britain* (London: Macmillan).

Solomos, J. and Back, L. (1994), 'Conceptualising Racisms: Social Theory, Politics and Research', *Sociology*, vol. 28, no. 1.

— (1995a), *Race, Politics and Social Change* (London: Routledge).

— (1995b), 'Marxism, Racism, and Ethnicity', *American Behavioural Scientist*, vol. 38, no. 3.

Sooben, P. (1990), *The Origins of the Race Relations Act* (Coventry: Centre for Research in Ethnic Relations, University of Warwick).

Sorel, G. (1908), *Reflections on Violence* (London and New York: Collier-Macmillan).

Spear, P. (1970), *A History of India*, vol. 2 (Harmondsworth: Penguin Books).

Sumner, W. G. (1906), *Folkways: A Study of the Sociological Importance of Usages, Manners, Customs, Mores, and Morals* (New York: Dover Publications).

— (1963), *Social Darwinism: Selected Essays*, with an Introduction by S. Persons (Englewood Cliffs, NJ: Prentice-Hall).

Stillwell, J. Rees, P. and Boden, P. (eds) (1992), *Migration Processes and Patterns: Population Redistribution in the United Kingdom*, vol. 2 (London: Belhaven Press).

Stone, C. (1985), *Class, State and Democracy in Jamaica* (Kingston: Blackett Publishers).

— (1993), *Democracy and Clientelism in Jamaica* (New Jersey: Transaction Books).

Spencer, H. (1967), *The Evolution of Society*, ed. with an Introduction by R. L. Carneiro (Chicago, IL and London: The University of Chicago Press).

— (1972), *On Social Evolution: Selected Writings*, ed. and with an Introduction by J. D. Y. Peel (Chicago, IL and London: The University of Chicago Press).

Stuart, O. (1996), '"Yes, We Mean Black Disabled People Too": Thoughts on Community Care and Disabled People from Black and Minority Ethnic Communities', in Ahmad and Atkin (eds).

Swann, Lord Michael (1985), *Education for All: Report of the Committee of Inquiry into the Education of Children from Ethnic Minority Groups,* Cmnd 9453 (London: HMSO).

Tandon, Y. (1973), *The New Position of East Africa's Asians: Problems of a Displaced Minority,* Report no. 16 (rev. edn) (London: Minority Rights Group).

Tatla, Dashan Singh (1991), *The Sikh Diaspora in the UK and Canada* (unpublished PhD thesis, University of Warwick).

Thatcher, M. (1988), *Britain and Europe: Text of the Speech Delivered in Bruges by the Prime Minister on 20 September 1988* (London: Conservative Political Centre).

Thomas, C. Y. (1974), *Dependence and Transformation: The Economics of the Transition to Socialism* (New York: Monthly Review Press).

Thomas, P. (1985), *The Aims and Outcomes of Social Policy Research* (London: Croom Helm).

Thomas-Hope, E. (1980), 'Hopes and Reality in West Indian Migration to Britain', *Oral History Journal,* vol. 8, no. 1.

— (1992), *Explanation in Caribbean Migration* (London: Macmillan).

Tinker, H. (1974), *A New System of Slavery: The Export of Indian Labour Overseas, 1830–1920* (Oxford: Oxford University Press).

Tomlinson, S. (1983), *Ethnic Minorities in British Schools* (London: Heineman Educational Books).

— (1989), 'Education and Training', *New Community,* vol. 15, no. 3.

Twaddle, M. (ed.) (1975), *Expulsion of a Minority: Essays on Ugandan Asians* (London: The Athlone Press).

van den Berghe, P. (1967), *Race and Racism: A Comparative Perspective* (New York: John Wiley).

Verma, G. K. (ed.) (1989), *Education for All: A Landmark in Pluralism* (London: The Falmer Press).

Virdee, S. (1995), *Racial Violence and Harassment* (London: Public Policy Institute).

Walvin, J. (1973), *Black and White: The Negro in British Society* (London: Allen and Unwin).

— (1982), *Slavery and British Society, 1776–1846* (London: Macmillan).

Walvin, J. and Edwards, P. (1983), *Black Personalities in the Era of the Slave Trade* (London: Macmillan).

Warnes, T. (1992), 'Temporal and Spatial Patterns of Elderly [sic] Migration', in Stillwell, Rees and Boden.

— (1996), 'The Age Structure and Ageing of the Ethnic [sic] Groups', in Coleman and Salt (eds).

Watson, J. L. (1977), *Between Two Cultures: Migrants and Minorities in Britain* (Oxford: Basil Blackwell).

Watters, C. (1996), 'Representations and Realities: Black People, Community Care and Mental Health', in Ahmad and Atkin (eds).

Weber, M. (1947), *The Theory of Social and Economic Organisation*, ed. with Introduction by Talcott Parsons (New York: The Free Press).

— (1995), *Max Weber: Selections in Translation*, ed. W. G. Runciman, trans. E. Matthews (Cambridge: Cambridge University Press).

Werbuer, P. (1994), 'Renewing an Industrial Past: British Pakistani Entrepreneurship in Manchester', in J. M. Brown and R. Foot (eds), *Migration: The Asian Experience*.

Wight, M. (1946), *The Development of the Legislative Council, 1606–1945* (London: Faber and Faber).

Williams, C. H. (1982), *National Separatism* (Cardiff: University of Wales Press).

Williams, E. (1950), *Education in the British West Indies* (Port of Spain: Guardian Commercial Printery)

— (1963), *British Historians and the West Indies* (London: Andre Deutsch).

— (1964), *Capitalism and Slavery* (London: Andre Deutsch).

Williams, F. (1996), ' "Race", Welfare and Community Care: A Historical Perspective', in W. I. U. Ahmad and K. Atkin (eds), *'Race' and Community Care* (Buckingham: Open University Press).

Woodham-Smith, C. (1962), *The Great Hunger: Ireland 1845–9* (London: Hamish Hamilton).

Wrench, J. (ed.) (1996), *Preventing Racism at the Workplace: A Report on 16 European Countries* (Dublin: European Foundation for the Improvement of Living and Working Conditions).

Wrench, J., Brah, H. and Martin, P. (1993), *Invisible Minorities: Racism in New Towns and New Contexts* (Coventry: Centre for Research in Ethnic Relations, University of Warwick).

# *Index*